P9-CAA-519

OTHER BOOKS BY THE AUTHOR

Known and Unknown
Rumsfeld's Rules

GERALD FORD

and the

RESCUE

of the

AMERICAN PRESIDENCY

WHEN THE CENTER HELD

DONALD RUMSFELD

FREE PRESS

New York   London   Toronto   Sydney   New Delhi

*f*P

Free Press
An Imprint of Simon & Schuster, Inc.
1230 Avenue of the Americas
New York, NY 10020

Copyright © 2018 by Donald Rumsfeld

All rights reserved, including the right to reproduce this book or portions thereof in any form whatsoever. For information, address Free Press Subsidiary Rights Department, 1230 Avenue of the Americas, New York, NY 10020.

First Free Press hardcover edition May 2018

Free Press and colophon are trademarks of Simon & Schuster, Inc.

For information about special discounts for bulk purchases, please contact Simon & Schuster Special Sales at 1-866-506-1949 or business@simonandschuster.com.

The Simon & Schuster Speakers Bureau can bring authors to your live event. For more information, or to book an event, contact the Simon & Schuster Speakers Bureau at 1-866-248-3049 or visit our website at www.simonspeakers.com.

Interior design by Joy O'Meara

Manufactured in the United States of America

10 9 8 7 6 5 4 3 2 1

Library of Congress Cataloging-in-Publication Data is available.

ISBN 978-1-5011-7293-9
ISBN 978-1-5011-7295-3 (ebook)

To my colleagues in the Ford administration,
who served a great man with honor and dedication,
and to the American people, who had the good fortune
that Gerald R. Ford was there when the need
was so great and that the center held

Contents

CONTENTS

Author's Note

Taos, New Mexico

This book is hardly the work of an impartial observer of history. Gerald R. Ford was my colleague in the U.S. Congress in the 1960s and a man I had known for more than a decade before he became our nation's thirty-eighth Commander in Chief. Of the four Presidents I have been privileged to serve, Gerald R. Ford was the only one who had been a longtime personal friend.

The circumstances that allowed me to come to know President Ford date back to the middle of the last century. After leaving the U.S. Navy in 1957, I served as the Administrative Assistant to Congressman David Dennison, a Republican from northeast Ohio. After Dennison, a fine and dedicated legislator, was defeated for reelection in 1958, I joined the staff of Congressman Bob Griffin, where I learned a good deal about his colleague from Michigan, Jerry Ford, and, before long, met Ford in person. Immediately after I was elected to Congress from Illinois in November 1962, Griffin recruited me to solicit support for Ford from the other newly elected members of Congress in his upstart bid to become the Republican Conference

Chairman, the number-three position in the House GOP leadership team. Ford was challenging the senior incumbent Congressman Charles Hoeven of Iowa.

I joined Ford's effort and our small team went to work. Ultimately, in a coup for the so-called Young Turks of the GOP, Ford won. During that time, I quickly came to appreciate what so many others have seen in Jerry Ford over his lifetime of service—his honesty, integrity, and basic human decency. Decency can be an underappreciated quality in general, but especially so in a competitive place like Washington, D.C., where brashness and sharp elbows are often heralded. Gerald Ford's kindness, midwestern politeness, and willingness to put other people's interests ahead of his own were so distinctive. Indeed, they were qualities that were desperately needed when he became President. As his political opponent, the Democratic Speaker of the U.S. House of Representatives, Tip O'Neill, later reflected, "God has been good to America, especially during difficult times. At the time of the Civil War, He gave us Abraham Lincoln. And at the time of Watergate, He gave us Gerald Ford—the right man at the right time who was able to put our nation back together again."

Perhaps because Ford's time in the presidency was brief—895 days—and was bookended by Richard Nixon and Ronald Reagan, sizable personalities far better known to the American people, he became, in a sense, the man in the middle. To this day his crucial service to our nation during an unprecedented time of testing has neither been fully understood nor appropriately valued. President Ford, of course, would never have believed he was owed anything. He did what he did out of his love of country and his deep respect for public service. That was at least in part what made him such a trusted figure at a time when trust for the presidency was at its nadir.

In American political history, the arrival of Gerald R. Ford to the presidency was what might be called a "Black Swan" event. Whoever would have contemplated that within two years of the landslide victory of the Nixon-Agnew ticket, both the duly elected President and Vice President would be swept out of office in separate corruption scandals? I would submit that Ford was likely one of the very few public servants able to lead America back from what careful observers characterized as the brink of civil and political collapse. Restoring public trust in the presidency and in the federal government was his "biggest" achievement, concluded historian Michael Beschloss, during a 2006 *PBS NewsHour* segment on Ford's legacy. Ron Nessen, Ford's second White House Press Secretary, added that it was President Ford's personality "that was . . . one of the contributions he made to healing and changing the mood of those times."[1] His demeanor, down-to-earth yet uplifting, heartened everyone who knew the gentleman from Grand Rapids, Michigan—all the way back to his college football teammates. Which brings me to the title of this book.

In football, the "center" is among the least glorified positions. Nonetheless, it is of central importance. In the middle of the offensive line, it is invariably the center's responsibility to handle the football at the start of every play on offense. If the play goes well, one of the other players on the team receives the plaudits—a tailback who breaks a long run, a quarterback who launches a Hail Mary pass, or a receiver who catches the ball and races for the winning touchdown. Though fans may take little notice, the center's teammates recognize and appreciate his importance.

From 1932 to 1934, Ford was the center on the University of Michigan varsity football team. In 1932 and again in 1933, the Michigan Wolverines went undefeated and became national champions. His final season, 1934, however, was tough. While the team won only one game, Jerry Ford—at center—remained its heart.

Many years later, in a time unique in the two-hundred-year history of the United States, our country was urgently in need of its "cen-

ter," and the largely unheralded Gerald Ford was on hand. Irish poet
William Butler Yeats might have been describing the chaos America
was experiencing in 1974 when he wrote back in 1919:

> *Turning and turning in the widening gyre*
> *The falcon cannot hear the falconer;*
> *Things fall apart; the center cannot hold;*
> *Mere anarchy is loosed upon the world,*
> *The blood-dimmed tide is loosed, and everywhere*
> *The ceremony of innocence is drowned;*
> *The best lack all conviction, while the worst*
> *Are full of passionate intensity.*[2]

In the wake of the historic Watergate scandal during the Nixon administration, it seemed our nation was hurtling headlong into an
abyss—a "widening gyre." With chaos at the highest levels of our
nation's government, some believed anarchy might be loosed upon
our country and, from there, possibly the world. The American people were deeply disillusioned and gripped by a lack of trust in their
government. Our "ceremony of innocence" was being drowned.

In that poisonous, ugly atmosphere in August 1974 stood a largely
unknown American. In stunning contrast to every other individual
who had ever served as our nation's President and Commander in
Chief, Gerald Ford's name had never appeared on a ballot either
for the presidency or for the vice presidency. He had fashioned and
tested no national campaign team, no seasoned group of policy advisors. He had neither organized nor managed anything larger than
his congressional staff and the U.S. House of Representatives' Minority Leader's office. He had neither sought nor earned a national
constituency. His base of support was Michigan's Fifth Congressional
District—the Grand Rapids area of the state. Yet suddenly, there he

was, thrust into a tumultuous, even desperate environment in which America's durability as a functioning democracy was being tested and questioned as never before.

Despite his decades of public service—aboard the aircraft carrier USS *Monterey*, in the Pacific theater during World War II, over two decades in the U.S. House of Representatives, and, only briefly, as an unelected Vice President—the former football star and Yale Law School graduate had never received a hero's laurels, nor had he ever sought them. He simply performed his duty while others received the acclaim.

As he took the oath of office as President of the United States on August 9, 1974, Gerald Ford was once again reporting for duty. Without fanfare, he would steady the ship of state, restore balance to our country, and lead his fellow Americans out of the national trauma of the Watergate scandal and the unprecedented resignation of both the elected Vice President and the elected President. In this case, fortunately, the poet Yeats's frightful vision went unfulfilled. To be sure, things were coming apart, but, to our nation's great benefit, the "center" held.

I was privileged to be at his side during that unprecedented juncture in our nation's history—first at the new President's request as Chairman of Ford's transition team, and then as his White House Chief of Staff and still later as his Secretary of Defense. As Chief of Staff during Ford's crucial first year or so in office, I had multiple conversations with him each day—in the Oval Office, at Cabinet and National Security Council meetings, on *Air Force One*, and during his domestic and foreign travels.

After each of our meetings, to keep the work of his presidency moving, I would immediately dictate a brief note that members of my outstanding staff—Brenda Williams and Barbara Hildreth—would promptly type up. Those many hundreds of quick action memos enabled me or my young assistant, Dick Cheney, to follow up on the

President's requests, to make notes to myself, to Dick and to key staff members, and also to keep my mind refreshed on what the President had been told and on what the President was planning or considering on a full range of subjects. What my notes—the many hundreds of action memos—in effect became was a real-time, raw, running log of the Ford presidency from its inception. They were largely unedited and were in no sense a journal. I make generous use of them in this book. They provide unvarnished insight into what was happening in those early months of the presidency of the only person to serve in the Oval Office having never been elected either President or Vice President. Many of these and others which have never been made public will also be included on my website, www.rumsfeld.com.

Knowing that those who are closest to a President and are seeing him frequently owe him their unvarnished advice, I was not sparing in offering suggestions. Gerald Ford had the self-awareness and the confidence to recognize that as a legislator he had not run a large department or agency. Apart from our friendship and our close working relationship in the House of Representatives, one of the reasons he insisted I leave my post as the U.S. Ambassador to NATO and return to the White House to assist him was that I had recently run two large organizations during the Nixon administration—serving for the better part of four years overseeing the Office of Economic Opportunity and the Economic Stabilization Program, and serving in the White House as a Counsellor to President Nixon before becoming U.S. Ambassador to NATO. Further, I was so solidly for President Ford's success that he had no doubt I was on his side; as a result, he encouraged me to offer the candid, personal opinions that thread through many of my memos.

Because they were not meant for anyone but me and my very small circle of aides, and because it was such a fast-paced environment, these memos contain numerous misspellings and grammatical errors. In many cases, standing alone, the comments lack context.

Some of these memos, out of necessity, have been lightly edited and, on occasion, modestly redacted to remove sensitive or clearly inaccurate or unfair references. They do however portray, indeed reveal, Gerald Ford as the impressive leader he became. Further, they provide real-life examples of the magnitude of the problems he was confronting on behalf of our nation from his first moments as President.

Today, we read and hear a good deal of talk about dysfunction in Washington, D.C., as if it were a new phenomenon. The 2016 election, we were repeatedly told, was the most divisive election ever. We are still, many months later, warned of "permanent gridlock." As of this writing, trust in our public institutions remains low. But, in truth, the Washington, D.C., of today is not entirely different from that of 1974, when for the only time in our nation's history an elected leader had resigned and surrendered the presidency to a man with whom little of our country—and even less of the world—was even passingly familiar.

This is that story, told by one who was privileged to have been there and who had the chance to see a friend rise to the occasion just when our nation needed him most.

WHEN
THE
CENTER
HELD

⚔ 1 ⚔

The Long National Nightmare

August 8, 1974, Washington, D.C.

There was a palpable unease in our nation's capital as the most talked about man on the planet prepared to address the American people for his final time from the Oval Office. A man who less than two years earlier had won re-election to the presidency in a forty-nine-state landslide was about to resign the presidency in disgrace.

For some time, no one was sure whether the combative Richard M. Nixon would, or even *could*, surrender the White House of his own volition. Only two days earlier, he had told some members of Congress that he would never quit regardless of the consequences. Then the bottom fell out. Republican stalwarts, including Senator Barry Goldwater (R-AZ) and House Minority Leader John Rhodes (R-AZ), had traveled to the White House with the unhappy task of urging the President to come to terms with reality. He would have to resign in the public interest, they advised him, or suffer an even more demeaning exit. Senator Goldwater told President Nixon that he hadn't counted more than a dozen U.S. Senators willing to fight against his impeachment, adding, in his refreshingly direct style, "I don't know whether I'd be one of them."[1]

The scandal driving Richard M. Nixon from the presidency—a job he had sought for much of his political life—had taken a terrible toll on the country, on those he had selected to serve with him in his administration, on his family, and most certainly on the thirty-seventh President's own health. He had reportedly slept two or three hours a night at most for weeks, even months.[2] Aides described him as "wretched and gray."[3] An hour earlier, in a meeting with friends from Congress, Nixon had had to leave the room abruptly as he began to break down in tears.[4]

Still, despite the dark bags under his eyes, he struggled not to show the stress he was enduring; certainly not to the outside team preparing the Oval Office for his address. Instead, in that tense, raw moment when he was about to abandon everything he had spent so many years working for, Richard Nixon, true to his nature, was both awkward and human.

"Hey, you're better looking than I am. Why don't you stay here?" President Nixon called out in jest to the television technician who was moving aside as Nixon strode into the Oval Office.[5] The spectacled technician had been serving as a stand-in, helping to test the lighting for the television cameras while sitting in the President's chair behind the Wilson desk. When Nixon approached, the young man jumped up and scurried over to the side of the room. Struggling to connect with someone, Nixon did not let the man escape so easily.

"Blondes, they say, photograph better than brunettes," Nixon remarked to the fair-haired man. "That true or not?"[6]

Without waiting for an answer, he earnestly asked the TV crew: "Have you got an extra camera in case the lights go out?" A technical glitch that evening would make what for him was a gut-wrenching experience even worse.

Oliver F. Atkins, the President's White House photographer, was on hand. "My friend Ollie always wants to take a lot of pictures," Nixon joked. Yet, his emotions in flux, the President soon displayed a flash of annoyance, directing "Ollie" to cease taking photos altogether. He also sternly ordered members of the Secret Service to leave the Oval Office before he spoke. Told that wasn't possible, Nixon claimed, with a grin, that he was "just kidding."[7]

History was now only minutes away. Before an audience of 150 million Americans—a number that dwarfed that year's record-breaking Super Bowl viewership—Nixon announced that he would resign the presidency at noon the next day. "Vice President Ford," he said, "will be sworn in as President at that hour in this office."

As he spoke of Gerald Ford in that evening's televised address, Nixon was solemn. "In passing this office to the Vice President," he told the American people, "I also do so with the profound sense of the weight of responsibility that will fall on his shoulders tomorrow and, therefore, of the understanding, the patience, the cooperation he will need from all Americans."[8]

What Nixon was passing over to Ford was a government so rocked by turbulence and trauma that it was a very real question whether the American experiment might be wrecked. Not since the Civil War had the institutions created by our country's Founders come into such doubt. Not since the depths of the Great Depression of the 1930s had the American people's confidence in its future been so eroded. Not ever in our nation's history had a leader of the United States been such a likely candidate for prosecution and imprisonment.

There was, to be sure, little cheer in the national mood. For more than a decade, the country had been suffering divisions, deep disappointments, and, more recently, anguish. High-profile assassinations had rocked America. The most consequential took place on November 22, 1963, when the youthful and charismatic President,

John F. Kennedy, in whom the hopes of many young Americans were invested, was shot and killed as he rode in his motorcade through downtown Dallas. Millions of Americans saw the entire traumatic episode unfold on their television screens—the stricken First Lady crawling onto the back of the convertible apparently to try to retrieve a piece of her husband's skull; his alleged assassin gunned down by a local nightclub owner; the President's young son memorably standing in salute as his father's coffin passed down Pennsylvania Avenue.

Then in April 1968, Dr. Martin Luther King, Jr., another beacon of hope and inspiration to millions, was killed on the second-floor balcony of the Lorraine Motel in Memphis, Tennessee. Two months later, U.S. Senator Robert F. Kennedy of New York, a younger brother of President Kennedy, was gunned down in the Ambassador Hotel in Los Angeles, California, just as he seemed to be gaining momentum in his bid for the Democratic nomination for President. On February 22, 1974, Samuel Byck, an unsuccessful small-business owner from Philadelphia, attempted to hijack a plane scheduled to fly out of Baltimore, with the intention of crashing it into the White House and killing President Nixon. (Byck committed suicide, shooting himself in the head, when police stormed the plane on the runway.) Just two months before Nixon's stunning resignation, in June of 1974, Alberta King, mother of the slain civil rights leader, was killed during a service at Ebenezer Baptist Church in Atlanta, Georgia.

Death and violence were constant companions in those difficult years, particularly as casualties mounted during the frustrating and painful stalemate in Vietnam. That long conflict had toppled the presidency of Lyndon B. Johnson, led to violent protests in our nation's streets and on a number of college campuses, and seemed to provide endless displays of carnage on television sets in homes across America. Even in August of 1974, after direct U.S. military involvement had been declared officially over, the war in Southeast Asia dominated headlines. America's long-suffering Vietnamese allies in the south of their country were losing to the Communists from the north, and partisans in the U.S. on both sides cast blame for the continuing difficulties and their consequences.

The U.S. economy was faltering. American workers were hurting. Unemployment was rising toward an unprecedented post–World War II record of 9 percent. In the aftermath of an OPEC oil embargo, Americans faced lengthy lines to fill up their vehicles' gas tanks, with waits sometimes over three hours. In some areas of Florida, gas could not be purchased at a station without making a reservation.[9] The U.S. inflation rate had soared from 3.3 percent in January 1972 to 10.9 percent by August 1974, the month Gerald R. Ford was sworn in as President.[10]

Of course, nothing contributed to the public's weariness and anxiety more than the scandals of the Nixon administration. Ford's predecessor as Vice President, Spiro T. Agnew, had had to resign in 1973 due to allegations involving bribery and kickbacks from when he had been governor of Maryland. Yet even the tawdry Agnew episode was dwarfed by the mother of all presidential political scandals.

The 1972 break-in at the Democratic Party's Washington, D.C., headquarters in the Watergate Hotel by individuals, some of whom were linked to Nixon's re-election campaign, and an attempted cover-up of the crime and of its links to the White House engrossed and angered the country. The string of misjudgments blew up in a spectacular fashion during nationally televised testimony in mid-July 1973, when Alexander Butterfield, who had been a senior White House aide, acknowledged that Nixon had maintained a tape-recording system in selected locations to document what he considered historic presidential conversations. The existence of the recording systems in the White House had been unknown to all but very few. After their existence became public, Nixon was implicated in one specific recording, the so-called smoking gun tape, which revealed that he had accepted advice to allow a cover-up of the break-in and to have the CIA slow an FBI inquiry. The multiple Watergate investigations eventually resulted in the indictments of more than sixty people, of whom forty-eight were eventually found guilty. Notably, that list included President Nixon's powerful and influential White House Chief of Staff, H. R. Haldeman, and his senior domestic policy assistant, attorney John Ehrlichman, on charges of perjury, conspiracy, and obstruction of justice.

The protracted public drama and the widely watched nationally televised hearings eroded confidence in the federal government to perhaps the lowest level in our history. The American National Election Study, today the oldest continuous series of survey data reporting on American electoral behavior, first began asking about trust in government in 1958.[11] Trust had reached an all-time high in 1964, at 77 percent, as the new Johnson administration received bipartisan support in the difficult months immediately after the assassination of John F. Kennedy. By 1974 that number had been driven down to 36 percent.[12] President Nixon's approval rating, at one point as high as 68 percent, had plummeted to 24 percent by the time of his resignation in August 1974, the lowest that has been recorded for a sitting president.[13]

Members of the media were openly hostile to President Nixon, with journalists engaging in heated exchanges with the President's embattled Press Secretary, Ron Ziegler. The additional revelation that Nixon kept an "Enemies List," and that some of those on the list were journalists, further increased the members of the media's animosity. (Nixon was also reported to have apparently maintained a "Freeze List" of political adversaries and an "Opponents List" of people who, specifically, were to not set foot inside the White House.[14]) The Nixon administration and *The Washington Post*, which was breathlessly chronicling the scandals, seemed to be in all but open warfare.

Nixon's White House was by various accounts in a state of constant siege, with the President veering into dark moods.[15] Earlier in 1974, when Nixon had visited NATO headquarters in Brussels, Belgium, while I was serving there as the U.S. Ambassador, I saw a glimpse of that mood. Thinking it would boost his morale in the midst of the Watergate scandal back in Washington, D.C., I had assembled the members of our U.S. NATO staff to greet the President upon his arrival at the Brussels airport. The President shook hands, took photos, and seemed friendly, courteous, and presidential. Immediately after, I followed the President and Secretary of State Henry Kissinger, who had accompanied the President, to the waiting limousine. There Mr. Nixon made an ill-informed and offensive remark about the members of the U.S. NATO staff. I pushed back hard, informing him that they were talented public servants, Defense Department officials, as well as seasoned Foreign Service officers, both military and civilian, serving our country well. As we stepped out of the President's car, Kissinger pulled me aside to offer a telling piece of advice: "Rummy, we don't argue with him anymore."

Even amid the tenacious attacks on Nixon by his political opponents, there were steadfast supporters, perhaps most notably California Governor Ronald Reagan. "As the Watergate cover-up closed in on the President, no Republican officeholder in the country defended Nixon more staunchly than Reagan," observed journalist Lou Cannon. In private, Reagan spoke of "a lynch mob" forming to get Nixon.[16] Notwithstanding that strong support, the specter of a sensational criminal proceeding loomed, a "trial of the century" in which the President of the United States, Richard Nixon, would be the defendant and might well be indicted, tried, and, potentially, imprisoned.

On the night of August 8, 1974, in his televised resignation address, President Nixon made some effort—though not nearly enough for most of his critics—to atone for what had happened and to begin to heal the nation's yawning divide. "I regret deeply any injuries that may have been done in the course of the event that led to this decision," he said. "I would say only that if some of my judgments were wrong—and some were wrong—they were made in what I believed at the time to be the best interests of the nation." He said he hoped his decision had "hastened the start of that process of healing which is so desperately needed in America." He urged Americans to "join together" in "helping our new president succeed for the benefit of all Americans."[17] After years of suspicion, mistrust, and partisan hostility, this was an all but impossible task for any person to carry out. But Gerald R. Ford—assuming power over an angry, divided populace amid unprecedented distrust, concerned about a precarious economy trending in the wrong direction, girded against international turmoil and the Cold War, and trying not to be overcome by the shadows of a disgraced presidency—had no choice but to try.

Moments after Richard Nixon informed Vice President Ford of his decision to resign, Ford headed back to his office in the Old Executive Office Building—the grand nineteenth-century edifice located in the White House complex—and made a telephone call to one of the few people who was "in the know" about what was about to take place.

Dr. Henry Kissinger had become a prominent fixture in Washington's social circles due in part to his close relationship with President Nixon, his charismatic persona, his memorable accent, and his proclivity—prior to his marriage to Nancy Maginnes—to be spotted with photogenic female movie stars. The son of German parents, Henry was born in the Bavarian region of Germany in 1923. He enjoyed a normal childhood—even playing soccer for one of the country's best youth clubs—until, in 1938, when Henry was fifteen, his family fled the Nazi persecution of the Jews and landed in New York City. Reportedly shy as a boy, he was hesitant to speak, which, ironically, may have contributed to his distinctive accent remaining with him to this day.[18]

Kissinger launched his academic career, receiving multiple degrees from Harvard. Eventually he grew weary of the insularity and occasional pettiness of campus life and hungered to test his theories on international relations in the real world. He befriended New York Governor Nelson Rockefeller, whom he advised on international affairs during Rockefeller's several unsuccessful bids for the Republican nomination for president in the 1960s. He was then tapped by Nixon, the victor in the 1968 presidential contest, to serve as his National Security Advisor. Four years later, in an unprecedented step, Nixon nominated him to the additional position of Secretary of State.

Given his experiences in academia, and later in government, Henry knew his subject matter well. Tough and effective in steering a challenging bureaucracy, along with his brilliance he also had a splendidly wry sense of humor. Mao Zedong had ostensibly been briefed on Henry's succession of public romances, which had reportedly included actresses Candice Bergen, Jill St. John, and Shirley MacLaine.[19] "You know China is a very poor country," Mao interjected during a meeting with Kissinger in Beijing in 1973. "What we have in excess is women." Kissinger, without pause, asked, "There are no quotas for those, or tariffs?"[20]

Ford would later write in his memoir, *A Time to Heal*, "It would be hard for me to overstate the admiration and affection I had for Henry."[21] In the aftermath of Nixon's resignation, Ford came close.

In his phone call hours before Nixon's resignation, Ford said to Henry, "I just finished talking with the President, and he gave me his decision, and we spent about an hour and twenty minutes over there. During the course of the conversation, he indicated that you were the only one in the Cabinet with whom he had shared his decision."[22]

"That is correct," Kissinger replied. Henry's reply had unambiguously given Ford a sense of Nixon's pecking order. Kissinger after all had been told that Ford would soon become the President before even Ford himself.

"I would hope we would get together sometime this afternoon," Ford suggested. In his recollection of the moment, Kissinger noted that Ford "in his modest unassuming way" had left the timing of this meeting up to him.

That same day, Ford tried getting in touch with the Chief Justice of the United States, Warren Burger, to discuss a swearing-in ceremony for the following day. Burger, he learned, was at a conference in the Netherlands. When they connected over the phone later in the day, Ford said, "I'd hate to interrupt your trip," wishing not to bother the Chief Justice. Burger replied that he would return to Washington immediately.[23] In the coming months and years, Ford's natural politeness would occasionally be misinterpreted as weakness. This was especially so in Washington, D.C., a city that had grown accustomed to a more muscular and imperial presidential style.

"I really want you to stay and stand with me in these difficult times," Ford told Kissinger during their call.[24] At their meeting later that afternoon, Ford reiterated this sentiment in blunt terms. "Henry, I need you. The country needs you. I want you to stay. I'll do everything I can to work with you."[25] The Secretary of State later noted Ford "made it sound like I would be doing him a favor by staying."[26]

"Sir," Kissinger somberly pointed out, "it is my job to get along with you and not yours to get along with me."[27]

Ford watched President Nixon's seventeen-minute resignation address later that evening with his wife, Betty, and members of his family. As the gravity of the situation bore down upon him, Ford had prayed for guidance.[28] A verse from the Book of Proverbs was a favorite. He had recited it before bed each night since his high school days in Grand Rapids: "Trust in the Lord with all thine heart, lean not on thine own understanding, in all thy ways acknowledge Him and He shall direct thy paths."[29]

Ford took care to avoid seeming presumptuous, even as Nixon's fate started to become clear. Not wanting to give up on the President, whom he considered a friend, Ford had not even packed for his coming move to the White House. There was no vice presidential residence back in 1974, so Ford intended to spend the first days of his presidency in the same place he'd lived for nineteen years—his modest two-story home on a quiet street in Alexandria, Virginia, across the Potomac River from Washington, D.C. As Nixon's speech ended, a cluster of reporters had gathered outside in the drizzle to await the first statement from the nation's incoming President.

Stepping out that evening into his small front yard, carrying neither notes nor a prepared text, Ford spoke from his heart. He called Nixon's resignation speech "one of the very saddest incidents that I've ever witnessed." Yet Nixon, Ford added, had made "one of the greatest personal sacrifices for the country and one of the finest personal decisions on behalf of all of us as Americans."[30] Ford pledged his best efforts to work with the Democrat-controlled Congress for "what's good for America and good for the world."[31] Very much sounding like the legislator I had first met more than a decade earlier, Ford explained that he had "a good many adversaries" on Capitol Hill, but could not name, or think of, a single enemy.

Not for a moment seeking to distance himself from the scandal-plagued White House, or pretending he had not been a part of the administration, as some politicians in his position might have been tempted to do, Ford instead expressed his respect for one of Nixon's most recognizable cabinet officials, Henry Kissinger. He announced there and then that Secretary Kissinger would stay on in his unprecedented dual roles of Secretary of State and National Security Advisor.[32]

"We've been fortunate in the last five years to have a very great man in Henry Kissinger, who has had to build the blocks of peace under President Nixon," Ford added.[33]

Such praise was not unwarranted. Henry was a highly skilled public servant who, along with White House Chief of Staff Al Haig, had played a crucial role in keeping the White House and the Nixon administration functioning throughout the months of turbulence during the Watergate scandal. He was also by then a seasoned diplomat who had been instrumental in helping to craft the Nixon administration's foreign policies: the opening to China and the so-called détente policy toward the Soviet Union, which despite its shortcomings had helped to stabilize East-West relations. President Ford undoubtedly also believed it made sense for him to identify his presidency with a figure considerably better known to foreign leaders across the globe than he was at the time, to project stability during what promised to be a challenging transition period.

Though Henry deserved considerable credit for his contributions to the Nixon administration, it was Richard Nixon who steered foreign policy. Normalizing U.S. relations with China, for example, had been one of Nixon's goals even before he had been elected President. Kissinger's role in that piece of historic diplomacy was important, but Nixon had brainstormed the strategy some time before and together they choreographed the moves. "Henry is a genius," Nixon had said to Ford on August 8, appending, "but you don't have to accept everything he recommends. . . . You can't let him have a totally free hand."[34]

Ford's strong desire to keep Kissinger on board created for some, including a number of Ford's friends, a worrisome perception of dependency that would linger. Coupled with his self-effacing nature, this occasionally led him to be underestimated.

Nixon, for one, had some reservations. He confided to Kissinger, and probably to others, that Ford would do an "adequate" job as Commander in Chief. As endorsements go, that was hardly resounding. The embattled President was also said to have believed Ford's confirmation as Vice President made it *less* likely that he—Nixon— would be impeached. "On several occasions," Kissinger recalled, thinking of Watergate, "the President mused that Congress would not dare to assume responsibility for replacing him with a man who had so little background in international affairs."[35]

Ford had not had any inkling that his life would move in this trajectory. To the contrary, he had agreed with Betty that he would run for one more term in the House of Representatives in 1974 and then retire from public life.[36] History of course had other plans, though sometimes those plans were far from obvious. Ford, in fact, had not been Nixon's first choice to replace Spiro T. Agnew as Vice President—a point Nixon made clear to Ford and to others. In 1973, Nixon had urged Presidential Counselor Bryce Harlow and Defense Secretary Mel Laird to try to carve a path through the Congress for John Connally, who was then the subject of an ethics investigation.[37] Enormously charismatic, Connally, the Texas Democrat-turned-Republican, had served as Secretary of the Navy in 1961 in the Kennedy administration, Governor of Texas from 1963 to 1969, and then Secretary of the Treasury in Nixon's first term. He was probably best known for having been wounded while riding in the President's limousine in Dallas in November 1963, when John F. Kennedy was assassinated.[38]

Anyone in close proximity to Nixon quickly saw he was unusually enamored of Connally, a man Kissinger pointedly observed was "the only person about whom I never heard Nixon make a denigrating comment."[39] The former Governor of Texas was so impressive to President Nixon that in Cabinet meetings I attended Nixon actually cheered him on. On occasion, when Connally said something Nixon particularly liked, the President would turn to others in the meeting with a look of pride.

Though Nixon was confident that the various controversies surrounding Connally would subside, which they in fact did, close aides managed to ease him toward the solid, well-liked, and easily confirmable Gerald R. Ford. Still, even after picking Ford, Nixon forthrightly told his new Vice President that Connally would be his choice for the White House in 1976.

In short, Gerald R. Ford entered the White House underestimated by a number of important people, including, quite possibly, himself.

Two days before Ford took office as the nation's thirty-eighth president, a surreal incident in New York City provided a distraction in an already surreal time. During the early morning hours of August 7, as President Nixon likely lay awake contemplating his dwindling future, a thin young man dressed in black slipped into a Manhattan skyscraper, made his way to the top floor, and with the help of some accomplices, slung a cable across to the neighboring building. Then, using a pole for balance, the man in black stepped out onto the cable and began to walk.

He was Philippe Petit, a twenty-five-year-old French acrobat. He was traversing the roughly 131-foot space between the newly completed twin towers of the World Trade Center. At the time, the towers were sitting unfinished and largely unrented. They just happened to be a project of David Rockefeller and his brother Nelson, who had recently resigned as Governor of New York and was soon to be nominated by President Ford to become Vice President.[40]

Suspended between the towers, 1,350 feet above the street for forty-five unnerving minutes, the thrill seeker walked the wire, stopping periodically to do knee bends and other stunts. Rush-hour traffic was snarled in the streets below as people craned their necks to watch. The acrobat eventually came down and was arrested, but charges were dropped on the condition that he perform a free show in Central Park. After an eventful morning, New Yorkers went back to their lives. But the story made headlines, a sideshow amid the Watergate circus to which the entire nation had tickets.

Nobody could have seen it at the time, but the French acrobat's stunt could be taken as merely the opener for an even more difficult balancing act of enormous importance to the world: holding our country together in the tempestuous wake of Watergate. That event opened two days later, and its star was Gerald R. Ford. When the gentleman from Michigan took office as president on August 9, 1974, he stepped out onto his own high wire. All eyes were trained on his every move. If he put a wrong foot forward, it could mean disaster, not just for him but for our country.

⇥ 2 ⇤

"Give Me Hell"

MEETING WITH THE PRESIDENT
(Dictated December 3, 1974)
Next we talked about the Nixon issue—the "CREEP issue"—dirty tricks . . . the
problem that Gerald Ford would have is the competence issue . . . governing
under the best of circumstances is tough . . . under the worst of circumstances,
which he has, is impossible—that we have one arm tied behind our back.[1]

Even the most harmonious presidential transition is a pressure-filled full-time undertaking, involving meetings between the outgoing and incoming officials, deliberations about Cabinet nominations and key White House Staff positions, preliminary discussions with foreign heads of state, intelligence briefings and national security updates, and initial exchanges with key members of the U.S. Senate and House of Representatives. In normal circumstances, the presidential transition process takes several months. Ford had little more than twenty-four hours.

Assuming the presidency at an extraordinary time, Gerald R. Ford made a number of necessarily quick but critical decisions about how to handle his unique circumstance. Most of those decisions were wise. A few caused some difficulties and required some adjustments later.

Gerald Ford began his first day as President the way he had begun most days—at his home in Virginia, pouring a glass of orange juice, popping an English muffin into the toaster, and retrieving the newspaper from his front porch in his pajamas.[2] Amidst that calm suburban setting, only *The Washington Post*'s front page suggested that August 9, 1974, was to be astoundingly different from the previous twenty-four hours: "NIXON RESIGNS," "FORD ASSUMES PRESIDENCY TODAY."[3]

> Gerald Rudolph Ford Jr., a Grand Rapids, Mich. lawyer, who never aspired to national office but had it thrust upon him as a result of two of the greatest scandals in American history, will become the 38th President of the United States at noon today. He will be the first American president not elected to national office by the people.[4]

Just minutes after noon on August 9, 1974, Ford took the oath of office as President of the United States in the East Room of the White House, where only minutes earlier a departing Richard Nixon had received a long standing ovation from his Cabinet and senior staff after delivering a largely extemporaneous, uncomfortable, and painful farewell. There, an emotional Richard Nixon quoted Theodore Roosevelt's 1910 "Citizenship in a Republic" speech, more commonly known by its famous line referencing "the man in the arena," called his mother a "saint," and discussed his father's humble, hard luck beginnings, saying he had "the poorest lemon ranch in California." Having listened to what he found a generally maudlin speech by his predecessor, Ford noted he was struck by one line in particular: "Always remember others may hate you, but those who hate you don't

win, unless you hate them, and then you destroy yourself." Ford felt
Richard Nixon might have avoided his tragic predicament had he
taken his own advice.[5]

Wisely, Ford struck a contrast to the tenor of Mr. Nixon's remarks. His eight-minute speech, written with the able assistance of
his speechwriter and senior aide Robert Hartmann, served several
purposes. It was an introduction, an exhibition of stability to the
sizable global audience, and an overture to all Americans urging
them to move past recent years of recrimination and bitterness. As
a symbolic demonstration of this new beginning, Ford's small vice
presidential staff thought to change the seating arrangements in the
White House East Room for the members of the media so that their
chairs faced in the opposite direction than they had when Nixon had
spoken earlier.[6]

Ford was keenly aware of the challenges he faced. Writing about
the moment in his memoir, he recalled a story that he had heard from
a *Chicago Daily News* reporter who had traveled to Greece during
its civil war in the 1940s. There the reporter had encountered a villager who was emigrating to the United States. The villager asked
his war-weary neighbors what he might send back from America
after he arrived—Money? Food? Clothes? No, his neighbors replied,
"You should send us a ton of tranquility." This was what Ford felt he
needed to strive to bring to America as he prepared to take the oath of
office—a sense of calm. The American people had lost faith in their
leaders. Many had lost faith in their institutions. "I knew that unless
I did something to restore their trust," Ford later recalled, "I couldn't
win their consent to do anything else."[7] What was needed was a gen-
tle nod to a scandal-ravaged, war-weary nation that everything was,
finally, going to be okay. This was the origin of what would be one of
his most famous rhetorical phrases.

"My fellow Americans, our long national nightmare is over," he
announced with confidence. "Our constitution works. Our great

Republic is a government of laws, and not of men. Here the people rule."[8] "I assume the presidency under extraordinary circumstances never before experienced by Americans," Ford acknowledged upfront. "This is an hour of history that troubles our minds and hurts our hearts." He offered listeners what he called "just a little straight talk among friends." And, in implicit contrast to his two predecessors, who each had acquired a reputation among many for dishonesty, he pledged "to follow my instincts of openness and candor with full confidence that honesty is always the best policy in the end."

Ford's remarks were viewed on television by tens of millions of Americans. I was one of the interested few not among them. At that moment, I was flying across the Atlantic Ocean from Europe to Washington, D.C., at the urgent request of my friend, the new President of the United States.

INFORM CONSULATES: PRESIDENT NIXON HAS JUST ANNOUNCED HIS RESIGNATION TO TAKE EFFECT AT 12 NOON WASHINGTON TIME FRIDAY, AUGUST 9. VARIOUS DETAILED INSTRUCTIONS WILL FOLLOW WITHIN THE NEXT FEW HOURS. VICE PRESIDENT FORD WILL BE SWORN IN AS PRESIDENT AT NOON FRIDAY WASHINGTON TIME.[9]

This was the flash telegram sent by the Secretary of State on August 8 to every U.S. diplomatic post across the globe. The telegram sent to me as the U.S. Ambassador to the North Atlantic Treaty Organization had arrived at the U.S. Mission to NATO at my office at the military alliance's headquarters in Brussels, Belgium, on Boulevard Léopold III. But I was not there to receive it.

Joyce, our children, and I had been largely isolated from the unrest in Washington, D.C., in the days, weeks, and months immediately preceding the Nixon resignation. My family had left for a brief vacation in Switzerland and northern Italy without me due to a crisis in the Eastern Mediterranean, which required me to stay at my NATO post in Brussels.[10] On July 25, a coup d'état had deposed Cypriot President Archbishop Makarios III. It had been ordered by the military junta in Greece, our NATO ally, and staged by the Cypriot National Guard in conjunction with the OKA-B, a Greek Cypriot paramilitary organization. Five days later, the Turkish military, another NATO ally, invaded, starting with an amphibious incursion into Pentemilli on Cyprus's northern coast.

On August 8, the day President Nixon announced he would resign, we had departed San Remo, Italy, by car. As I was driving, Joyce caught up on the news, reading the Paris *Herald Tribune*. At one point, she urged me to find a place to stop the car and pull over to read the newspaper account of the historic events that were taking place in Washington, D.C. I drove through Cannes to St. Tropez, where we found a place to stop. Only then did I pause to read the paper. I quickly understood what Joyce had been intimating, but had not wanted to discuss in front of our young children, each of whom had met President Nixon during my time in his Cabinet. The reports left us both with the unmistakable impression that the U.S. government was unraveling.[11]

Having served in the Nixon Cabinet and as Counsellor to the President in the White House, it came to my mind that I might be able to be helpful to the new President during his transition. As it happened, the same thought had occurred to him. That evening we drove from St. Tropez to Grimaud in southeastern France, where we had been scheduled to spend time with André de Staercke, the Belgian Ambassador to NATO and the Dean of the NATO Council. There, I received a call from Leona Goodell, my assistant in my office at NATO Headquarters in Brussels, telling me that Vice President Ford had requested that I return to Washington, D.C., immediately.[12]

The next twenty-four hours were a whirlwind. I slept a few hours at Ambassador de Staercke's home in Grimaud, France, got up at 4:30 a.m., made the two-hour drive to the Nice airport, where at 7:00

a.m. I boarded an Air Force T-39 Sabreliner that had been ordered by the White House and headed for Heathrow Airport in London. There I caught a Pan Am flight to Washington, D.C., where I arrived at Dulles International Airport at 1:55 p.m. Friday afternoon, shortly after Vice President Gerald R. Ford had been sworn in as President of the United States.[13]

Three people were waiting for me at my arrival gate at Dulles Airport. One was a man dispatched by Ford's office with a note from the new President requesting that I serve as Chairman of his transition to the presidency. The second individual was John King from the State Department, one of the talented foreign service officers who had been assisting me in Washington, D.C.[14] The third was my young former aide and friend, Dick Cheney, whom I had asked my office to call and request that he be available to give me a hand in my new assignment assisting the new President.

Though the Nixon White House had been officially focused on salvaging his presidency and refusing to even entertain the idea of resignation, I was informed that a small unofficial group of the Vice President's aides and friends had met quietly to begin to think through what a transition to a Ford presidency might require—if it were to happen. The group had been assembled by Phil Buchen, Ford's former law partner in Grand Rapids, Michigan. Other than the three or four members, no others were aware of the team's existence—not President Nixon, not his key lieutenants, and, as I understand it, not even Vice President Ford.[15] Once Ford had been informed by President Nixon he would become President, he urgently began to organize his official transition team, consisting of individuals he knew well and trusted, all from his days in the Congress: former Pennsylvania Governor and former Congressman Bill Scranton; former Maryland Congressman and Nixon's Secretary of the Interior Rogers Morton; my friend, former Democratic Congressman from Virginia and former Assistant Secretary of Defense Jack Marsh, who was by then serving on Vice President Ford's staff; and finally he asked me to serve as the Chairman.

When I entered the Cabinet Room of the White House for the first meeting of our transition team with the brand-new President, having just landed from my flight to Washington, D.C., from Europe, I took special note of my friend. He was in one sense his familiar self—his receding dark blond hair graying at the temples—flashing his open, expressive smile. But he had, in tangible and intangible ways, been transformed by his new position and what he must have sensed were its unmatched burdens and responsibilities.

This was my first glimpse of Gerald Ford as President of the United States. I hadn't known quite what to expect. The weight of the office, and literally the world, had suddenly fallen on his shoulders. How would he handle it? Might he be shaken? In fact, I found him to be very much the same person I'd known since my early days in Congress.

Like many others, I found the Nixon-Ford contrast remarkable. A distant and often secretive man, Richard Nixon was a deep thinker, a strategist immersed in and fascinated by the nuances of policy, a person interested in, and on occasion suspicious of, the motives of others, opponents, even advisors and friends. Kissinger, who had worked closely with President Nixon, had been struck by how difficult it could be to gauge his intentions. "When I saw Nixon," Henry told me, "I figured whatever he said was not what was going to happen. . . . You never knew what game Nixon was playing."[16]

As President, Gerald Ford was determined to be accessible and, due to his nature, he was naturally un-Nixon-like. One of the first symbolic things he did was to order the removal of any recording devices—which apparently had been in existence in various forms and locations off and on since the presidency of Franklin D. Roosevelt—from all White House offices.[17] He instructed his aides to cut down on the playing of the grandiose "Hail to the Chief" when he appeared at ceremonial events; the University of Michigan fight song—"Hail to the Victors"—would suffice.[18] He referred to his sleeping quarters in the White House as "the residence," instead of the term that had been in vogue during the Nixon years—"the executive mansion." And he even urged his Secret Service agents to smile once in a while.[19]

Prior to the formal proceedings of our transition team, the new President walked around the Cabinet Room's long, oval table, which was positioned under the two golden, nineteenth-century Empire-style chandeliers that had been installed at President Nixon's request. Ford looked each member of his personally selected transition team in the eyes and shook their hands. He then opened our initial session by acknowledging that it was a difficult time and thanking those of us present for our assistance to the nation. Be willing to "give me hell," he urged the small group of his friends and former colleagues—an instruction I knew he truly meant. But from my experience in the Nixon White House, I also knew well that for most individuals giving a President of the United States "hell" was easier said than done.

After some preliminary discussion, it became evident our transition team's role was not to fashion policy proposals, at least at the outset. Instead, the new President asked us to promptly tackle the key organizational and personnel matters. His priority was to energize the White House staff and leadership across the executive branch of the federal government.[20]

One of the early issues he asked us to address was the circumstances of the embattled senior members of the Nixon White House staff, whom Kissinger had likened to "shipwrecked sailors thrown together on some inaccessible island."[21] These were individuals known for their skills, their experience, their accomplishments, and their loyalty to President Nixon. Among them were Pat Buchanan, a talented speechwriter and close advisor who famously called President Nixon, his longtime friend and patron, "the old man"; John

McLaughlin, the highly visible speechwriter and former Catholic priest who had cautioned that a "parade of horrors" would follow should Nixon be impeached; Alexander Butterfield, the solid Deputy Assistant to the President who, during televised testimony before Congress, accurately revealed the existence of President Nixon's secret taping system; and Rosemary Woods, Nixon's longtime secretary and confidante, who had taken responsibility for what had become known as the Watergate tape's 18.5-minute gap.

The unraveling of the Nixon presidency, coupled with the arrival of the few largely untested members of the Ford vice presidential staff, made the transition less cordial than one might have expected or hoped. Ford himself found that some of Nixon's people seemed defensive, territorial, and suspicious. "Their man was going down," as he put it to me.[22] He fully understood their feelings. It was not an easy time for either team. And Ford was reluctant to replace these seasoned, loyal public servants. He worried that having them quickly follow Nixon out of the administration might unfairly taint them with the Watergate stigma.

Privately, I suggested to Ford that he nonetheless consider taking an approach that would unambiguously establish a Ford presidency. "Mr. President," I said, "I can't argue with your position that if someone in the Cabinet is doing a good job they shouldn't be removed. But let me argue it anyway."[23]

I emphasized that—in the earliest hours and days of his new administration—the taint of the Watergate scandal would quite understandably call for a fresh start. "It is tough to govern in the best of times. This is the worst of times," I told Ford. Not fashioning a new, fresh "Ford administration," I feared, could lead to a perception that it was business as usual.[24] He listened to my argument, but disagreed.[25] He thought stability was more important than optics, and, in time, I came to realize he was probably right.

Ford did bring into the White House several people with whom he had previous relationships. Bob Hartmann, who had been his Chief of Staff while Ford was Vice President, was promptly named the President's chief speechwriter and political advisor. He was born in Rapid City, South Dakota, the year America joined World War I. A Stanford graduate, Hartmann worked at the *Los Angeles Times*, enlisted in the Navy, and served in the Pacific during World War II as a public information officer for two outstanding naval officers— Admiral Chester W. Nimitz and, later, for Admiral William F. Halsey. After the war, Bob returned to the *Los Angeles Times* where, for more than two decades, he was an editorial writer, Washington bureau chief, and Middle East bureau chief. In 1966, he went to work for the House Republican Conference before becoming the senior aide to then Congressman Gerald Ford. A highly skilled speech-writer, Bob had the major role in many if not most of Gerald Ford's finest speeches.

Jerry terHorst, a veteran journalist with the *Detroit News*, was announced as the new White House Press Secretary. The son of Dutch immigrants, he was born in Grand Rapids, Michigan, in 1922. He received a degree from the University of Michigan in 1946, after serving in the Marine Corps in the Pacific theater during World War II. TerHorst, then a member of the press, had happened to be in the presidential motorcade during the assassination of President Kennedy.

Jack Marsh, a former Democratic Congressman from Virginia and National Security Advisor to then Vice President Ford, was named Counselor to the new President. Marsh, born in Winchester, Virginia, in 1926, enlisted in the Army in 1944 and was selected for Officer Candidate School at age eighteen. He served in the Army of Occupation of Germany and was a long-serving and dedicated member of the U.S. Army Reserve. Jack graduated from Washington and Lee in 1951, served with distinction in Vietnam, and then was elected as a Democrat to the U.S. House of Representatives from Virginia's Seventh District serving from 1963 to 1971. When we were in Congress, Jack's and my office were only a few doors apart, and we had become good friends. Jack was nominated to be the Assistant Secretary of Defense for Legislative Affairs in 1973, a position he held for just short of a year before being asked by Ford to join the Office of the Vice President. President Ford and I had both come to respect Jack enormously while we had served together as colleagues in the U.S. House of Representatives.

Marsh's appointment inadvertently demonstrated the tensions that lingered in the White House. When Ford announced in a meeting that Jack Marsh would become Counselor to the President—and focus on foreign policy and defense—I noticed Al Haig wince. Haig, whom Ford had announced he would keep on as his White House Chief of Staff, was sensitive to the fact that designating Marsh's responsibilities in that manner could be seen as infringing on Kissinger's carefully guarded portfolios as both the National Security Advisor and the Secretary of State. Jack Marsh was equally sensitive to the problem and immediately suggested to the President that his title not include a focus on foreign policy and defense.[26]

Haig had been President Nixon's second White House Chief of Staff following H. R. (Bob) Haldeman. Born near Philadelphia, Al earned degrees from the U.S. Military Academy, Columbia Business School, and Georgetown. He went on to a successful Army career, serving during the Korean and Vietnam Wars, rising to the rank of General after holding high-level positions in the Department of Defense and on the National Security Council in the Nixon White House. Replacing H. R. Haldeman, General Haig had earned praise for providing crucial leadership during the hardest days of the Nixon administration, when the President was increasingly embattled, isolated, and distracted.[27] Leon Jaworski, the second special prosecutor appointed during the Watergate investigations, and no Nixon partisan, later wrote, "In my own view, General Haig . . . performed in the highest and noblest tradition."[28]

Ford, who had gotten along well with Haig while he served as Vice President, overruled detractors within his camp and in the media and announced immediately that the general would remain in the role of Chief of Staff, continuing to manage White House staff access to the President, assisting in setting the executive agenda, and managing relationships with the Cabinet and the various executive agencies. As talented and experienced as these men were, and each was both experienced and highly skilled in their roles, some critics noted that the discredited Nixon's two most visible aides—Kissinger and Haig—would be continuing in the White House in the same exact roles.

MEETING WITH THE PRESIDENT
August 9, 1974
5:30 to 6:30 p.m.
Cabinet Room
The President indicated that he planned to start the day a little before 8:00 a.m., and as a regular thing have a CIA briefing with Jack Marsh present, see Bob Hartman [sic], do some office work, see Marsh on legislation, some press things, and at 10:00 a.m. start his visits. He said he was a better listener than a reader and that he did like to have things to read at home at night.[29]

The President explained that he intended to have an open Oval Office door for Cabinet officers—provided they had something substantive and important to discuss. The definitions of "substantive" and "important" he left to those seeking the meetings. He was notably uncomfortable with the public characterization of the Nixon White House as having had an "imperial character," which had been attributed to Nixon's senior aides Bob Haldeman and John Ehrlichman. They, along with Kissinger, had been given the moniker "the Berlin Wall," for seeming to be ferociously guarding access to the President. My view was different, having served in the White House and in the

Nixon Cabinet during most of the first four years of the Nixon presidency. I had observed and believed that Kissinger and Haldeman were without a doubt each performing in a manner that was what President Nixon requested and expected, though I was not as knowledgeable as to whether that was the case with Ehrlichman.

In any event, Ford was determined to upend what he saw as this insular approach. In his view, too few people with access to the Oval Office meant too few opportunities to broaden the knowledge of a President and of those of his key advisors. "The President has made it clear," attested Dr. Bob Goldwin, whom I had brought in as the Ford administration's unofficial "intellectual-in-residence," "that he wants to be an accessible President with a steady flow of information, opinions, and imaginative suggestions reaching the White House."[30] Ford called his preferred style a "spokes of a wheel" approach, with the President at the center and a range of advisors reporting to him.

In this new setup, a good many senior officials (the spokes) would theoretically each enjoy ready access to the singular President (the hub). That was the approach he had used with considerable success in the Congress as the Republican Leader. On a great many more than one occasion, I cautioned the President that that approach would not work well in the White House and that he could be "consumed" by it.[31] So many people would have access to him, each understandably believing his or her respective issues were of the upmost importance, that he would have little time to assure that the administration's key executives were concentrating on his priorities. Continuing with the "spokes of the wheel" analogy, I reminded him that what could happen was that the lubricant at the hub of the wheel would overheat and that the wheel might need to be replaced. My recommendation was that he get the U.S. government working off his "outbox"— his priorities—rather than he, as the President, working off his "inbox"—everyone else's priorities.

Ford had been Vice President for only eight months—246 days, to be exact, and had never served in an executive position. Conversely, since his service in the Navy in World War II, he had been a legislator for almost a quarter-century. As such, the Congress was his frame of reference when it came to decisions about management, organization, and personnel. As a member of Congress, he had not been required to manage a staff larger than perhaps a dozen or so people. As a result, the "spokes of the wheel" approach had been a well-developed pattern for him. Indeed, as a legislator and the leader of a group of elected legislators his role was to listen to them and lead. The presidency—needless to say—is an entirely different situation, with dozens of senior officials from the executive departments, agencies, boards, and commissions, plus the senior members of the Congress, as well as a great many important individuals outside of the government all vying for a President's attention and each, more often than not, with an understandably strong sense of urgency.[32]

The next morning at ten o'clock, I joined the President as he held his first Cabinet meeting. All of us were Nixon holdovers. But anyone there could sense that things were different. One change was cosmetic, but telling. On the wall in the Cabinet Room during the Nixon presidency were portraits of three Presidents: Abraham Lincoln, Woodrow Wilson, and Dwight D. Eisenhower. Nixon's affinity for Dwight Eisenhower, whom he had served with as Vice President, was understandable, as was his respect for Abraham Lincoln. Woodrow Wilson, a liberal Democrat who was an intellectual force behind a powerful and large federal government, was a bit puzzling. Ford decided to replace the Wilson portrait with that of a man who he believed better fit his approach, the plainspoken midwesterner Democrat Harry S. Truman, a "people's president," as President Ford called him.[33] Truman had also served as Vice President and become President by a historical event not of his choosing—the death of Franklin Roosevelt.

One of Nixon's most memorable Cabinet meetings, at least for me, had occurred immediately after his landslide re-election in 1972, when he had won forty-nine out of fifty states. Fresh from his historic triumph, Nixon entered the Cabinet Room to rousing cheers and an extended standing ovation. But rather than enjoying the moment and expressing warm appreciation to his team, the President began a meandering yet colorful lecture with seemingly no clear point. He spoke of various British Prime Ministers he admired, tossing in unusual comments, like, "Richard Nixon doesn't shoot blanks." Then he mentioned "exhausted volcanoes," a phrase he said Benjamin Disraeli had used to describe public servants drained of their energy and inspiration. As the session ended, Nixon exited the Cabinet Room to more muted applause and a few confused looks as to exactly what had just transpired, leaving his powerful Chief of Staff, H. R. Haldeman, to promptly—and without preface—ask each of the Cabinet members to tender their resignations and, moreover, to provide summaries of their responsibilities that could be helpful to whoever might replace them.[34]

A similar request might well have been anticipated by members of the Nixon Cabinet during their first meeting with President Ford. Instead Ford caught them by surprise. He thanked all of them for their service and then said he was counting on them to stay on. Going further to make his point absolutely clear, he said he would not accept any resignations that might be tendered.[35]

Of his predecessor, Ford expressed a surprising level of admiration and affection. In his first speech to the nation, he had closed by asking his fellow citizens to pray for Nixon and his family: "May our former President, who brought peace to millions, find it for himself." His instructions to the Cabinet were in keeping with that tone, adding that nothing about his administration should reflect negatively upon the previous administration. Ford also put forward an assessment of the political atmosphere that differed sharply with the one many pundits and political analysts were providing. He said he believed there was a reservoir of sympathy for former President Nixon across the country. He further suggested it would last—and possibly even increase—particularly if Nixon's adversaries were to continue efforts of harassment or revenge.

With respect to any legal steps he might take with respect to Mr. Nixon, the President phrased his comments carefully. He simply advised, "Time is a healer." He closed his remarks by requesting those gathered not to speculate about a "pardon," though talk of a pardon was clearly in the air.[36]

It was characteristic of Ford to feel sympathy for the beleaguered former President. Nixon had been through a great deal, Ford believed. He and his family had been disgraced. But Ford's basic human decency may have led him to not fully sense the lingering anger and deep disappointment of a great many Americans and, for some, how much they had come to disapprove of the former President. To many, Nixon's departure was taken not as a denouement, but as a beginning.

After his remarks on Nixon, Ford opened a discussion of his plans for selecting a Vice President. He indicated he had asked the Republican National Chairman to solicit suggestions from GOP leaders across the country. He requested suggestions from the Cabinet members and from his senior advisors, asking that they be funneled through Al Haig.[37]

After Ford concluded his remarks, Kissinger, as Secretary of State and the senior Cabinet member, was the first to speak. He pointed out that an opportunity to perform a national service was what had initially brought people to serve in the federal government. He assured the President he could count on total loyalty and unflagging support from the members of the Cabinet. As his final comment, he forcefully advised that "the fate of the country—and the world" depended upon the success of the Ford administration.[38]

Peter Brennan—then Secretary of Labor—said we all owed allegiance to the new President and needed to get on with the tough task of piecing the country back together. Agriculture Secretary Earl Butz suggested a need to prevent erosion of conservative support on Capitol Hill. The President shifted the tone, demurring that he had not had time to think about the politics of the situation.[39]

In words that almost certainly hadn't been uttered in the White House in years, the President then urged members of the Cabinet to improve the administration's relations with the media, to be less defensive, and to be more "affirmative."[40] To underscore this, he led by example, moving smartly from his first Cabinet meeting as President to the White House press room to personally introduce to reporters Jerry terHorst, the man he had selected to be his new Press Secretary.

At least a few Nixon veterans resentful of the media must have considered the President's hopeful tone a bit naïve. Many had been hunkered down in struggles against what they saw as the liberal media for years. When he was Nixon's Vice President, Spiro Agnew memorably called the members of the press corps "nattering nabobs of negativity." But the gesture was pure Jerry Ford. He had enjoyed excellent relations with reporters as a member of Congress and sincerely believed that should and could continue. Yet the move also likely involved a calculation—and a shrewd one on his part—that such unexpected openness and candor might help to bleed some of the prior administration's lingering toxins from the political bloodstream.

President Ford's strikingly different approach proved effective. As he began his new administration, there was a sense of optimism in the public and even among many in the media. "[I]n the person of Gerald Ford, the United States just may have proved itself once again to have the greatest of national assets: good luck," wrote the liberal columnist Anthony Lewis. "When President Ford took the oath of office and said his few words of reassuring modesty, it was as if a cloud had lifted. Words once more had a simple, direct meaning."[41]

The New York Times, a leading critic of Richard Nixon, opined, "Out of the morass of Watergate, the nation has planted its feet on solid ground once again. Out of the tragedy of Mr. Nixon has evolved the triumph of America."[42]

Defying the bitter atmosphere of the moment, Gerald R. Ford's open and earnest approach earned him an impressive, and almost unimaginable 71 percent approval rating upon his taking office.[43] The American people, and even the Washington, D.C., press corps, seemed willing to give the new guy a chance, though it wasn't clear for how long.

3

The Pardon

MEETING WITH THE PRESIDENT

October 9, 1974

11:00 a.m. to 12:00 Noon

I said I didn't want to get in the subject with him but I did feel that he should know that I received a phone call on 10/4/74 from Haig on the pardon and that Haig had said that it was going to get dirty and I will blow the place wide open if I have to and it'll be a goddamn bloody mess and no more of these second rate people around the President are going to challenge my integrity and devotion to my country and I've got Nixon, Garment, Buzzhardt, Ziegler and others with me and I've got verbatim records and I'll do it. . . . I stopped Haig and said, Look, I've taken enough and that he was very friendly to me. I said I didn't want to get in to the subject and that I thought the President ought to be aware of it. A. Because Haig obviously called me so I would tell the President about it, B. because I felt that the President ought to be aware of Haig's comment that he has "verbatim records." The President started to discuss it with me and I said, look, Mr. President, I don't need to get into it—I simply wanted you to be aware of that message.[1]

On September 5, 1974, a U.S. Air Force jet touched down at Marine Corps Air Station El Toro in the black of night, the midnight arrival adding to a sense of intrigue. For the past six years, El Toro had been a frequent stop for U.S. military aircraft, in part because of its proximity to a mid-sized California city whose most prominent resident was now back home, trapped in an exile largely of his own making.

After the jet came to rest on the tarmac and its plug door opened, a thirty-six-year-old man emerged, tired and jetlagged, but prepared to quickly head to La Casa Pacifica, former President Nixon's compound on the beach in nearby San Clemente.[2] Benton L. Becker, a former prosecutor, had practiced law for less than a decade, having graduated from American University's Washington College of Law in 1966. He had been on the staff of the House Judiciary Committee where he came to know and gain the confidence of the then Minority Leader, Congressman Gerald R. Ford.[3] So much was he trusted by Ford that he was one of only a handful of people aware that the new President was considering a pardon of his disgraced predecessor. A draft of a pardon was now tucked in Becker's briefcase on its way to meet with the former President.[4]

Accompanying Becker on the flight was Nixon's personal lawyer, Herbert J. Miller. A pioneer of white-collar criminal defense, Miller had earlier served as chief of the Justice Department's criminal division from 1961 to 1965, successfully prosecuting Teamsters leader Jimmy Hoffa and some members of organized crime families.

A few days earlier, Miller had met with Phil Buchen and several other Ford administration officials in Washington to discuss the wording of a letter that outlined a proposed federal facility near San Clemente to store Watergate papers and tapes. At one point, however, Buchen noted that Ford was giving consideration to granting Nixon a pardon. Buchen recommended that, to reciprocate, Miller persuade his client, Richard M. Nixon, to agree to a statement of genuine contrition. Miller allowed that such a statement, one admitting involvement in Watergate, was appropriate given what would surely prove to be a momentous and contentious action. Yet Miller was not optimistic about extracting one.[5] He believed that Nixon's "... ability for objective mental recollection on that subject [Watergate] [was] poor."[6] To help him make the case, Miller asked the administration to send with him an emissary—Mr. Becker—to present the case to the former President and his team personally.

Some in the new Ford administration considered Becker's mission doomed from the start. "You'll never get it," Chief of Staff Al Haig advised.[7] Haig had stood by Nixon during the long struggle against his political and legal opponents and lived through multitudes of Nixonian denials and self-justifications. It was simply impossible for Haig—and undoubtedly anyone in Nixon's inner circle—to imagine the former President affording his "enemies" the penitence they sought and believed was appropriate. Still, Ford instructed Becker to evaluate Nixon's readiness to offer an acknowledgment of his conduct. "Be very firm out there and tell me what you see," he advised, arm on Becker's shoulder, before he left the White House on his confidential assignment.[8]

Arriving at San Clemente in the early morning hours, Becker and Miller first met with Nixon's former White House Press Secretary Ron Ziegler, an experienced political operative and spokesman who had earned his reputation as among Nixon's most stalwart loyalists.[9]

Armed with what Becker believed to be "inside" information from Haig about what Ford was considering, Ziegler quickly moved to take ownership of the terms of the meeting. "I can tell you right now," he declared, "that President Nixon will make no statement of admission of complicity [regarding Watergate] in return for a pardon from Jerry Ford."

To Becker, this assertion had the "ring" of having been rehearsed.[10]

The fact that Ziegler called Nixon "President" and referred to the actual President by just his last name also wasn't lost on Becker.

To test what he hoped was Ziegler's bluff, he asked for a way to contact his pilot about prepping the plane for an immediate return to Washington. At this point, Ziegler softened his position, tensions eased a bit, and their discussion proceeded. If Ford was considering granting a pardon, Becker insisted that there needed to be some acknowledgment of a sense of guilt on Nixon's part for what the nation had been through. The first draft of Nixon's acceptance of the pardon, as prepared by Ziegler, was wanting. (Ford later would recall it as "disastrous.")[11] It read, in its entirety, "In accordance with the law, I accept this pardon."[12] Becker sent Ziegler back to the typewriter. Nixon's Press Secretary went through three more drafts. Becker found none of them satisfactory.[13]

Later that day, Becker finally was given an audience with Nixon. Meeting in a sparsely furnished room in his San Clemente home, Becker found what he saw was a broken man—a haunting image that left him with a lingering feeling of "freakish grotesqueness."[14] "I was shocked," he noted in a memo on the meeting. The former President was rail-thin, giving his head an outsized appearance. He appeared frail and even almost frightened.[15] "Had I never known of the man before and met him for the first time," Becker wrote of the then sixty-one-year-old former President, "I would have estimated his age to be 85."[16] In their brief conversation, Nixon appeared to drift in and out. Pained to discuss the topic of a pardon, he kept trying to change the subject to safer matters or "trivia," like football. [17]

Searching to give the lawyer a parting gift—perhaps a presidential tie clip or cuff links as he might have were he still in the White House—Nixon came up empty. "I don't have anything anymore," he conceded. "They took it all away from me. Everything I had is gone."[18] He finally gave Becker a set of cuff links and a tie pin from "my personal jewelry box." "There aren't any more of these in the world," Nixon said. "You got the last one."[19]

The scene offered Becker what he called "the most sad, pathetic frame of mind I've ever seen in my life."[20]

Nixon, it became clear, would not agree to a full statement of contrition that Ford wanted and believed that the country needed. Nixon may well have been incapable of it. Ford made plans to go forward anyway, in what would be one of the most consequential—and politically calamitous—decisions of his nascent presidency.

Nearly one month earlier, on August 9, 1974, the day Ford had been sworn in, aides to Leon Jaworski, then the special prosecutor in the Watergate case, had drafted a memo weighing the pros and cons of prosecuting Richard Nixon. "In our view," the memo argued, "there is clear evidence that Richard M. Nixon participated in a conspiracy to obstruct justice by concealing the identity of those responsible for the Watergate break-in and other criminal offenses." The memo continued: "There is a presumption (which in the past we have operated upon) that Richard M. Nixon, like every citizen, is subject to the rule of law. Accordingly, one begins with the premise that if there is sufficient evidence, Mr. Nixon should be indicted and prosecuted. The question then becomes whether the presumption for proceeding is outweighed by the factors mandating against indictment and prosecution."[21]

The main arguments the aides cited in favor of Nixon's arrest, indictment, and prosecution were: the "principle of equal justice"; that the country would remain divided without a final disposition of charges; that the lack of action might encourage a future President to commit acts of lawlessness; and that a resignation alone might not be "sufficient retribution" for such criminal offenses. Among the factors cited that weighed against arrest, indictment, and prosecution were: that the embarrassment and disgrace associated with resignation would be punishment enough; that prosecution would "aggravate" the nation's divisions; and that pretrial publicity might make it hard, if not impossible, for Nixon to receive a fair trial.[22]

From the outset, Ford indicated that he was sympathetic to the latter view. He knew a trial of a former President would not only be unprecedented, but also would reopen wounds and divisions over the Watergate scandal. Ford had asked White House Counsel Phil Buchen to inquire of Jaworski just how much time a criminal prosecution would take. Jaworski responded that, with various legal considerations, it would be at least nine months before Nixon was even brought to trial.[23] Then the trial itself, if it were to take place, would last an indeterminate amount of time, and could conceivably lead to additional unsavory revelations about the Nixon administration. It would surely be a protracted, drama-filled affair in which there would be very few, if any, "winners."

Also, driving Ford were the questions from the members of the media at his first press conference, which had taken place on August 28. Ford had prepared to field a wide variety of questions, from the pending negotiations with the Soviet Union on a nuclear arms agreement to the precarious situation in Cyprus. Instead, his encounter with White House press corps was dominated by inquiries about Nixon and Watergate. The very first question, from reporter Helen Thomas, was whether Ford believed Nixon should receive immunity from prosecution. That was followed by a grilling about what Ford believed should be Nixon's fate, including whether the President was considering a pardon. Was this, the President later asked an aide, what he was going to face every time he met with members of the media?[24]

There was also a human element to consider. Ford, as noted, had made no secret of his sympathy for his longtime friend, who was in declining health, by some reports both mentally and physically. At the White House, we received periodic reports that the former President was despondent over his predicament. Kids were throwing what was euphemistically referred to as "dog dirt"—actually dog excrement—from the beach onto Nixon's property in San Clemente.[25] Pat Nixon, too, felt under siege in the community. "She disappeared from public view," noted historian David Lester, "secluded behind the high walls and impenetrable trees and shrubbery of the 5.9 acre estate where they had gone to live."[26] Ford heard disturbing reports that Mrs. Nixon needed to wear wigs and disguises just to go out shopping.[27]

Adding to his problems, Nixon, soon after leaving office, suffered a blood clot in his leg, a painful ailment that he had experienced on other occasions. As his situation deteriorated, a physician who had examined Nixon advised reporters that the former President was "a ravaged man who has lost the will to fight" and characterized his condition as "critical."[28] Nixon had never been known to pay much attention to his health, Ford, the former football player and excellent athlete, once mentioned to me. As a result, Nixon, who had been a workaholic, didn't have much reserve to rely on when he needed it.[29] To Ford, pardoning Nixon was what he believed was the humanitarian—and the Christian—thing to do.

As he had remarked during his first Cabinet meeting, Ford believed there was a reservoir of sympathy for Nixon's plight across the country. "We are not a vengeful people," he told himself. Regardless of the passions of the moment, he did not believe the country truly wanted to see an ex-President behind bars.[30] To a segment of the Republican Party, those who had stuck with Nixon until the end, that was certainly true. But public polling indicated that most of the country felt otherwise. A significant majority—56 percent in one poll—believed that Nixon ought to be tried.[31]

Only a very small number of Ford's closest aides knew that a pardon for Nixon was being considered. They included Phil Buchen, Benton Becker, Henry Kissinger, Al Haig, Jack Marsh, and Bob Hartmann.[32] Kissinger, Ford later noted, made an "impressive" argument for the merits of a pardon, arguing that the trial of a former President would damage America's standing abroad.[33] Having left Washington, D.C., and returned to my post overseas as the U.S. Ambassador to NATO in Brussels, Belgium, I was not aware of any of these discussions or considerations.

When Ford made his final decision to pardon Nixon, he did it without making any political calculations. He did not, for example, share his intention with any Republican members of Congress, where he certainly would have been able to find some support. Nor did he take any steps to prepare a media strategy. To the contrary, on learning of Ford's decision to pardon Nixon, the newly appointed White House Press Secretary, Jerry terHorst, promptly submitted his resignation thirty minutes before Ford was scheduled to address the nation on his decision. For a month, the former newsman had rebuffed the White House press corps' suspicion that a pardon might be forthcoming. In his resignation letter to President Ford, which he unhelpfully released to the press, terHorst wrote, "So it is with great regret, after long soul-searching, that I must inform you that I cannot in good conscience support your decision to pardon Richard Nixon even before he has been charged with the commission of any crime. As your spokesman, I do not know how I could credibly defend that decision."[34]

This very personal rebuke from a friend did not dissuade President Ford, who, as I knew well, was firm, even in some cases unmovable, once he had come to a decision. "Once I determine to move, I seldom, if ever, fret," Ford later noted. "I have confidence that my lifetime batting average is high, and I'm prepared to live with the consequences."[35] Hand-wringing and second-guessing were foreign concepts to Gerald Ford, a trait I admired.

On September 8, 1974, Ford delivered a ten-minute address to the nation, which he believed, or at least hoped, would put the Watergate scandal firmly in the past. It was a bit after 11:00 a.m. and was preceded by Sunday services at St. John's Church across Lafayette Square from the White House.

From behind the Wilson desk and with thick, gold curtains and the leafy South Lawn as the backdrop, the President spoke to the nation in a calm, deliberate tone. "I have learned already in this office that the difficult decisions always come to this desk," he began. Trying to get ahead of criticism about the timing of the decision—one that came before Nixon had even been charged with a crime—he said, "To procrastinate, to agonize, and to wait for a more favorable turn of events that may never come or more compelling external pressures that may as well be wrong as right, is itself a decision of sorts and a weak and potentially dangerous course for a President to follow." Of the Nixon family, Ford said, "Theirs is an American tragedy, in which we all have played a part. It could go on and on and on, or someone must write the end to it. I have concluded that only I can do that and, if I can, I must."[36]

What may have most offended Nixon's opponents was the passion of Ford's defense of his friend, as the sound of Sunday church bells could be heard in the background. "It is common knowledge that serious allegations and accusations hang like a sword over our former president's head," he stated, "threatening his health as he tries to reshape his life, a great part of which was spent in service of this country and by the mandate of its people."[37]

When his remarks ended, Ford walked down to the office of his Assistant for Legislative Affairs, Bill Timmons, to learn the reactions from his former colleagues in Congress. Pipe clenched between his teeth, Ford stood, ironically, under photos that still depicted Nixon as President and Ford as Vice President. Even after a month, they had not yet been changed.[38] Ford's talented and ever-present Pulitzer

Prize–winning photographer, David Hume Kennerly, who became a surrogate son of sorts to the Fords, was in the room with the President both before and after his address. "What I found shocking," Kennerly recalls, "was that almost everyone who called in that morning privately told the president that he had done the right thing, but publicly went out and lambasted him."[39]

Democrat Tip O'Neill, the House Majority Leader, who was a friend of Ford's, asked bluntly, "Jesus, don't you think it's kind of early?"[40] One of the most shocked members of the "establishment" was *Washington Post* reporter Carl Bernstein, who along with his colleague Bob Woodward, had participated in reporting on the Watergate scandal. "You're not gonna believe it," Bernstein said to Woodward. "The son of a bitch pardoned the son of a bitch!"[41] Senator Edward Kennedy, then contemplating his own bid for the presidency in 1976, blasted the decision in a speech in Los Angeles. "So we operate under a system of equal justice under the law?" he sarcastically asked his audience. "Or is there one system for the average citizen, and another for the high and mighty?" However, an unexpected source of support came from Georgia Governor Jimmy Carter, Ford's future Democratic rival.[42]

The outsized negative reaction may have been prompted not necessarily by the issuance of the pardon itself, but by the fact that it seemed to exonerate Nixon without an admission of guilt. "Mr. Ford's decision was not unexpected, in light of his previous statements that he thought the former President had suffered enough by being forced from office," *The New York Times* reported. "Yet the unconditional nature of the pardon, taken without the recommendation of Mr. Jaworski, was more generous to Mr. Nixon than many had expected."[43]

A number of pundits had anticipated that the resolution of Mr. Nixon's situation would dovetail with that of his former Vice President, Spiro Agnew. When Agnew was being forced to resign the previous October, he pled "no contest" to a charge of tax evasion and agreed to a bill of particulars that detailed a number of other serious charges, such as accepting bribes from engineering contractors while he was Governor of Maryland. Even after becoming Vice President, Agnew had brazenly continued taking cash payouts—bribes—in white envelopes while sitting in the Office of the Vice President of the United States in the Old Executive Office Building—right in the White House complex.

To broker the removal of Vice President Agnew, Attorney General Elliot Richardson reportedly offered to recommend a nonprison sentence for Agnew in return for his resignation and a declaration of culpability.[44] (Agnew's "no contest" plea was in effect an acceptance of the charges against him.) As early as December 1973, *The New York Times* had reported rumors of a so-called Agnew deal in which President Nixon similarly "could arrange to step down, that is, in return for certain assurances from President-to-be Ford that indictments or other legal actions would not be pursued in the case of a private citizen named Richard Nixon."[45]

Unfortunately, Nixon's statement accepting the pardon proved less than satisfactory to much of the country, despite Ford and Becker's efforts. "Looking back on what is still in my mind a complex and confusing maze of events, decisions, pressures and personalities," the statement read in part, "one thing I can see clearly now is that I was wrong in not acting more decisively and more forthrightly in dealing with Watergate." And while he accepted fault for some of the impact of the scandal, he resisted specifically conceding that he had contributed to the scandal. "I know many fair-minded people believe that my motivations and action in the Watergate affair were intentionally self-serving and illegal," he said. "I now understand how my own mistakes and misjudgments have contributed to that belief and seemed to support it. This burden is the heaviest one of all to bear. That the way I tried to deal with Watergate was the wrong way is a burden I shall bear for every day of the life that is left to me."[46] In short, Nixon had refrained from acknowledging that any of his actions or decisions were illegal.

Though many members of the press—and the public—were understandably deeply dissatisfied with Nixon's lack of clear public contrition, some of the things the former President *did* acknowledge utterly astonished at least one of his longtime and closest senior aides. Al Haig, after seeing Nixon's proposed pardon statement, asked Becker whether he had put a gun to the former President's head.[47]

In Ford's mind, Nixon had not gotten off scot-free. Ford had come across a 1915 Supreme Court case, *Burdick* v. *United States,* which ruled that a pardon carried an "imputation of guilt," and, therefore, accepting a pardon was, as such, "an admission of guilt."[48] For a time, to justify his stunning decision, Ford kept a clipping of the *Burdick* case's ruling in his wallet.[49] One biographer noted that *Burdick* "had redefined the whole concept of a pardon. Issuing a pardon did not mean exoneration of the recipient, as many people thought. Instead, a pardon rendered a verdict without a trial—or punishment. Ford, believing that was the case, seized on the point."[50]

Convinced his was the right decision, Ford saw no reason to hang around the White House on a Sunday afternoon to second-guess it. Instead he headed to Maryland for a round of golf with his friend and former colleague from the Congress Mel Laird, who had served as Nixon's Secretary of Defense. Speaking to reporters afterward, Laird offered a defense of Ford's timing, noting that the furor would have been far greater had Ford waited until Nixon had been indicted to issue the pardon.[51] Back at the White House, "angry calls, heavy and constant" began jamming the switchboards.[52]

Throughout the rest of Ford's presidency, fomented by Nixon critics in the media where they were thick in number, suspicion about the circumstances surrounding the pardon lingered. A whopping 71 percent polled by *Time* magazine believed then that Ford may not have told the country the whole truth about the circumstances of the pardon.[53] The suspicion was that in exchange for stepping down, Nixon might have been promised that he would be exonerated by his successor. The optics were, of course, unfortunate—closely consulting with only a very few key aides, as well as with the two most prominent Nixon officials, Haig and Kissinger. Also, as House Speaker Tip O'Neill noted, Ford had pardoned the former president in a manner that seemed to many to be too hasty—thirty days after taking office. Gerald R. Ford, as honest and as forthright a human being as one could ever meet in a lifetime, repeatedly stated both before and after the pardon that he had not entered the presidency with any kind of an understanding to pardon his predecessor. To those who knew Ford well, there is no question as to whether that was true.

I had already returned to Brussels to my post as U.S. Ambassador to NATO. As a result, I was as caught off guard by the momentous decision as anyone else. Nonetheless, I knew the personal mettle and integrity of Jerry Ford and had seen it up close for years. The American people had not. And with the first major decision of his presidency, many were not ready to give him the benefit of the doubt. As a result, much of the goodwill the new president had achieved with the American people and the media evaporated. A Gallup poll at the time of the pardon found that a significant majority of the nation—55 percent—believed Ford's decision was the "wrong thing" to do, as opposed to only 35 percent who felt it was "the right thing."[54] In any event, as a result of the pardon, Ford's approval rating began a steady decline, falling from his high of 71 percent in August 1974 down to 40 percent by December 1974.

It's easy for someone to say in retrospect, but there were a number of things I might have advised Ford to do before announcing the pardon to soften its impact. Had he surfaced his thinking to a larger group of trusted friends—of which he had a great many on both sides of the aisle in the Congress—many might well have been prepared to support his decision and to help him find a way to make his decision more acceptable to the nation. He also might have gotten a better sense of the outrage his decision could provoke, even within his own party. Many Republicans were angry at President Nixon for his role in the Watergate scandal, and for not being truthful or forthcoming with those who had supported him. Had I been in Washington, D.C., and had Ford asked my opinion about a possible pardon, I'm not sure what I would have counseled. After I returned to the White House that October, in fact, Ford expressed to me his interest in calling an ailing President Nixon, who had been in the hospital. I argued against the call, telling Ford that I understood his sympathy for his predecessor but that Nixon had misled the American people regardless of his concern for what's right and wrong—and I noted "he had damaged hundreds of human beings by betraying them. Further, he betrayed the goals that all of them were working for." I said that I personally had felt angry and betrayed. Ford listened carefully to this, and while he might have been caught off guard by my reaction, he certainly understood it. The President didn't call Nixon that evening.[55]

With his reputation hurt and the credibility of the presidency once again badly damaged, the President's already formidable hurdles to getting the country back on track became extraordinary. And despite President Ford's completely honorable intentions, the ghosts of Watergate did not depart as easily or quickly as he had hoped.

One week after the presidential pardon, on September 16, 1974, my father, George Rumsfeld, died in Illinois at the age of sixty-nine. My dad had been suffering from Alzheimer's disease, which had been stressful for all of us, especially my mother. She had been the one who had to go out to find him when he became lost and disoriented and to comfort him when he became frightened and didn't know where he was or recognize those around him. Despite his heavy burdens, the President had periodically asked me about my father's declining health, and upon hearing the news, he and Betty sent a note of condolence. "Our hearts go out to you and your family in the loss of your father. Betty and I share your sorrow and we pray that God's love will comfort you and your loved ones at this sad and difficult time."[56] I flew back from my post in Belgium to help my mother and sister with arrangements and to attend the funeral service. I was scheduled to return promptly to my responsibilities at NATO, but President Ford called me in Illinois, and requested that I come to the White House to meet with him before heading back to Europe. As it turned out, what he had in mind was someone to replace Al Haig as Chief of Staff.

General Haig, who was understandably used to a more orderly and structured chain of authority, was feeling the frustration of the new President's more relaxed management style. Knowing what I'd known about Ford's "spokes of the wheel" management philosophy, I had neither the interest nor the intention of leaving NATO to return to the White House. My family and I were relieved to be out of Washington, D.C., and out of the White House after my seven-plus years in the Congress and my almost four years in the Nixon Cabinet. But of course I needed to hear him out and offer whatever advice I might have had. Perhaps I could think of others who might be able to help.

On Sunday, September 22, I traveled to Washington and spent an hour and a half with the President in the Oval Office. Though controversy about the pardon had not dissipated, Ford was relaxed. We spent the early part of our meetings talking about our dads. Ford's adoptive father, Gerald R. Ford, Sr., was a hardworking man of integrity and compassion—Ford once said of him that he "loved me as much as he loved his own three sons"—and had informed the President's perspective of people and the world.

Our talk turned to the White House. Ford was open about the

fact that things were not working as well as he wanted or had hoped. There were personnel issues smoldering that required attention. To the President's annoyance, Jerry terHorst, the Press Secretary who had resigned in protest over Ford's pardon of Mr. Nixon, was now back at the *Detroit News* and Ford felt he was lacing his columns for his paper with information acquired during his brief White House stint.[57] The President's two closest key aides, Al Haig and his former vice presidential Chief of Staff Bob Hartmann, were feuding, which bothered the President greatly—though he, accurately, saw that the barbs being leaked to the media were flowing largely from Hartmann.

I had sympathy for both Hartmann's and Haig's predicaments. As Ford put it, moving with him to the presidency "had been a tough transition for Bob." For years, Bob had been Ford's right-hand man—in the Congress and then in the vice presidency. And now suddenly he was not. As Ford had noted on a number of occasions, Bob liked to "stir the pot."[58]

Haig, meanwhile, knew that Bob was leaking negative stories to the media about the man Hartmann saw as "the holdover Chief of Staff." "You've got to get this guy under control," Haig had, rather bluntly, notified President Ford. "Otherwise, I can't serve you."[59] In Hartmann's view, Haig was stonewalling Hartmann's access to the President, while Haig understood there could be only one Chief of Staff at a time.

Ford, however, told me that he wasn't certain Haig had enough fuel left for the tough job ahead of him. Watergate understandably had taken its toll. Haig's name was surfacing frequently in media discussions about the Nixon pardon. Al was a man of the military and, understandably, appeared to be growing "weary of White House intrigue."[60] Haig wanted to move on, Ford said, and the President, as was his way, was as direct as possible with me about whom he insisted he needed as Haig's replacement.

For my part, I was equally direct. I told the President that I wanted to be as helpful as I could, but I absolutely did not want that job. We talked at some length about the fundamental differences between his role as the Minority Leader and that of the President. We had an extensive conversation about how the White House needed to operate, which was fundamentally different from his congressional leadership office. I stressed, again, the need for him to replace the dysfunctional "spokes-of-the-wheel" approach, which he had employed so successfully in the Congress, but which was clearly draining his time and energy. He urgently needed to institute a more traditional structure of a kind used by Eisenhower's and Nixon's Chiefs of Staff—Governor Sherman Adams and Bob Haldeman. "There has to be order," I emphasized. The presidency cannot afford disorder and the country cannot afford disorder in the White House.

Ford remained uncomfortable with his impression of the Haldeman model. Specifically, he had been advised that every paper from a Cabinet officer to Nixon did not necessarily reach the President. Rather, senior White House staff would often provide cover memos that characterized the Cabinet officer's request or a preferred position. This sort of system made Ford uneasy. "I do not like agreed positions," Ford said, meaning presenting him a formed consensus before he'd heard the facts.[61] Ford would rather have senior officials offering their views to him so that he could then weigh the pros and cons himself. He did not want all the issues being decided before the matter was brought to his attention.

But President Ford's less restrictive approach was essentially the opposite of the Nixon approach. It had resulted in the President's struggling to try to manage his schedule and referee a range of differences and competing views.

Nonetheless, Ford would not relent with his request that I come back to the White House. About an hour into our discussion, I sensed he was softening on the management ideas he had adopted. He insisted that he wanted me to become his "chief White House coordinator." He preferred that title over "Chief of Staff," since it sounded less like what he saw as a discredited Nixon model. Further, he told me that he only needed me in the White House for the early portion of his presidency.

"Come on, Rummy," he finally pleaded. "Say yes."

I responded with a laugh and a smile. And he knew he had me.

Fully aware that I would need whatever help I could get, I went about an important task: finding the right person to become my deputy. Dick Cheney, then thirty-three, had worked with me in various capacities in the Nixon administration, first when I was the Director of the Office of Economic Opportunity, then when I served as Director of the Economic Stabilization Project and in the White House in my role as an Assistant to President Nixon and a member of the Cabinet. I had come to rely on him for his consistently excellent judgment and his unflappable demeanor. I knew from close observation that the tougher the assignment, the better Dick performed. So after I briefed the President and secured his approval, Dick agreed to come on board. It was one of, if not the, best decisions I made in my new role.

At Ford's behest, I began an effort to reduce "White House trappings." This involved, for example, cutting back on some of the perquisites of office, including the use of government vehicles.[62] The size of the presidential staff had ballooned under President Nixon, from 250 when he took office in 1969 to 540 when I returned to the White House in September 1974. Ford had agreed with my recommendation to start paring the staff down, particularly when it came to the large number of "floaters" whose duties seemed to me to be poorly defined. However, this led to considerable staff resistance. Even the President balked when I suggested that the staff cuts I was proposing would include the First Lady's East Wing staff.

My wife, Joyce, and I had known Betty Ford for many years. She was a fantastic person, charismatic, good-humored, and full of life. She could also be a tough adversary, even when she was a friendly one. When I asked the President to inform his wife of my proposed cuts for her office, he smiled. "Don, this is your idea. You go to Betty and tell her." The size of Mrs. Ford's staff remained largely unchanged.

Inefficiencies in any part of the White House operation would lead to avoidable problems down the line. There were even some relatively minor issues that never seemed to get resolved. I was astounded one day to find an open bar in the White House staff lounge at 8:00 a.m. I had gone there to get some coffee, and sitting out in plain view—while the President was hosting visitors, no less—were two pitchers of cold Bloody Marys.[63] That practice was promptly discontinued.

Compounding our challenges, Watergate remained a lingering, seemingly permanent, and notably unwelcome presence in the White House. There was a heightened sensitivity to even the suggestion of impropriety by federal officeholders. Thus we knew we needed to be scrupulously careful to ensure that ethics, as well as perceptions, in the Ford White House were beyond question, let alone reproach—even when it came to totally innocent situations.

A few small moments demonstrated the heightened sensitivities. In one instance, I was set to begin my official White House responsibilities as the Assistant to the President and a member of the President's Cabinet on Monday, September 30. On the Saturday before, I started the process of moving into the Chief of Staff's office in the West Wing that had been occupied previously by Bob Haldeman and then later by Al Haig. We cleaned out the place from top to bottom. "I wanted to make sure," I noted in a memo, "that there was nothing in the place that I didn't want there, such as recording equipment, telephone bugs or the like." That's when we encountered a locked safe that had apparently been there since the days of Bob Haldeman. General Haig apparently had never opened it.

Concerned it could contain sensitive documents—or even materials that might be relevant with respect to one of the many various Watergate investigations and prosecutions which were under way—I decided to arrange for the appropriate authorities to take it in hand. To make extra sure that the Ford administration would not be implicated in anything even remotely connected to what someone might contend was a cover-up, I requested that the removal process be monitored and documented with transfer receipts. We learned later that the safe had been blown open and found to be empty.[64]

We also moved with caution after my assistant Brenda Williams came across fourteen recording tapes in one of the secretarial desks.[65] Not long afterward, Don Lowitz, a trusted consultant to the White House on legal and ethics matters, found twenty-five cartridges of MT/ST tapes, each encased in a plastic IBM container. By this point, "there was a well-established procedure for handling these sorts of 'discoveries,'" White House counsel Phil Buchen informed Lowitz.[66]

After White House photographer David Kennerly told me of his intention to purchase a two-hundred-dollar golden retriever for the President, I called White House Counsel Phil Buchen to see if there was a regulation about staff members providing gifts of value to more senior officials.[67] Lowitz expressed concern, noting that such a gift would not at the time meet certain exceptions.[68] Ultimately the Counsel cleared it, and the eight-month-old Honor's Foxfire Liberty Hume, better known as "Liberty," became a welcome member of the First Family that fall.

It was not long before members of the Congress and reporters began to scrutinize and discuss the size and cost of the former President's staff operation in San Clemente. Both in the White House and up on Capitol Hill there was a growing concern that a resigned President, the first in U.S. history, and one who had been accused of having committed crimes, should not be entitled to a replication of the White House staff, albeit a smaller version. In response to a request from the Senate Appropriations Committee, the Ford White House staff put together a list of the by then thirty-three individuals assigned to Mr. Nixon's so-called transition staff. They ranged from Coast Guardsmen to personnel from the General Services Administration and the National Archives to personal aides like his loyal close associates Ron Ziegler, Rosemary Woods, Jack Brennan, and Diane Sawyer, before Nixon began to assume more of the cost burden.

President Ford's justification for his pardon decision also was coming under continuing scrutiny, buttressed by new reporting. Journalists began to raise questions, for example, about whether Mr. Nixon's health was as poor as was being publicly portrayed. *The New York Times* had quoted Richard Nixon's brother, Donald, who had unhelpfully said soon after visiting the former President that he found him "in extremely good health and spirits."[69] He undoubtedly said it to try to be supportive of his older brother. Further, wildly inaccurate allegations, suspicions, and rumors persisted of an alleged secret deal supposedly brokered by Al Haig, whom President Ford had since nominated to serve as Supreme Allied Commander in Europe, once he had left his post as White House Chief of Staff. In one major newspaper, Haig was quoted as warning Ford in late August that a pardon was essential to avoiding "a personal and national tragedy"—an allusion to the possibility of a complete physical breakdown by Nixon.[70]

Jerry terHorst claimed publicly that President Ford spent too much time "placating the sensitive feelings" of Haig, who was allegedly pushing for a pardon.[71] "Nixon's preoccupation with Watergate had magnified Haig's authority in the White House and the executive branch of government," terHorst reported. "For most of the final Nixon year, as Haig himself would agree, he was the acting President of the United States."[72] In an effort to quiet rumors that his Chief of

Staff was behind the pardon, Ford felt compelled to issue a statement to the press: "Al Haig never discussed with me the mental or physical condition of former President Nixon prior to my decision to grant the pardon."[73]

For his part, Haig was justifiably angry that his conduct and integrity were being put into question. Shortly after I had succeeded Haig, he telephoned me from his new post in Belgium in a heated mood. "This is going to get dirty," he said, "and I'll blow the place wide open if I have to and it'll be a goddamn bloody mess and no more of these second-rate people around the President are going to challenge my integrity and devotion to my country."

Haig, who had talked to Nixon regularly since Nixon's resignation,[74] gave me, and in effect asked me to give President Ford, the ominous-sounding warning that "I've got Nixon, Garment, Buzzhardt, Ziegler and others with me and I've got verbatim records and I'll do it." I had no idea what he was talking about. My guess was he thought the Ford forces, particularly Bob Hartmann, were trying to hang him out to dry unfairly, and he wanted the President to know he wasn't going to put up with it.

The President had his own view of what Haig might have been concerned about. He told me that when Richard Nixon offered him the vice presidency in the Oval Office, Al Haig was present and that that meeting was probably taped. He indicated that Nixon had said that Ford would be his nominee for Vice President but that John Connally would become President. It was something that might prove a little embarrassing if it was later revealed publicly. After John Connally had some ethical questions raised, President Nixon said to Ford, "It's a new ball game."[75]

In any event, I finally said to Haig, "Look, I've taken enough of this." Haig had always been friendly and cordial to me, and I understood he was agitated. I told him bluntly that I didn't want to get into the subject and that I thought he ought to talk directly to President

Ford. The unusual outburst from Haig seemed to be a sign of how much the pardon issue still hung, to use Ford's words, like a dagger over the White House, as well as the considerable stress Haig had been under.

To make absolutely clear he had nothing to hide and nothing to apologize for, President Ford agreed to the most unusual step of testifying before the Congress as a sitting President. His bold, continuing efforts to pull his administration out of the Watergate thicket was a lingering frustration for him, particularly in that his new administration faced so many pressing national concerns—foreign crises, arms control negotiations with the Soviet Union, and a sluggish economy that had begun to worsen.

Public Enemy Number One

MEETING WITH THE PRESIDENT

November 6, 1974

8:30 to 9:07 a.m.

Oval Office

Alone

The doctor who's the most brilliant on venereal disease, who talked about it all the time, suddenly becomes thought of as the venereal disease man. And that's not a happy image.[1]

If the most serious constitutional crisis in American politics since the Civil War was beginning to recede by the fall of 1974, our country's economy was rapidly worsening, driving prices of everyday goods so high that millions struggled to afford them. As Ford entered his presidency in August 1974, inflation was reported at its highest level since the year 1919. Opinion polls consistently cited inflation as the nation's top problem, at one point mentioned by up to 80 percent of the public.[2]

The spiraling inflation in the fall of 1974 meant that a ten-dollar bill was not purchasing nearly as much in groceries or gas as it had only months before. From October 1974 through May 1975, the American economy experienced one of its steepest economic declines since the Great Depression back in the 1930s.[3] Few were immune to the pain of the economic downturn. The "Misery Index," named by Dr. Arthur Okun, who had been the Chairman of Lyndon Johnson's Council of Economic Advisors in the late 1960s, quickly became a telling analytical tool.

Economists were using the term "stagflation" to describe the unusual toxic brew of rapid inflation coupled with high unemployment and declining economic growth. Until the mid-1970s, many if not most economists had viewed inflation and recession as mutually exclusive. If products were getting more expensive, it was generally because demand was high and the economy was growing. But this seemed to be a new era, one in which the traditional monetary tools for fixing one problem, such as the Federal Reserve tightening the monetary supply to reduce inflation, could create another problem, in this case, by reducing economic growth and increasing unemployment.

Stagflation's underpinnings seemed to be easier to understand than to remedy. The United States faced a $25 billion deficit in 1968 due to President Johnson's decision to accelerate spending on both "guns *and* butter" without increases in revenues. President Nixon then adopted wage and price controls in August 1971, which had the federal government trying to control wages and prices in a free enterprise system, the folly of which I saw up close during my time as the Director of the Cost of Living Council.

Since the end of World War II, a good deal of U.S. manufacturing had moved overseas, squeezing the middle class, the backbone of the American economy. The year 1971 had been the first since 1888 in which the U.S. had experienced a trade deficit, importing $2.26 billion more in goods and services than was exported.[4] Further, OPEC's oil embargo, which began in October 1973 in response to the Yom Kippur War and lasted until March 1974, had quadrupled the price of oil. Because oil is necessary in the production of so many products, the prices of a great many things rose—some sharply.

Having served in Congress for decades from a state where the chief industry, automobiles, was closely tied to the nation's economic trends, Gerald Ford was particularly sensitive when it came to economic issues. He was a master of the complex process in the Congress that governed federal spending, having served for years as a senior member of the powerful House Appropriations Committee. Because of Congressman Ford's role on that committee, President Harry Truman once took him on a tour of the White House to demonstrate the pressing need for funds to shore up rooms that were on the verge of collapse. Truman had been so persuasive, saying at one point that the ceiling of the State Dining Room was staying up only out of force of habit, that Ford, then a freshman member of Congress, broke his antispending campaign pledge and voted for every penny President Truman had requested.[5]

Now in the presidency himself, Ford knew the American economy was in a precarious state. Many Americans were hurting in very direct ways, having less to spend on the necessities for their families. He wasted no time in addressing the issue. His first major economic address—which was also his first appearance before a joint session of the Congress as President—was on Monday, August 12, 1974, three days after he had been sworn in as President. There he asserted that, having traveled more than 118,000 miles and participated in some fifty-five press conferences as Vice President, he was convinced "the unanimous concern of Americans is inflation."

"My first priority," Ford continued, "is to work with you to bring inflation under control. Inflation is domestic enemy number one."[6]

As had been proposed by Senate Majority Leader Mike Mansfield the previous week, the President directed the Joint Economic Committee of Congress to provide its findings on the best ways to combat the issue in six weeks rather than the six months that had been initially planned. The American people, Ford affirmed, "are as anxious as we are to get the right answers."[7] Still finding his footing as the country's new chief executive, he was confident enough to know he didn't have all the answers, and that combating inflation wasn't something that any chief executive could take on alone from the Oval Office. His early speech was a punt, but a useful one.

Meanwhile the economic situation was worsening. In a September 19, 1974, memo to the President, Alan Greenspan, the new Chairman of Ford's Council of Economic Advisors, advised the President that the Consumer Price Index (CPI) had recorded "the largest monthly increase since August 1973 and the second largest since during the Korean War. All major categories of the CPI—food, nonfood commodities, and services—contributed relatively equally to the advance."[8]

At the end of September, the President convened a two-day "summit conference" on the economy and inflation, attended by, in Ford's words, "some of the best economic brains from labor, industry, and agriculture."[9] As he convened the group that weekend, he received some unwelcome personal news that almost certainly distracted him. His beloved, Betty, who had discovered a lump in her breast, was being operated on. Late that morning, Ford received a call from a doctor, informing the President that Betty's cancer was malignant and that her surgical team would proceed with a full mastectomy. The news shook Ford. With his friend Bob Hartmann present and sympathetic, the President broke down in tears at his desk in the Oval Office.[10] Mrs. Ford, sharing her husband's penchant for openness, publicly disclosed her battle with breast cancer—the first time the medical condition was ever discussed by a sitting First Lady. Her efforts undoubtedly led to an increase in awareness of breast cancer and may well have helped to save the lives of a number of women who sought mammograms as a result.

After visiting Betty in the hospital that afternoon, September 28, the President returned to the economic conference with an address in which he previewed what he labeled the "WIN Program," a "volunteer citizens program" to "whip inflation now." He petitioned the American people for support. "Right now, make a list of some ten ways you can save energy and you can fight inflation . . . and I urge you and ask you to send me a copy."[11] Maybe it meant driving less to save more on gasoline. Or maybe it meant buying less expensive groceries. The speech did not include specifics. Ford's entreaty may have been one of the first crowd-sourced presidential initiatives in American history.

This call to service and sacrifice, though genuine, raised questions. It left some feeling that the President might be shifting the onus of solving the country's economic woes, not totally onto the American people, but certainly to some extent away from the White House, the government, and the nation's elected officials. It seemed to be a shift from his August speech, in which he had forthrightly charged Washington, D.C., with supplying leadership. The WIN plan led to one of the first real policy debates inside the still-young Ford administration.

On the morning of October 8, with the President scheduled to speak that evening before a joint session of Congress to publicly unveil the so-called WIN program, the twentieth-largest bank in the nation had collapsed. Founded in 1926, New York–based Franklin National Bank, which had lost $63 million in the first five months of 1974, would become the first major financial institution in U.S. history to be wound down by federal regulators.[12] Although the bank's fate was seen as primarily the result of fraud and mismanagement, the stunning news heightened apprehension about the health of the economy and its prospects. Some wondered if this might be the first of many dominoes to fall and whether a full run on America's banks could be at hand.

The proposed final draft of the President's WIN speech arrived on my desk only hours before the President was scheduled to deliver it. I found it worrisome. In the speech, Ford was to explain to Congress that since the summit, he had "evaluated literally hundreds of ideas, day and night," relaying there was "only one point on which all advisors have agreed: We must whip inflation right now." He outlined what was described as "a grand design" to whip inflation, which consisted of ten areas where the executive and legislative branches could work together to solve the problem. It was fiscally conservative in orientation, calling for $4.4 billion in spending cuts to hold the federal budget to $300 billion and imposing a one-year 5 percent surtax on corporations and upper-level individual incomes. It also laid out plans to encourage food production and to stimulate the housing industry.

But what stood out was the call for volunteerism to tame spending and increase savings, elaborating on his tease of the "volunteer citizens program" he had mentioned two weeks earlier in his inflation summit press conference. He announced that, in a week in Kansas City, before the Future Farmers of America, he would elaborate upon "how volunteer inflation fighters and energy savers can further mobilize their total efforts." The idea of WIN, as Ron Nessen noted, "was that ordinary citizens could play a role in stifling inflation by such steps as cutting back on their spending, planting gardens to grow their own food, riding bicycles to work . . . cutting back on electricity, and so forth."[13] The President's draft remarks concluded with him stopping just short of asking Congress to declare "war" on inflation, in terms similar to Lyndon B. Johnson's so-called war on poverty.

The draft of the speech was plagued by rhetorical discrepancies and confusing lists of policy proposals. With only a few hours before the President left the White House for the speech, I felt a responsibility to caution Ford about what I was concerned could be its impact.

Knowing how the Ford White House speech shop tended to operate, I was concerned that the speech may not have been fully coordinated with the relevant Cabinet officials and senior White House economic advisors. In a normal presidential speechwriting process, a major address would be fact-checked and vetted and would receive a signoff from the relevant departments and agencies. I soon learned that Alan Greenspan, the White House's top economist, had not seen a semifinal draft until eight o'clock the previous morning, at which point he had found five or six factual mistakes. The speechwriting team had unveiled the WIN campaign and distributed sample buttons to him. It was Greenspan's first such experience in the White House, and one that almost sent him "racing back to New York." "It was surreal," he recalled. "I was the only economist present, and I said to myself . . .'What am I doing here?' "[14] The President's senior economic staff advisor Bill Seidman, Treasury Secretary Bill Simon, U.S. Trade Representative Bill Eberle, the Chair of the Federal Reserve Bank, Dr. Arthur Burns, and noted economist Dr. Paul McCracken, all of whom would be needed to professionally discuss, explain, and support the program, had also received their copies of the landmark economic speech only hours before it was to be delivered.[15] I saw a problem in the making—but unfortunately not the first I had witnessed from the new White House communications and speechwriting team in my very brief time as the new Chief of Staff.

The White House Press Office had not been functioning well in the later months of the Nixon administration nor in the early days after Gerald Ford had assumed the presidency. The slumping morale suffered an additional knock after Jerry terHorst resigned over the Nixon pardon. But the speechwriting operation posed still another problem.

The shop was headed by Bob Hartmann. Having been so close to Ford for years, Hartmann felt his thunder was being stolen by Ron Nessen, who had left NBC News as a correspondent to become the President's Press Secretary, replacing terHorst. After accepting the

White House appointment, Nessen asked the President whether he would also be a senior advisor. "Of course," Ford replied. Hartmann, who was present at that meeting, spoke up. "You'd better tell him, Mr. President, that I have a lot of experience in the [press relations] field and that I'm going to be looking over his shoulder a lot."[16] Not an auspicious beginning.

Personal rivalries, which understandably concerned the President, on occasion led to leaks and unflattering newspaper articles, which concerned Ford even more.[17] Zealously guarding his role as the President's message crafter, Hartmann would resist circulating drafts of speeches or coordinating with White House policy experts. I told the President that the process was not sufficiently professional and, as a result, was having the effect of making the White House seem hapless.[18] On a number of occasions, I had to ask Dr. Robert Goldwin to set aside other tasks to take a crack at trying to improve late speech drafts.

Ford understood the problem well. As mentioned, he had referred to the "Bob Hartmann issue" when he urged me to take over as the Chief of Staff. Still, the existing process, as clumsy as it might be, had worked for him before, the President told me. And indeed it had when he was in Congress, where speeches were often delivered extemporaneously and received little to no national attention. But the presidency is a different stage and the stakes were considerably higher.

The President thought the WIN program had been devised by the head of the White House's editorial department, Paul Theis, who reasoned that a voluntary citizens' program needed a campaign with a symbol. Ford further noted he was sold on the program by Bob Hartmann, who argued that WIN was "a great idea."[19] As to who was the progenitor of the voluntary citizens' program, that remained something of a mystery. "I'm not sure who dreamed up the WIN program," Ron Nessen later reflected. "Nobody claimed credit."[20]

(Apparently, the White House speechwriting office—with the assistance of New York–based advertising agency Benton & Bowles—had developed the idea and the branding behind WIN.)

Just hours before the President was scheduled to head to Capitol Hill for his nationally televised address, and armed with the information that the speech's contents had likely not been fully vetted with the policy experts, I made a last-ditch effort to try to persuade the President to consider delaying the speech. I told him I was concerned the program might not provide the degree of confidence the country needed. I argued that instead he consider taking five minutes of prime time and state that the program being developed to deal with inflation was not yet good enough. I argued that the economy was too important for a less than fully vetted proposal. I lost. "Well, I think it's a good program," Ford told me. Understandably, he was reluctant to reverse a decision he'd already made, especially at the last minute. He also undoubtedly also knew such a reversal would reflect poorly on his close aide and friend, Bob Hartmann. The President got in the motorcade and headed to the U.S. Capitol, where he would deliver the speech.

The content of the speech was what it was, but arguably an even greater problem might have been the optics. The President strode to the rostrum, conspicuously wearing a WIN button. In the minds of some, the President seemed to be pinning the success of his anti-inflation program on a voluntary citizens' program. No matter what else he said, listeners would remember the WIN button. Earlier the morning of his address to the joint session, we had all looked at the button. Ron Nessen and Russell Freeburg, Coordinator to the Citizens' Action Committee to Fight Inflation, wanted the President to wear it. I did not want him to wear it and told him so.[21]

The President's address—in particular the notion that small acts in your home could tame the broader economic forces—perplexed a number of our country's top economists. Some reactions were stinging. "While some of his measures are good and some are question-able," read a *New York Times* editorial, "they in no sense add up to a program for an emergency, and it is an emergency that confronts the nation and the world."[22] If the WIN program seemed to some to lack persuasive economic reasoning, that, in my view, was because it did. In his memoir, Ford guardedly recollected that "some" of his economic advisors were "skeptical," but wrote "most" agreed WIN was worth a try.[23]

Looking back, the President very well might have been right to press forward on the issue. To my amazement, although the media reaction to the speech was lukewarm at best, the initial public response to the WIN program was positive. A tiny staff in the White House faced 1,000 telephone calls a day and had to handle the more than 200,000 letters addressed to the President. In the first nine days alone, 101,240 WIN enlistment papers arrived in the White House, and the number of requests for WIN buttons was staggering.[24] "What we have been doing so far," said Russell Freeburg, who was in charge of the WIN program, "is like building an airplane in mid-air."[25] Hartmann went so far as to unfairly accuse Nixon administration holdovers of torpedoing the WIN program using "every dirty trick in their considerable bag to make it fail," which of course was not the case.

There were also, it should be noted, some truly heartwarming responses to President Ford's call to action. For example, Girl Scouts in eastern Tennessee held the price of their cookies during the January 1975 sale at the same level as the previous two years despite the higher cost of sugar. In Ohio, employees of the Gold Circle, a discount department chain, wore "Humbug on High Prices" buttons to remind shoppers to look for the lowest possible prices.[26]

But this support proved short-lived, especially as media criticism dominated. Shortly before Thanksgiving 1974, Ron Nessen, President Ford's replacement Press Secretary, appeared before reporters

wearing what was by then an increasingly familiar piece of administration paraphernalia: a "WIN" button. Yet there was something
obviously amiss about Nessen's button; it was upside down, reading
instead "NIM." When asked what that stood for, he replied with
good humor, "No Immediate Miracles."[27] President Ford, he added,
"had warned that there would be No Immediate Miracles in curing
the nation's economic ills."[28] Nessen's comment was an attempt to
make light of the situation. Regrettably, the program had become the
butt of some late-night-show jokes.

By late December, WIN's staff consisted of only two full-time volunteers and two part-timers—with one hundred thousand letters to
Ford remaining unanswered, some of which the speech shop farmed
out to volunteers and typists on loan from other offices. "WIN was
what the advertising world would call an over-promise," noted Edward Block, an Illinois Bell Telephone Company executive from
Chicago who had taken over as WIN's volunteer executive director.
"More was anticipated than was reasonable to expect."[29]

Still, President Ford was to be admired for making the effort.
Inflation was a real and serious concern for millions of Americans.
Even though no President could fix the problem overnight, no President who cared about working families, as Ford did, could ignore it.
I was concerned about the scattershot approach in some elements of
the White House operation in those early days, where messaging and
speeches of this import continued to be less than fully coordinated
and not vetted by the key policy experts. There were other aspects
that suggested that the new White House was still a less than fully
professional operation. An amusing example was that once in the
Oval Office, when the President pounded the table for emphasis, Bob
Hartmann popped into the room. Apparently the buzzer system in
the President's desk was overly sensitive. Another example occurred
when the President requested some sort of a curtain at the back windows of the Oval Office, because the sun came in in the morning,

right on his head and face, and was a problem. It took forever, it seemed, for us to get that problem fixed.[30]

Shortly after his WIN speech, I expressed a concern to the President. As I noted at the time, I advised him that "the White House needs running, and he's not doing it, and no one can do it for him, unless he decides that it has to be done by someone."[31]

By the start of 1975, a number of prominent economic thinkers, from both inside and outside of government, had captured the President's ear, convincing him there may well be better ways than volunteer efforts to achieve his goals. The economic numbers had not improved as much as had been hoped and concern was palpable. The White House had received various reports from around the country that the administration's economic agenda was "destroyed," "killed," or "dead."[32] In December 1974, Robert Werner, then President of the Washington Forum, penned a scathing letter after visiting with dozens of the country's largest investment institutions. The overriding concern, he conveyed, was "the Administration's economic policies—its apparent failure to anticipate the deep recessionary characteristic."[33]

The President continued to declare that fighting inflation would remain the centerpiece of his economic agenda. I mentioned, first, that the unemployment component of the stagflation equation was accelerating. Second, and more important, I was concerned that he risked being seen as a Johnny One Note on "inflation," a problem he wasn't going to be able to solve—or at least solve in such a way that he would be seen as deserving of credit. I said to him, "The doctor who's the most brilliant on venereal disease, who talked about it all the time, suddenly becomes thought of as the venereal disease man." I added "that's not a happy image."[34] Given his focus on inflation, I doubted that it would be helpful for him to become known as "the inflation man."

Heading into the midterm elections of 1974, the first national elections since the Nixon resignation, President Ford had wisely set expectations low. With Nixon consumed in his political crisis and Ford focused on restoring confidence in the presidency, the Republican Party had, in large measure, been without the most valuable asset, the bully pulpit of the White House. Although Ford had spent several days on the stump in the months before the election, logging thousands of miles and visiting some twenty states prior to the November midterm elections, his words and demeanor were missing the fire to energize the party. His heart wasn't in red-meat attacks. After Watergate—and after his pardon of Richard Nixon—President Ford saw a need to be largely nonpartisan, even postpartisan, to help heal the country's continuing divisions. A number of his conservative friends had urged that he attack Democrats to boost the party's chances. But Ford, given his courteous nature, was inclined toward restraint. He was persuaded that robust campaigning could backfire. The American people, he felt, were looking for leadership more than politics.[35]

A number of his advisors, including me, agreed that the President should not spend too much time on the campaign trail. GOP political advisors were resigned to Republicans taking a walloping. A grim postelection statement was prepared in late October, more than a week before voters had headed to their ballot boxes. The Ford campaign team, which was beginning to be assembled with the presidential election only two years away, was concerned that some in the party might use a sizable loss as reason to challenge Ford's leadership. They knew that political capital was a valuable commodity for a President. Wasting it on what seemed certain to be a losing effort was an unnecessary risk. But Ford disagreed. He thought a President, who is also the leader of his party, has a responsibility to campaign for his team regardless of the likely result or impact. More to the point, many of the members of Congress running were his personal friends. And Jerry Ford stood by his friends.

On November 5, the day of the election, preparations were made for a long and difficult evening. Those responsible for the White

House mess were instructed to be open through the night to provide food for those who would inevitably be working late. Three television sets, coffee, and light snacks were brought into the Roosevelt Room across the hall from the Oval Office so staffers could come and go without creating disruptions in the President's office. Most of the senior staff watched the all-too-expected returns until 12:30 a.m.[36]

The Democrats indeed steamrolled the GOP. Back on October 8, Bill Timmons, the President's wise Assistant for Legislative Affairs, had predicted the GOP would lose fifty seats in the House.[37] He was close. The results showed the Democrats had made a net gain of four seats in the Senate, giving them a majority in that chamber, and they had gained forty-nine seats in the House, giving them a majority above the two-thirds mark in that chamber. The Democrats also picked up a net of four governorships. In state legislatures, Democrats increased their control by 14 percent in the lower houses and 12 percent in the upper houses.[38] "Watergate and the Agnew scandal," several historians later noted, "had taken their toll on the reputation of a party that not long before had been considered more honest and upright than the Democrats."[39]

In the days after the 1974 election, members of the GOP engaged in extensive discussions about how best to move forward. As for President Ford, his instinct was to be the same person he had always been. I suggested that he place the legislative burden on the Democrats. "We should let it be known we took a licking—that we are down—that they have an overwhelming majority—that they have responsibility," I noted in a memo on November 6, 1974. I pressed this point by suggesting that events would inevitably arise at home and abroad that would require leadership—the type of leadership that only the White House can provide. Congress, on the other hand, would remain culpable: "a collection of 435 in the House and 100 in the Senate individual human beings with very poor leadership and no structure and no drive."[40]

• • •

On January 13, 1975, two days before his State of the Union address, the President delivered a televised speech to the American people. "This speech," I penned to Ford, "will almost certainly be the most important of your Presidency." I recommended "bitter medicine" as the theme, to reflect the number of difficult policy decisions he had made—and he was going to have to make—to cope with stagflation. Individuals rewriting and editing the draft of the speech had gotten "cold feet" and were attempting to "sugar-coat" those difficult decisions. "A first step in restoring confidence," I suggested, "is to convince the American people that you understand the seriousness of the current situation and share their assessment of it."[41] That was step one. Step two, I believed, was filling the void left by the President's anti-inflation campaign, which was increasingly being characterized as long on rhetoric and short on solutions.

The U.S. economy was by then declining even deeper into recession. Unemployment was increasing. Modestly reducing the prices of goods and services would hardly satisfy folks without much income. The administration had to take steps that would get people back to work. Before his first joint session of Congress in August 1974, the President had announced that while the state of the economy was "not so good," the state of the union was "excellent." In his January 1975 State of the Union message, he conceded: "I must say to you that the state of the Union is not good: Millions of Americans are out of work."[42] "Without wasting words," Ford had begun, "I want to talk with you tonight about putting our domestic house in order. We must turn America in a new direction. We must reverse the current recession, reduce unemployment, and create more jobs."[43]

Some within the White House suggested it was less the words and more Ford's delivery that was lacking. I thought he was most persuasive when he was himself. Others counseled the use of image gurus.

The latter camp won out. In response to his January 13 address, one critic suggested someone must have talked the President "into gesturing with his hands and otherwise [acting] like a Dale Carnegie student"—a pointed reference to the prominent self-improvement guru and author of the book *How to Win Friends and Influence People*.[44] Press reports reinforced that impression. The *Los Angeles Times* ran a story that quoted Ford's top speechwriter, Bob Hartmann, unhelpfully explaining publicly that he had coached Ford with a teleprompter six times, and emphasized the importance of using his hands.[45]

It's not as if the President didn't already face enough opposition from the left. The "Watergate Babies," as the recently elected new members of the Democratic-controlled Congress were dubbed, threw their considerable weight around, further limiting the President's policy options. As one of the largest classes of freshman Democrats ever elected to the House, they pushed for massive spending to create government jobs, especially after unemployment rose to 7.2 percent in December 1974.[46] Frustration, nevertheless, inspired one of the most fruitful and potent revolutions in U.S. economic history.

In December 1974, an obscure, thirty-four-year-old economist named Dr. Arthur Laffer sat down with me and Dick Cheney at the Two Continents restaurant on Fifteenth Street in Northwest Washington, D.C. Venting about the administration's flagging WIN campaign, he pulled a pen from his pocket and sketched on a napkin a "curve" illustrating the relationship between the tax rate and tax revenue collected from salaries, corporate profits, and investment income. The concept was, very simply, that at a zero tax rate the federal government would receive zero revenue, and at a 100 percent tax rate, the federal government would likely also receive zero revenue, having eliminated any incentive to work or produce. However, at some tax rate in between zero and 100 percent, revenues can be maximized. There, in a few sentences and a drawing, was what became known and heralded as the "Laffer curve" and "supply side" economics, which, over time, turned Keynesianism, the standard of economics of the twentieth century, on its head. Supply side economics, in dramatically reduced form, advocated the idea that tax cuts—especially for businesses, the "suppliers"—partially paid for themselves by boosting economic activity. To spark growth, consumers and corporations needed the ability to spend money. "What we had to do," recalled Ford, "was reverse completely the economic strategy."[47] The word *reverse* wasn't an exaggeration. When a reporter asked whether the new economic agenda constituted a 180-degree shift, Ron Nessen sardonically responded it would be "only a 179-degree shift."[48]

In his State of the Union address on January 15, 1975, President Ford proposed a one-year $16 billion tax reduction. In March, only weeks later, Ford signed the Tax Reduction Act of 1975, which called for a $22.8 billion tax cut. The stage had been set for the impressive and previously unanticipated recovery that occurred on President Ford's watch and presaged the Reagan Revolution and the economic boom of the 1980s. As for the WIN buttons, Nessen confirmed they "went into desk drawers, never to reemerge."[49]

Ford, before leaving office in January 1977, managed to lasso the stormy trends that had threatened, and he did so during the expensive but needed defense investments to counter the Soviet Union's military investment and buildup. Unemployment, though still high, was heading down. Inflation had been more than cut in half from an annual rate of 12 percent to 4.8 percent. "[T]he economic recovery is on track after all," the *Wall Street Journal* reported in late 1976, calling the signs "a vindication of the general thrust of Gerald Ford's economies policies."[50]

5

Choosing Rockefeller

MEETING WITH THE PRESIDENT

December 19, 1974

6:05 to 6:58 p.m.

Oval Office

Rumsfeld and the President

I gave the President the memo that Jerry Jones had worked up on the respon-sibility of the Vice President under Executive Orders and statutes. Pointed out that it was very thin—said that there are other options—Productivity Commission, the WIN thing, the economy, energy conservation. I said if he went with just what was statutory or already in Executive Orders that it would be really perceived as a real let-down. And that you'll really want to carefully craft this and we'll need something much more creative. I said if you want a creative idea why don't you make him Secretary of the Treasury, give him a Department to run—Department of Transportation. 1 said I've always believed that the job [of VP] was a non-job and that there is nothing wrong at all with having the Vice President run a Department.[1]

S piro T. Agnew was not an impressive Vice President. He did, however, make great efforts to look the part. "Never let your back touch the back of the chair," he lectured some White House staff members in his zeal to avoid wrinkles in his jacket.[2] During the early years of the Nixon administration, I was in many meetings with Vice President Agnew. Other meetings, such as those for the President's Committee on School Desegregation, of which on paper Agnew was the Chairman, he seldom attended. Though he rarely contributed much in the way of substantive thought in meetings when he *was* present, Agnew seemed to always sport perfect creases in his well-pressed, unwrinkled pants. His taste for panache carried over into his public performances. He cultivated a reputation as a bold public speaker, in part due to his alliterative assaults on journalists, labeling them "pusillanimous pussyfooters," "hopeless hysterical hypochondriacs of history," and, most famously, in a speech written by my friend, the skilled wordsmith William Safire, describing members of the media as "nattering nabobs of negativism."[3]

A former Governor of Maryland, he was not well known when he had been selected by Richard Nixon as his vice presidential nominee at the GOP convention in 1968 over at least a dozen better qualified contenders, including then–California Governor Ronald Reagan and—as fate would have it—Gerald R. Ford.[4] There may well have been an allure to President Nixon to pick someone who would jolt and surprise the so-called Washington Beltway establishment. But Agnew soon underscored the political dangers of selecting a relatively unknown and untested candidate. Not sufficiently vetted by the FBI, the media, or the Nixon political operation, and unknown to most of the public outside of Maryland, Agnew had a propensity for corruption that had been undetected.

In August 1968, I was a thirty-six-year-old third-term Congressman from Illinois and had been a supporter of Richard Nixon in his competition for the presidency with Nelson Rockefeller. Immediately after winning the nomination for President, he invited me to a 2 a.m. meeting in his top-floor suite in a Miami Beach hotel to participate in his deliberations on his selection for the nomination for Vice President. There I sat, a relatively junior member of Congress, along with fifteen or twenty others—prominent Governors, U.S. Senators, former presidential candidates Senator Barry Goldwater and Governor Thomas Dewey, and even the highly respected Reverend Billy Graham. Throughout the early morning meeting it became clear the candidate was moving the discussion in a specific direction. As Nixon asked the participants for their thoughts, he periodically brought the discussion back to two governors: John Volpe, who was serving his second nonconsecutive term in Massachusetts, and Spiro T. Agnew, then the Governor of Maryland and the former Maryland Chairman of the Nelson Rockefeller presidential campaign committee. Nixon specified directly that he favored a centrist figure—not a vice presidential nominee from either the left or the right. He effectively turned the discussion away from political figures such as John Lindsay, Nelson Rockefeller, or Senator Charles Percy of Illinois on the left and from Senator John Tower on the right. When the discussion turned to others, Nixon would ask: "What about John Volpe?" or "What about Spiro Agnew?" His eventual choice of Agnew changed history, though certainly not in a way either Nixon, or Agnew, for that matter, intended, anticipated, or desired. Agnew's eventual successor, Gerald Ford, certainly took the lessons from Mr. Nixon's unhappy experience to heart as he selected the nation's third Vice President in the space of two years.

As Gerald Ford assumed the presidency, the vacancy in the office of the Vice President was a pressing concern. President Ford had indicated his intention of consulting leaders on Capitol Hill and in the Republican Party before deciding on his selection. He wanted a nominee who could help him lead the administration and strengthen the GOP ticket for his upcoming presidential election campaign. Under the Twenty-fifth Amendment of the Constitution, ratified in 1967 to clearly establish the lines of succession should there be a vacancy in the office of the vice presidency, whoever Ford selected would have to achieve a majority vote in the U.S. Senate and the U.S. House of Representatives, both of which were then under the control of the Democratic Party. During a morning meeting in the Oval Office, while I was still serving as Chairman of his transition to the presidency, Ford had told me I was one of three candidates he was considering to replace him as Vice President. The other two, he told me, were Nelson Rockefeller, the four-term former Governor of New York, and George H. W. Bush, a former two-term Texas Congressman and then the current Chairman of the Republican National Committee.[5] Each of us had filled out the extensive required legal and financial forms and had been vetted by the FBI.

On August 13, 1974, four days after Nixon had resigned, and well before I had been told that I was under consideration, I had hand-delivered to Ford a memo he requested and I had drafted, suggesting several "criteria" he might consider when selecting a Vice President. I noted that the individual's "personal behavior" should meet the "considerably higher standards now required in this post-Watergate period." Next, he or she should complement Ford "by virtue of a different background and appeal," which in my view ruled me out. I appreciated the President's consideration of me, but I was certain there was little to no possibility I would be his choice given our common midwestern and congressional backgrounds. I offered no geographic balance and would bring no particular national political strength to the ticket. (Back in those days, more so than in recent political history, geography tended to be an important factor in vice presidential nominees.)

In his deliberations on who he would recommend to become his Vice President, Ford was clear about what he did not want to do.

When President Nixon nominated Ford for the vice presidency back in October 1973, the announcement had been a dramatic, drawn-out guessing game, and what Ford labeled "an oddly exuberant" affair, considering that the event followed the embarrassing departure of Agnew.[6] The announcement of Ford came after several days of news stories about other possible candidates, which the Nixon White House clearly had floated—Rockefeller and John Connally were among others who received prominent mention. Adding to the drama, Nixon retreated to Camp David to deliberate on his choice. His visit there was followed by a surprise prime-time announcement live on television and radio from the East Room of the White House, during which Ford emerged before a crowd of dignitaries feeling like a game show contestant.[7] Now, as President, Ford wanted to do something that was more businesslike and dignified. On August 20, meeting with members of the Cabinet in the Roosevelt Room, the President without much fanfare announced that he intended to send the name of Nelson Rockefeller to the Congress for its consideration and approval.[8]

I later learned that Nelson Rockefeller had been Nixon's recommendation. In fact, according to President Ford, Rockefeller was Nixon's sole recommendation.[9] Perhaps Nixon believed Rockefeller, a well-known national name, would add stature to the Ford administration. It is also conceivable that Nixon, ever the chess player, may well have surmised that the left-leaning, big-city scion of one of America's richest families, who was energetically detested by many conservatives, would pose less of a challenge in 1976 to Richard Nixon's hoped-for successor John Connally.

Rockefeller, then sixty-six, was born in affluent Bar Harbor, Maine, to a more-than-affluent and prominent family. After graduating from Dartmouth College in 1930, he became involved with family-related businesses and nonprofit organizations. In a step toward politics, he was appointed to be the head of the Office of the Co-

ordinator of Inter-American Affairs in Franklin Roosevelt's administration. He stayed in the nation's capital for several years to work in
various capacities under President Truman and then later President
Eisenhower.

Rockefeller was elected Governor of New York in 1958 as a Republican and re-elected in 1962, 1966, and 1970. An activist Governor,
he was known as a liberal spender, particularly on public works proj-
ects. In 1960, just two years into his first term, he sought the Republican presidential nomination but lost to Richard Nixon. Four years
later, he ran again for President and was once again defeated for the
nomination, this time by conservative Senator Barry Goldwater, who
represented the new Sunbelt, limited-government character of the
Republican Party. Rockefeller's reputation was marred for some by
his controversial divorce and second marriage as well as by criticism
of dealings he made to use the New York state police to suppress the
Attica Prison riot in 1971, which left forty-three people dead, including ten correctional officers and civilian employees.

The Rockefeller family had a history of sharing its wealth with
employees, arguably, in the view of some, to garner or solidify political support and loyalty. Those practices would prove to be hard
habits to shake. Besides enjoying his sizable inherited wealth,
Rockefeller presented other unique concerns as Ford's vice presidential selection.

Rockefeller's personality, for example, was an issue. As I came to
know him, he seemed almost to be two different people. On the one
hand, he could be open, engaged, friendly, and enthusiastic. One of
his favorite words was "fabulous!" Experienced in state government
and modestly in federal government, he came to the vice presidency
leaning forward and seemingly eager to help President Ford.

On the other hand, Rockefeller was accustomed to being in charge
and to getting his way. Aggressive personalities and the vice presidency of the United States are rarely an easy mixture, especially for a

man who had sought the top job for himself more than once. Perhaps knowing this about himself, Rockefeller had, publicly at least, expressed reluctance to be Vice President, noting that he wasn't suited to be what he properly characterized as "standby equipment."[10] Rockefeller denied he still harbored presidential ambitions of his own. This led former President Lyndon Johnson's aide Bill Moyers to memorably quip, "I believe Rocky when he says he's lost his ambition. I also believe he remembers where he put it."[11]

The relationship between Presidents and Vice Presidents can be delicate. There have been times in recent history, such as during the Kennedy-Johnson administration, when the two men saw each other as rivals. And there have been other occasions when Presidents bridled at the idea of giving their Vice Presidents too much responsibility, or even the perception of influence. President Ford, rather atypically, had none of those concerns. In fact, in offering Rockefeller the nomination, Ford had apparently left Rockefeller with the impression it was to be a "partnership." He offered him a broad portfolio in domestic matters. This was a typically generous and astute decision by the President, at least at the outset: Ford knew that Rockefeller brought a different kind of experience to the administration from his years as Governor of New York State and therefore had dealt with a wide array of issues from a different perspective than Ford had as a former legislator. Ford saw Rockefeller not as a threat, but an asset.

Unfortunately, Ford underestimated, as we all did, Rockefeller's tendency to seize the bit in his teeth, turning any ambiguity to his full advantage. His new portfolio seemed, at least in Rockefeller's mind, to include most everything except foreign policy and national security affairs. Those were the domain of Henry Kissinger, who had previously been recruited by the Rockefeller family and by Rockefeller himself in various capacities for some period of years. But this arrangement, at least envisioned by Rockefeller, posed an obvious problem. If Kissinger was seen as the leader in foreign affairs, intelligence, and national security matters, and Rockefeller saw himself as the leader on domestic issues, then what was left for President Ford? Belatedly, Ford realized the seriousness of this misunderstanding.

Former President Nixon, the first outsider to hear the news of the selection, told Ford in a phone call that Rockefeller's name and stature would help him internationally. The "extreme right wing," Nixon noted, would be upset by the choice, but Nixon suggested there was nothing Ford could do to satisfy them anyway.[12] A story had run in *Newsweek* about a meeting Nixon had allegedly had with Rockefeller in the White House when Nixon was still President. According to the article, presumably related by Rockefeller, Nixon had looked at his Oval Office desk and asked Rockefeller, "Can you imagine Gerald Ford sitting in this chair?" Nixon denied to Ford that he'd made that remark, though Ford may not have been completely persuaded.[13]

In any event, even Nixon had underestimated the GOP's conservative opposition to Rockefeller. Rockefeller, a highly visible northeastern liberal, was the perfect target for conservative dissatisfaction with the establishment. As one conservative leader, *National Review* publisher William Rusher, later noted, "Every movement needs a villain. For the GOP right, Nelson Rockefeller was it."[14] Rumblings of disapproval instantly arose. Senator Jesse A. Helms of North Carolina organized a group of conservatives in the Congress who vowed to fight the nomination.[15]

Overtures to mollify conservative dissatisfaction flowed in. An apprehensive Lee Edwards, a historian and a founding member of Young Americans for Freedom, sent a letter in early November outlining ways to retain the support of not only the "Conservative Establishment," but also "those Americans who voted 'conservative' and for Richard Nixon in 1972." One idea he suggested, wisely foreshadowing an approach Donald Trump used decades later when his conservative credentials were questioned, was preparing a list of "constructionist" jurists from which, if the situation were to arise, President Ford would choose for appointments to the Supreme Court.[16]

Democrats had their own concerns about the Rockefeller choice. In *The New York Times*, the columnist R. W. Apple reflected the mood of some on the left when he opined, "President Ford's nomination of Nelson A. Rockefeller as Vice President completes a reversal of national political tides of potentially historic proportions. Ten days ago, politicians were asking whether the Republican Party could survive; today, they were asking how the Democrats were going to mount a challenge in 1976."[17] Echoing these fears, the Democrats, who then had majorities in both houses of the U.S. Congress, vowed vigorous and extensive hearings. Even though Rockefeller had been a household name for decades, the Democrats were exacting in their examination and vowed to review every word Rockefeller had ever uttered and every piece of paper he ever touched.

The extended hearings on the Rockefeller nomination, which went on for months, led to embarrassing though not disqualifying revelations. One hit rather awkwardly close to home. In early October 1974 it was revealed that Rockefeller had given tens of thousands of dollars in gifts to various Republican figures over the years.[18] Shortly after that, Rockefeller disclosed that the Rockefeller fortune had financed a negative biography of one of his political opponents, the former Supreme Court Justice Arthur Goldberg, which had been published during their 1970 battle for Governor of New York.[19] (According to news accounts, 100,000 copies of the 116,000 sold had been purchased and distributed by the Rockefeller re-election campaign.) Learning of the revelation, by then years after his defeat for governor, Goldberg blasted Rockefeller for "belatedly admitted misconduct and its cover-up."[20] By the middle of December 1976, nearly four months after he had been nominated, a bruised but not broken Rockefeller was finally confirmed by the House and Senate.

When it was becoming clear that Rockefeller would eventually assume the vice presidency, I asked the President how he wanted to handle Rockefeller and Rockefeller's staff. As I noted at the time, "[Ford] said when he came in the Nixon people were defensive; their man [Nixon] was going down, Ford was popular. He wants a good feeling. He wants us to embrace [Rockefeller], make him feel at home, not have reservations, make him part of it."[21] I did my best to help carry out the President's instructions. In fact, I even offered the President a suggestion, as I noted in a December 19, 1974, memo, to give Rockefeller a Cabinet post in addition to the vice presidency. "A guy who is energetic and active, I think, would like it," I noted.[22]

On December 21, two days after Rockefeller was confirmed, the President and the new Vice President conferred in the Oval Office. Ford was in a warm, welcoming mood. He said this was a historic meeting and it offered a unique opportunity for the administration and the country. He noted that we all had the same aims, but, undoubtedly reflecting on his own experience under Nixon, he observed that "history shows a lot of staff jealousies" between presidential and vice presidential staffs.

"Nothing bothers me more than problems within a staff or between staffs," Ford said.

At some point during the discussion, Vice President Rockefeller commented on how nice the Navy people had been in connection with the new vice presidential residence that was being established at the site of the old U.S. Naval Observatory. After the meeting, I went to Rockefeller and offered a cautionary suggestion. "Mr. Vice President, a lot of people are going to want to be very nice to you. You are a very powerful man," I said. "The danger is that they'll be nice to you through ignorance. That is to say, it's not their money that they're being nice to you with. It's taxpayers' money."[23]

Still in my mind was an article written many years earlier by columnist Jack Anderson when I had been serving as the Director of the Office of Economic Opportunity (OEO) in the Nixon administration. Anderson said later he had received a rumor that I had made expensive renovations to my government office. Despite the fact that it was flat not true, the story carried in Anderson's widely read column and dogged me for some time. (Anderson, years later, publicly admitted his error—saying it was one of the worst he had ever made—before a congressional committee.)

In any event, I advised Rockefeller, "You and your staff have to make conscious decisions as to whether or not you want people to do things for you in the bureaucracy because you can get yourself in an awful lot of trouble real fast."[24] He nodded and said he agreed.

Shortly thereafter, I had another lengthy meeting with Rockefeller. He did most of the talking. I came away remarking in my note, "He's such an enthusiastic, decent person." This was an initial characterization that I would later have cause to revise.

6

Morning Coats and Wolf Furs:
Ford Abroad

MEMORANDUM FOR THE FILE

November 20, 1974

He never protects himself from having other people see him in a relaxed situation.

Can a great leader let down and still inspire?[1]

At seventy years of age, the "shy, frail, white-haired man," as President Ford recalled, greeted the President's delegation warmly.[2] In itself this was a small moment in a busy day, but a remarkable, even unprecedented, moment in the history of free people. Only three decades earlier, Emperor Hirohito was the scourge of the Western world and the sworn enemy of Americans enlisting in World War II after Japan had bombed Pearl Harbor—men like a young Gerald Ford, and so many others, including my father, George Rumsfeld, each of whom served aboard a ship in the war against Japan. Now Ford and Hirohito faced each other, not as enemies, but as tested allies—critical allies, in fact, in the middle of the Cold War. This historic meeting, however, would start on a modestly discordant note.

The President's Far East trip—with important meetings in Japan,

South Korea, and the Soviet Union—was Gerald Ford's first set of meetings as President outside North America. (He had been to Mexico the previous month, but only for a day.) So it was, not surprisingly, noted by the press as "his first major test in personal diplomacy."[3] His weeklong trip through East Asia offered the first glimpse many would have of this new, unknown, and untested President of the United States.

In Washington, Ford's decision to even make the trip had come under scrutiny. A few critics wondered publicly if the President, so new to the presidency, might need more time to become comfortable in the position before launching into high-stakes diplomacy. The tremors from the Watergate scandals were still causing ripples in and around his new administration, a recession was emerging, and Nelson Rockefeller had not yet been confirmed by the Congress as Ford's successor as Vice President. Because of the vacancy in that post, if something terrible happened on the trip, Ford's successor as President would have been Carl Albert (D-OK), the Speaker of the U.S. House of Representatives and the third American President in less than four months. Seizing on such concerns, Senator Robert Byrd of West Virginia bluntly stated, "I don't think this trip is necessary."[4]

The President discounted those concerns. He believed that this was a time to let the world see that, despite the unprecedented turmoil surrounding the Watergate scandals and the double resignations, America was not shirking its responsibilities abroad. In fact, his view was that a demonstration of American resolve was desirable if not essential.

The President's trip to Japan aboard *Air Force One* had been a rough ride, running into severe turbulence during a portion of the fifteen-hour flight, which left some reporters—situated, per tradition, in the rear compartment of *Air Force One*—slightly the worse for wear.

Although the U.S. had officially returned control of Okinawa to Japan in 1971, militant left-wing groups continued to oppose the presence of U.S. military forces remaining on the U.S. base there. Four days before we arrived in Tokyo, militants had carried out a firebomb attack against the U.S. Embassy there. About two miles from the airport, an estimated 2,000 far-left activists clashed with some 400 helmeted Japanese police.[5] The Japanese government had mobilized 160,000 police officers, the equivalent of ten infantry divisions, for the duration of Ford's four-day visit.[6] In Tokyo alone, 25,000 police officers were assigned to the President's entourage each day.[7] The President's Secret Service detail, of course, had a say with respect to the President's itinerary, and it successfully argued against several events that had been prepared, including an exhibition baseball game between the New York Mets and a Japanese team.[8]

From the airport, helicopters whisked us on the ten-minute trip to the Akasaka Palace not far from the Imperial Palace near downtown Tokyo. Built on the site of the old Edo Castle, the Akasaka Palace was the former residence of the Japanese Crown Prince. It somewhat resembles Buckingham Palace, but its three floors of brick and granite evoke Versailles. In 1967, the Japanese government had decided to make the Akasaka Palace Japan's State Guest House. President Ford and his delegation were the first official state guests to stay in the recently renovated structure.

After a welcome overnight respite, the official arrival ceremony was held on Tuesday in the front garden of the State Guest House. There, the honor guard from the Japan Self-Defense Forces played the national anthems of the U.S. and of Japan. Below a bright blue sky, it also honored Michigan's Maize and Blue by serenading the President with "Hail to the Victors," the football fight song of the President's alma mater.[9]

President Ford's arrival in Tokyo, on November 18, 1974, ended what the Associated Press dubbed "a historical absurdity."[10] Gerald R. Ford was the first sitting U.S. President who had ever visited Japan. President Nixon had prepared to visit the island nation in 1973, an event all the more important and sensitive because the Japanese had come to feel slighted that the Nixon administration had made a decision to keep private his highly secret overtures to the People's Republic of China. While a date for President Nixon's visit had still been active on the calendar, Nixon's presidency was not. After Nixon's resignation, Ford thought it desirable to follow through on the planned presidential visit. Japan, for both economic and security reasons, as widely noted in the media at the time, was then and remains today "America's major ally in East Asia."[11] It became President Ford's task to personally demonstrate to Japan and to the world the seriousness and sincerity of America's commitment to the Land of the Rising Sun. In his visit, he did this and he did it well, but with one problem—a minor but visible wardrobe malfunction.

The requisite attire for the occasion was the most formal of formalwear, that reserved for only the most elevated venues, such as the Royal Ascot in England—morning coats, black-and-gray-striped trousers, gray vests, wing-collared shirts, and black and gray ascot ties.[12] Most of us with President Ford were able to find suitable stand-ins, and avoided what was for us highly unusual attire. The President could not. Unfortunately, the trousers in the President's outfit he had been provided by the tailor were short by about two inches, ending a bit above his ankles.

When I saw President Ford step out in his getup, I was concerned. He would have had every reason to be furious over this slipup, and to take out his frustrations on anyone who happened to be near him. Other Presidents might very well have done just that. But while this was a far from ideal situation, Ford, who did occasionally have a temper, saw no purpose in that. Having no time for any adjustments, and without even a hint of embarrassment, the President did what he had to do, and he did it well and with good humor. "I'm going out there," he said. He gamely met not only the many assembled dignitaries—

but, unfortunately, a U.S. traveling press corps always eager for a story.[13]

Ford handled the awkward moment as well as anyone could. Noting that he was a former Eagle Scout, the President joked that "on occasion I still go around in short pants."[14] Of course, this did not satisfy some in the media who found in the incident, which was most certainly not in any way his fault, the beginning of a theme they would repeat, quite unfairly, to criticize President Ford throughout much of his term: a sense of haplessness.

To little avail, Press Secretary Ron Nessen complained about the press corps' eagerness to focus on such trivial matters. Helen Thomas, of UPI's White House Bureau, expressed the media's typical perspective and approach to news, asserting, "The president's pants being too short was a big story, and you can't expect us not to write about it."[15]

There was a bright side to the incident. Gerald Ford's relaxed demeanor, coupled with his even-humored response to his minor wardrobe problem, only enhanced his image and reputation as an upfront and cheerful American leader. He had made the most of the situation by handling it with the grace of a seasoned diplomat. And he worked his personal charm on the man who had been there to greet him.

Emperor Hirohito, the leader who personally had surrendered to the Americans three decades earlier, appeared precisely at 9:30 a.m. to welcome the U.S. President. Dignitaries who had visited Japan on previous occasions often had found it hard to keep up a conversation with the Emperor, who, as a largely ceremonial figure, did not discuss or engage in political matters. But Ford, who had spent his adult life successfully establishing human connections, found that he easily connected with the Emperor. For one thing, they shared a common love: baseball. And the President, having learned beforehand that the Emperor was one of the world's leading authorities on jellyfish and corals, had read up on a bit of marine biology.[16]

After the arrival ceremony, the President met with the besieged

Prime Minister, Kakuei Tanaka, who was engaged in fending off corruption charges. (He would have to resign only days later.) Ford later described Tanaka as a "burly, aggressive man." He said he couldn't warm up to him easily, and that Tanaka "never let diplomatic niceties stand in the way of blunt speech."[17] His career was on the ropes, but Tanaka, a strong-minded patriot and a senior member of the Diet, whom I had dealt with a number of times over the preceding decade as one of the founders of the U.S.-Japan Parliamentary Exchange, was still dedicated to serving his country. Japan was wrestling with soaring living costs, diminished food supplies, and a spike in oil prices after an OPEC embargo. The two leaders agreed on a need to reconvene General Agreement on Tariffs and Trade (GATT) talks as soon as possible. Ford importantly assured Tanaka that he was a proponent of fair trade—reciprocal trade—as opposed to free trade and that he would not bow to U.S. domestic pressures to impose new quotas on Japanese goods.[18]

On Thursday, the President traveled to Kyoto, Japan's ancient capital from AD 794 to AD 1868, and the country's third-largest city. There were hundreds of protesters in Kyoto, but they rarely got close to the President's party. The President visited the old Imperial Palace of Flowers where Emperor Hirohito had been enthroned in 1928, the 371-year-old Nijo Castle—a white-walled compound built for the Shogun—and the Buddhist lakeside Temple of the Golden Pavilion, covered in twenty-two-carat gold foil.[19]

That evening, the President's delegation enjoyed five-hundred-year-old historic Kaiseki cuisine at Kyoto Tsuruya restaurant.[20] The ten-course meal featured delicacies including dried fish soup and skewered sparrow. Geishas attended the group during the meal and danced at the conclusion, but not before engaging our visiting U.S. delegation in a parlor game that involved passing a straw held from their upper lips and noses to ours. The ever-present White House photographer David Hume Kennerly was there and snapped a few

memorable photos. Several ended up in the media. And for a couple
of years, one of a geisha giggling at my antics was on the packet of
Tyrrell's wasabi-coated peanuts.[21]

Kennerly was on the President's team so his documentation of
the visit was both skillful and in good humor. The same could not
be said of the U.S. reporters with respect to some of their coverage
of the President's trip. It's widely thought the President's "reputation
as a blundering klutz"—as *Time* magazine asserted—began after his
injured knee from his college football days gave out and he tumbled
down a few of the *Air Force One* steps after landing in Salzburg, Aus-
tria, in June 1975.[22] In my view, that misimpression started earlier,
during Ford's time in Japan, with a media effort to portray the President as less than competent. Of course, there was the issue with his
trousers being a bit short, which was blown way out of proportion.
Next, Fox Butterfield, reporting for *The New York Times*, felt it was
newsworthy that the President "seemed to have some difficulty" with
the slippers required to enter the Golden Pavilion in Kyoto. "On another occasion," Butterfield continued, "the visitor from Grand Rapids, Mich., appeared to have a language problem. A question about
the date of a well-tended garden elicited from a guide the answer
yes, a polite ambiguity that puzzles foreigners." The "occasion" was
inconsequential, but a reporter from *The New York Times* was apparently trying hard to portray the President as parochial and out of his
depth by referring to him as "the visitor from Grand Rapids, Mich."[23]

Frank Cormier of the Associated Press piled on. He wrote that
the President, while touring Nijo Castle, was asked to try playing
a koto, a traditional stringed instrument, but the picks didn't fit his
fingers. "He tried his hand at it, but the noise he produced was not
exactly musical."[24] Further, an article in *The New York Times* featured a large photograph of Ford dining with a geisha at his side who
had a somewhat skeptical look on her face. "Here," read the snidely
phrased caption, "the President is experiencing some of the West-

erner's usual difficulties in handling chopsticks."[25] The President felt different. "I even became fairly adept in handling the chopsticks in my left hand," he wrote in his memoir. Ford added, "I was enjoying myself thoroughly."[26] The President was indifferent to what was being said about him. He informed the potshot-taking press that he thought his visit to Japan was "going wonderfully" and that it "couldn't be better, substantively and otherwise."[27]

On Friday, the President's last day in Japan, he took a U.S. Marine helicopter for the short trip back to Tokyo. Emperor Hirohito was at the State Guest House to say good-bye to the President. Ford moved down a line of what seemed to be a hundred foreign diplomats and shook hands. A band played a medley of tunes, including the 1933 sports anthem, "You Got to Be a Football Hero," and Rudy Vallée's 1930, "Betty Co-ed," in tribute to the First Lady, who was still recovering from her breast cancer surgery back in the U.S.[28] We commuted to Tokyo Haneda Airport and then flew westward three hundred miles in *Air Force One* to Osaka before continuing to South Korea.

Kissinger told the press corps that the President's visit to Japan had achieved "the optimum of what one had hoped for."[29] As usual, Henry's diplomatic performance was excellent. His intelligence and wit had impressed his audiences.

As I look back on that first state visit, President Ford's instincts and intellect served him well. He had, in fact, achieved all the objectives laid out before he had left the White House. Ford had restored confidence in our ally, Japan, that the U.S. would maintain trade and our important military alliance commitments.

It is useful to note that President Ford's success was not simply the result of his careful preparation. Importantly, he possessed personal qualities that were helpful in achieving his goals. He benefited from his long experience in dealing with parliamentarians from many backgrounds and many nations. As I was with him throughout the trip, it was clear to me he enjoyed meeting, visiting, and being on the move—and those with whom he met genuinely reciprocated. He was in his element—an engaging and highly successful former legislative leader, briskly shuffling from one element of a constituency to another, eager to discover unique personalities and to grapple with new challenges. It helped that he sincerely liked and was interested in other human beings.

The President then flew from Japan to the Republic of Korea, an important American ally. President Park Chung-hee met President Ford and his delegation at the airport in Seoul. Park declared the U.S.–South Korea alliance had been "confirmed in blood" during the Korean and Vietnam Wars, and he termed President Ford "our partner" in the effort to establish security in Asia.[30] The President affirmed that the purpose of his visit was "to reaffirm our friendship and to give it new life and meaning."[31] He had been to a war-ravaged South Korea as a member of Congress in 1953. He was the third sitting U.S. President to visit that country, after Presidents Dwight Eisenhower in 1960 and Lyndon Johnson in 1966.

The South Korean people seemed ecstatic to have the President of the United States visiting their country. The visit had been declared a national holiday. An estimated two million people—an amazing 40 percent of Seoul's population—lined the motorcade's twelve-mile route to the hotel. If, in Japan, there might have been some modest lingering resentment on the part of a few toward their old victorious foe from decades before, I did not sense it. However, in South Korea, there was absolutely nothing but genuine gratitude toward the nation that had sent hundreds of thousands of our forces across the ocean to fight for the freedom of the Korean people.

Police officers were posted every fifty feet on the outskirts of the city and every fifteen feet downtown. The President's arrival and his motorcade were carried live on television. Large portraits of Presidents Ford and Park were displayed seemingly everywhere, and a stamp was even issued to commemorate the occasion.[32]

After a short break at the hotel, we traveled by helicopter northeast of Seoul to Camp Casey near the Demilitarized Zone (DMZ) to meet with the U.S. Army's Second Infantry Division. Several Generals were on hand, including Richard G. Stilwell, who had fought in Normandy, commanded the Fifteenth Infantry Regiment during the Korean War, and served as General William Westmoreland's Chief of Staff in Vietnam. Ford was sporting a varsitylike sweater emblazoned with the insignia of the Second Infantry Division and delivered rousing remarks. The troops responded enthusiastically. They were clearly fine examples of military discipline and dedication. Most ran four miles every day before breakfast and played combat football, a sport the object of which was to get a ball into the opposing team's goal through "any means short of an actionable felony."[33]

We took a helicopter back to Seoul, where the President met for two hours with President Park Chung-hee, "[a] trim, poker-faced man who doesn't mince words."[34] Park was seeking a pledge from the U.S. to increase our military assistance for the modernization of South Korea's military and also for President Ford to agree to maintain U.S. troop levels at thirty-eight thousand. In 1971, the U.S. had promised $1.5 billion over a five-year period after deciding to transfer the Seventh Infantry Division from Camp Casey back to its former garrison at Fort Ord in California. U.S. congressional budget cuts had held up delivery of the aid. Ford pledged that U.S. troops would stay and that there would be no future slowdowns. He then arranged to have a private meeting with President Park.[35]

The President of South Korea was an authoritarian. Some went so far as to claim that Ford's presence in South Korea, albeit brief, was a stamp of approval for their government. Dr. Edwin O. Reischauer, Harvard professor and the former U.S. Ambassador to Japan back in the early 1960s, unhelpfully called the decision to go to Korea "an awful blunder."[36] Secretary Kissinger had usefully and pointedly tackled the minor controversy, saying that the visit was the "natural consequence" of a trip to Asia, explaining correctly that circumvention would have raised doubts about U.S. security commitments.[37]

When Ford was alone with President Park, he spoke with him about the important but politically sensitive issue of human rights. The President left with the impression that the South Korean government under Park might modify some of its more criticized policies. Park Chung-hee's government was certainly less than democratic. Indeed, there had never been a democratic government on the Korean Peninsula—and very few in all of Asia. My personal view was that South Korea was prosperous and a success for the U.S.— and that the situation, while not perfect by our standards, was vastly better than the alternatives of anarchy or Communism.[38] During the Cold War, American Presidents of both political parties understandably sought allies where they could find them.

The Soviet Union, now decades behind, was still a potent force back in the mid-1970s, determined to outlast the capitalist systems and aggressive in its efforts to export its brutal socialist revolution across the globe. And the USSR had at that time as its leader a wily dictator, who likely looked forward to testing Gerald Ford and determining his mettle.

President Ford's journey to the Soviet Union from Seoul demonstrated the unusual, and occasionally hostile, relationship that the Communist empire had with the free world. Because the Soviet Union had supported its fellow Communists, the People's Republic of China and North Korea, during the Korean War, it did not officially recognize the existence of the Republic of Korea. So to travel to the USSR from Seoul, South Korea, the President's aircraft was required to execute a diplomatic pirouette. *Air Force One* had to fly from the Republic of Korea back to Tokyo's Haneda Airport, touch down, taxi, and then take off again.[39] Moscow would not have "recognized" President Ford's inbound flight had the aircraft departed directly from the Republic of Korea.

We arrived at a military airfield near Ussuriysk in the USSR—conspicuously close to the North Korean and Chinese borders—during the afternoon of Saturday, November 23. There the well-known Minister of Foreign Affairs, Andrei Gromyko, the Soviet Union's Ambassador to the U.S., Anatoly Dobrynin, and the leader of the USSR, General Secretary Leonid Brezhnev, were on hand to greet President Ford. Snow was everywhere. The airport was desolate. It brought to my mind scenes from the film *Doctor Zhivago*.[40]

Brezhnev, whose formal title was General Secretary of the Central Committee of the Communist Party of the Soviet Union, had been in power for a decade, assuming his powerful position from the ousted Nikita Khrushchev. Once he was in charge of the Soviet Union, its military investment and capabilities had expanded significantly. A large bear of a man, whose face was adorned with unusually prominent eyebrows, Brezhnev became the author of the so-called Brezhnev Doctrine, which declared that any effort to convert a socialist/Communist state to capitalism was a direct threat to the USSR. As such, he and the Soviet Union were quick to support Communist regimes and guerilla movements across the globe—from North Vietnam to Cuba to Angola, to Eastern Europe and Central America.

Like other Soviet leaders, Brezhnev had a penchant for fashioning a cult of personality. One way he did so was to have awards presented to himself—reportedly more than one hundred during his tenure. When he turned sixty, he bestowed on himself the honor of "Hero of the Soviet Union." And he gave himself that same honor three additional times. When he turned seventy, he was named Marshal of the Soviet Union, the highest military honor the Communist regime awarded a Soviet citizen.

Brezhnev, Nixon, and Kissinger had developed a seemingly good relationship, or at least as good as relations between the world's leading capitalist and the world's leading Communist nations could have been. The men had met at three summits during Nixon's presidency, and both sides were keen to pursue arms limitation agreements. Brezhnev went to some lengths to flatter the more-formal Nixon, cracking jokes and lauding his intellectual prowess.[41]

By contrast, Ford and Brezhnev had not known each other. They had met in Washington, D.C., the previous year when Ford was still the Minority Leader of the U.S. House of Representatives, but only briefly. This summit was an opportunity for Ford and Brezhnev to establish a personal rapport.

It is a measure of how vast the Soviet Union was that Brezhnev and his entourage had traversed four thousand miles through seven time zones to meet President Ford at this distant location, yet they had never left the territory of the Soviet Union.

"I understand you are quite an expert on soccer," President Ford said as he shook hands with the General Secretary.

"Yes, I play the left side," Brezhnev replied, "but I haven't played in a long time."

"I haven't played football for a long time, either," Ford said, adding, "I wasn't very fast, but I could hold the line."[42]

We boarded an ornate green- and gold-colored train from the airfield to travel to the site of the two-day summit: a spa on the outskirts of the Siberian port city of Vladivostok, a facility used by state officials and trade union members. (Although the meeting would become known as the Vladivostok Summit, it actually took place in the small town nearby called Okeanskaya.) The ride from the airfield was an hour and a half, and the only scenery was snow-covered hills.[43] Henry Kissinger helped break the ice, at least metaphorically.

We were huddled around a linen-covered table featuring cookies, pastries, and mints. "Henry simply couldn't resist them," President Ford later recalled. Over ninety minutes, and to the great amusement of the Soviets, Henry finished off three plates.[44]

As we arrived, and were being escorted to our dacha, Brezhnev joked with Ford, "Why did you have to bring Henry Kissinger here?"

"Well, it's just very hard to go anywhere without him," Ford replied in jest.

"Kissinger is such a scoundrel."

"It takes one to know one," Ford quickly replied.[45]

The Soviets had reportedly spent ten days laboring to spruce up the spa with fresh paint. But as Ford later noted, "It still looked like an abandoned YMCA camp in the Catskills."[46] The U.S.–Soviet summit commenced at 6:00 p.m. The meeting was held in a conference room overlooking a glass-enclosed garden. The two delegations sat across a long table, communicating through translators, while smoke from Ford's pipe and from Brezhnev's ever-present cigarettes filled the room.[47]

The overriding purpose of the summit was to try to establish the basis for a ceiling on strategic offensive arms, a key element in a new Strategic Arms Limitation Treaty (SALT), which was a priority for the President. Kissinger found Ford to be a different kind of negotiator than Nixon. As Ron Nessen later recounted, "He said Ford was more personable and seemed to get along well with the gregarious Brezhnev. Henry told me that while Nixon preferred to follow a prepared script, Ford was comfortable with a genuine give and take. Kissinger added that for some reason President Nixon seemed not to look foreign leaders in the eye."[48] Hedrick Smith, a reporter with *The New York Times*, echoed that assessment. "In some ways, Mr. Ford with his outgoing personality and his reputation for easy-going candor is personally more akin to the ebullient, joke-telling Soviet Communist party leader than was the more aloof Mr. Nixon."[49]

In their discussions, Ford sat through what was standard procedure among Soviet (and Russian) leaders: a long, less than stimulating
lecture about the failures and evils of the United States that seemed
designed more for an internal Soviet audience. Ford listened to it all
with a patient expression, waiting for his time to respond.

After one of their sessions, President Ford invited Kissinger, Nessen, and me to his dacha for a late-night bite. But first the President
wanted to discuss his impressions of the meeting. Because all of our
rooms were certainly bugged, that meant all confidential conversations had to be held outside in the cold. So we walked along a dark
road to talk, our breath forming clouds of vapor in the frigid tem-
perature.[50]

Ford believed the sessions the previous day had "far exceeded"
his expectations.[51] Ford had taken Kissinger's suggestions in the
meetings—to be polite, but firm on our positions. Ford, for example,
had calmly refused demands to cancel production of our B-1 bombers
scheduled to replace our aging B-52s. The Soviets, Kissinger advised,
eventually would bend. Indeed, Ford and Brezhnev achieved what
earlier had been less than certain, an agreement on numerical equivalence of missiles. The U.S. and the Soviet Union were each to limit
their nuclear arsenals to a total of 2,400 long-range offensive missiles and bombers. Further, no more than 1,320 of the missiles could
be made capable of carrying multiple independently targetable war-
heads (MIRVs). "It was," as Ron Nessen later noted, "one of the rare
times in history when adversaries had mutually agreed to limit their
arsenals."[52] The two delegations sat down to a late lunch of bear meat
and venison, which was followed by an official signing ceremony and
champagne toasts.[53]

That evening, Ford accompanied Brezhnev in the backseat of a
Russian limousine for a tour of Vladivostok thirteen miles away. On
the way back, Brezhnev reached over and held Ford's left hand. He
squeezed harder and harder as he spoke. He explained that he wanted

to save his fellow citizens the pain they suffered during World War II and that he wished to finish what they had started. Ford assured him he felt the summit was an important step toward avoiding "a nuclear holocaust."

"I agree with you," Brezhnev answered, adding, "This is an opportunity to protect not only the people of our two countries but, really, all mankind. We have to do something."[54]

On our departure from Russia, a train took the President back to the airfield near Ussuriysk, where Ford demonstrated a gracious act of diplomacy.

Throughout their encounter, President Ford had sensed that General Secretary Brezhnev had admired his rather unusual coat. Made of mottled gray, brown, black, and white Alaskan wolf fur, the large, shaggy coat had been given to the President by Jack Kim, a furrier and personal friend, during a refueling stop at Elmendorf Air Force Base in Anchorage, Alaska on the way over. As Brezhnev escorted the President up the ramp to *Air Force One*, Ford took off his coat and presented it as a gift to Brezhnev, who seemed delighted and grateful.[55]

Ford's trip to East Asia was in every sense a success, but particularly the summit with the Soviets. Exhausted, Nessen downed a bit of vodka during the train ride to the airfield. Shortly after takeoff in *Air Force One*, he told reporters that what was agreed and signed at Okeanskaya was "one of the most significant agreements since World War II." Then, before heading to the VIP lounge and going quickly to sleep on a couch, he boasted, "Richard Nixon could not achieve this in five years. President Ford achieved it in three months."[56] Unfortunately, but not surprisingly, his offhand comment became the lead for the 11:00 p.m. news the following day. President Ford was too pleased with his trip to express his views to his enthusiastic Press Secretary.

* * *

U.S. News & World Report branded the East Asia trip "a historic journey" in which Ford "achieved the primary goal of his first venture in global diplomacy," adding, "The President proved that he was ready to take over in his own right the world-leadership role Richard Nixon held until he was toppled from office." *Time* magazine confirmed that "as he traveled, he was visibly performing as a global leader and dramatizing the fact that on the world stage, no one is more important than the U.S. President."[57] I had noted during our visit to Japan: "He probably would be good in a crisis and could be seen as great in that event."[58] Over the next six months, the President would be given the chance in spades to demonstrate his skill, starting almost immediately with a situation in the Pacific Ocean that was the stuff of Cold War lore.

As for the President, I observed that he didn't particularly enjoy orating or wrestling with abstractions. Yet I also observed he was unflappable, likable, and impressively persuasive, whether one-on-one or in larger groups. He looked relaxed and fit. He was serene in his manner and charming in personal conversation. Reporter John Herbers in *The New York Times* attested that President Ford was "smiling through it all," "showed no sign of fatigue," and "Went about his activities with . . . good humor."[59] I had great faith in the President. But I did wonder whether there might be a bit of a disadvantage to his characteristic down-home relaxed demeanor. I noted privately at the time: "He never protects himself from having other people see him in a relaxed situation. Can a great leader let down and still inspire?" I asked myself.[60] In fact, looking back I may well have underestimated the positive impact of the President's natural approach. That he was completely comfortable with himself seemed to be seen, accepted, and even valued by those he dealt with.

The President, in the face of some doubts at home, had performed skillfully his responsibilities as Commander in Chief, demonstrating and projecting confidence. His demeanor, absent artifice or hesitation, proved to be his way to sway foreign as well as domestic audiences and led one and all to come to the realization that the United States of America had honest, credible, competent leadership. Ford had taken his oath of office as President only four months earlier, at a time when foreign allies and adversaries alike had reason to question whether America had veered off the rails. By the time Gerald R. Ford returned from East Asia to Washington, D.C., after his week abroad, he had made it clear that our country was firmly back on track. The center was holding.

$$\div 7 \div$$

Neither Confirm nor Deny:
The *Glomar Explorer* and the Crisis
in the CIA

"It started out as a bad day," the President said to me as I met with him in the Oval Office the morning of March 19, 1975, "and it's getting worse."[1]

In the dozen-plus years I had known Gerald Ford, that was one of the rare times I had seen him down—even dejected. An epic problem was erupting, one that threatened to damage the country he led and consume the energy of his still young administration. It involved national security, specifically, and the public disclosure of revelations concerning an extremely sensitive top-secret CIA mission to recover a sunken Soviet submarine and its contents from the floor of the Pacific Ocean.

"You haven't heard the half of it," I replied. "Wait until you read the *Evening Star*."[2] I handed him a copy of the latest edition of what was then Washington's evening newspaper of record. Weeks earlier, the *Los Angeles Times* had speculated about a covert submarine mission in a front-page article. (Its headline: "US REPORTED AFTER RUSS SUB.")[3] The *Evening Star*'s follow-up article stated that the mission had been "approved at the very highest level—by Henry A. Kissinger."

One of the nation's closely guarded secrets being thrust into the glaring light of public scrutiny was more than enough to exasperate a Commander in Chief. Most worrisome, of course, was what was threatening to come next: the release of highly classified information that would do damage to America's international relations. The story had begun seven years earlier when an unpublicized catastrophe on the high seas led to one of the most daring and innovative intelligence operations of the Cold War.

On March 8, 1968, when Lyndon Johnson was president and Gerald Ford and I were still in Congress, *K-129*, a Golf II–class diesel-electric-powered Soviet submarine, was sailing fifteen hundred miles northwest of Hawaii when it sank, killing ninety-eight Russian sailors aboard. The Soviet Union promptly launched a frantic effort to locate the sub, which contained their classified codebooks and three SS-N-4 nuclear-armed ballistic missiles. They failed. The U.S. Navy, alerted to the spike in Soviet activity in the area, initiated a secret mission to try to find the Soviet sub. They succeeded. Actually retrieving the wreckage of the ship and its sensitive contents, nonetheless, proved an undertaking of an entirely different magnitude.

Indeed, it wasn't until 1971 that President Johnson's successor, Richard Nixon, gave a green light to a nascent CIA project, codenamed AZORIAN. The highly classified mission involved constructing a vessel capable of clandestinely retrieving the Soviet sub *K-129*. Construction of the impressive new vessel took more than three years. It was designed and constructed by Global Marine Development at the Sun Shipbuilding and Drydock Company, a subsidiary of the Summa Corporation. The company was owned by the reclusive billionaire Howard Hughes. A whopping 619 feet long and 36,000 tons, the ship featured a giant mechanical claw, the "capture vehicle"—lovingly called *Clementine*—designed to grasp and then raise the 1,750-ton, 132-foot-long Soviet submarine from the depths and then tuck it into the belly of the ship.

In a careful effort to conceal the true purpose of the American ship as it sailed the Pacific Ocean, an elaborate cover story had been devised. The CIA arranged with Howard Hughes to claim his company was building the vessel to mine "manganese nodules" from the ocean floor. Theoretically, the mineral deposits could in turn be refined and sold to form alloys in steel production. As part of the audacious and commercially dubious mining mission, the vessel was overtly christened the *Hughes Glomar Explorer*. ("Glomar" was a truncated form of the name of the Global Marine Development Company). Security surrounding the *Glomar Explorer* was extremely tight. Only a small number of clearances were granted. Even then, only a small percentage of those involved in construction knew the *Glomar* was actually a classified instrument of the Cold War, rather than another pet project of an eclectic industrial titan.

President Nixon had given approval to launch the AZORIAN operation on June 7, 1974, two months before he resigned and only three weeks prior to his trip to Moscow, during which he would sign the Threshold Test Ban Treaty, prohibiting tests of nuclear devices with yields exceeding 150 kilotons. To avoid damaging the Nixon-Kissinger trademark policy of détente, one of his administration's key foreign policy initiatives, Nixon expressly instructed that the effort to recover *K-129* not begin until after his return from the Soviet Union.[4] The treaty was signed on July 3, 1974, and the *Glomar Explorer* arrived at the recovery site the next day.

The salvage operation was carried on for more than a month, and twice was within a hair's breadth of being exposed. The first close call came when a nearby British merchant ship requested medical assistance for a stricken crew member—which U.S. personnel aboard the *Glomar* provided. The second, and more ominous, occurred when a Soviet missile range instrumentation ship, the *Chazhma*, made its way toward the remote site of the recovery effort. Amid concerns that the Soviets might have discovered their mission, and might even attempt to seize the *Glomar Explorer*, the American crew was ordered to quickly destroy all of their classified material in case of a boarding by the Soviets.[5]

The *Chazhma*'s behavior, which was unusual, only added to the tension. The Soviet vessel was equipped with a helicopter, which made several low-level passes while photographing the *Glomar*. At one point, the Soviet vessel sent a message to the Americans.

"We are on our way home and heard your fog horn. What are you doing here?"

"We are conducting ocean mining tests—deep-ocean mining tests," replied the crew of the *Glomar*.

"What kind of vessel are you?"

"A deep-ocean mining vessel."

"How much time will you be here?"

"We expect to finish testing in two to three weeks."

Finally, after what must have seemed like an eternity to the American crew, the *Chazhma* communicated, "I wish you all the best."[6] The vessel steamed away.

Despite that fortunate break, project AZORIAN did not go entirely according to plan. On *Glomar*'s attempt to raise the Soviet's *K-129* submarine, more than three-quarters of the vessel broke off and plunged back to the ocean floor. Only a thirty-eight-foot-long forward section made it into the *Glomar*. As it happened, the failed recovery effort took place on August 9, 1974—the day Richard Nixon resigned the presidency. If the attempt to recover a sunken sub at the risk of triggering a superpower crisis sounds like a story plot, there's a reason. The *Glomar* episode inspired, at least in part, two: the 1977 movie rendition of Ian Fleming's *The Spy Who Loved Me* and author Tom Clancy's 1984 debut novel, *The Hunt for Red October*. Revelation of America's real-life salvage endeavor, however, was an unwanted real-life drama for the new president, who had inherited not only a serious publicity nightmare but an intelligence coup that threatened to be undone by media exposure.

On August 10, Gerald R. Ford's first full day as President, he convened a National Security Council meeting. The meeting primarily dealt with roles and responsibilities. But after the meeting, I put only a very vague cryptic reference to a submarine matter in my notes— purposely so, for reasons of security. The next day, Ford gave the go-ahead for the recovered section of *K-129* to be brought back to Long Beach, California, on a classified, close-hold basis.[7]

For months, a few reporters had been asking around about the operation, having caught wind of it after a bizarre robbery of a safe at the Summa Corporation's California headquarters. Bill Colby, the CIA Director, had managed to convince reporters to hold off on printing any story in the interest of national security. That understanding began to fall apart in December 1974, when other disclosures about covert American intelligence activities came to light, creating a growing national security problem for the new administration.

On December 22, 1974, *The New York Times* ran an explosive front-page article, stating that the CIA, under then Director Richard Helms, had spied on American citizens during the Nixon presidency. The article asserted that "the Central Intelligence Agency, directly violating its charter . . . conducted a massive, illegal domestic intelligence operation during the Nixon Administration against the antiwar movement and other dissident groups in the United States."[8] Under pressure, Helms's successor, Bill Colby, and the CIA General Counsel briefed the Justice Department nine days later. They disclosed eighteen so-called skeletons in the closet, adding they were "trying to track down more details about the various skeletons." Among other revelations, the CIA was said to have wiretapped some journalists, physically surveilled reporters, and "plotted" the assassination of foreign leaders. According to the article, the Agency had even conducted warrantless break-ins and entries at the homes of former CIA employees.[9] The undocumented allegations reawakened questions about a possible CIA role in the Watergate break-in and cover-up. Colby, the paper also reported, was considering recommending legal action against those allegedly involved in domestic spying.[10]

The disclosures, unsurprisingly, led to a public outcry, and a number of individuals in government took steps to try to save their careers. Leaks occurred left and right. So many revelations were coming out simultaneously that many officials began wondering whether the U.S. government would be able to keep any of its classified information out of the press. Classified guidance on delicate arms control negotiations with the Soviets, for instance, ended up in the pages of *The New York Times*.[11] Still only a few months into the Ford presidency with very few new personnel in place, it wasn't certain who in the White House touching classified papers had received the necessary security clearances.[12] Career and non-career officials seemed to have discovered how it was possible to anonymously preempt, weaken, or even shift a President's policy position in a negotiation with a timely leak to the media.[13]

Henry Kissinger, rightly concerned about the international implications of America's secrets hitting the media, urged President Ford to launch an FBI investigation into the series of damaging national security leaks. That was an understandable impulse. But President Ford expressed concerns about the previous administration's handling of leaks, when investigative agencies were requested to engage in investigations to advance political interests. Indeed, "stopping leaks" was a primary goal of the infamous "plumbers" operation that was a part of the Watergate scandal. President Ford decided it was best to assign responsibility for dealing with the leaks to the relevant Cabinet officers, rather than conducting investigations from the White House.[14]

With sensitive matters being leaked to the media, the situation was serious, and the President knew he needed to take determined action to quell concerns among the American people. At that same time the Watergate drama was being rekindled. The trials of Nixon's former top aides and my former colleagues, John Mitchell, Bob Haldeman, and John Ehrlichman, were under way, with them ultimately being convicted of a series of felonies for their roles in the Watergate cover-up, including obstruction of justice, conspiracy, and perjury.

Meeting with top aides in the Oval Office on the evening of January 3, 1975, President Ford directed us to assemble a presidential panel to examine the charges revealed in *The New York Times* and to investigate the actions and activities of the CIA to ensure the agency was operating within the law.[15] My hastily written note from that meeting included the following:

MEETING WITH THE PRESIDENT
January 3, 1975
10:45 to 11:10 a.m.
Oval Office
Nessen, Marsh
We talked about the CIA. The President, Marsh, Buchen and Kissinger met on the subject this morning and agreed on the approach . . . that the President will call in the appropriate Department and Agency heads early next week, tell [them] how he wants their departments and agencies managed with respect to this subject, ask them to get back to him with assurance that that's the way they are presently being administered, that he will take the appropriate governmental action to see that any wrongdoing is referred to the Department of Justice. . . .

That he will create a special panel of citizens to look into the matter with respect to the past to assure him as to what the status is at the present and to make any recommendations to him with respect to safeguards for the future. . . .

That in the event that the Congress creates a Joint Committee on the subject of or even with respect to their present oversight Committees, he assures them that the Administration and the Citizens panel will cooperate fully with them. . . .

That the President . . . feels that this is an important subject because of the importance of an intelligence gathering capability to the United States of America in the world environment that exists. On the other hand he also feels that it is important that that intelligence gathering activity continue on a basis that is consistent with the laws and with the political code of the country and he intends to see that that is the case.[16]

While I certainly agreed that "the CIA had to operate in a lawful manner and ways consistent with statutes," I discussed with the President the CIA's need to "to engage in covert activities," given the nature of the world. In other words, transparency can become dangerous at a certain point. People who understood that critical balance were needed on the proposed panel. "We didn't have time to horse around with this thing," I noted at the time. "It could do great damage to the country if all covert activities in the US government were subject to public scrutiny . . . and the United States foreign policy would be undermined."[17]

Ford summoned CIA Director Bill Colby to the Oval Office on January 3, 1975. Jack Marsh, Counselor to the President, was also present. Marsh noted that Colby was visibly nervous. Because Colby had been required to spend so much time testifying on Capitol Hill, at one point he accidentally called the President "Mr. Chairman."[18] Colby was defensive but forthright in backing many of the claims in the *New York Times* account. "We [the CIA] have run operations to assassinate foreign leaders," Colby said, adding, "We have never succeeded." He cited Fidel Castro of Cuba, for one.[19]

The next day the President was informed that Colby's predecessor, Richard Helms, was "irate" at Colby for his public disclosures of activities that occurred on Helms's watch and made "verbal ultimatums" that seemed to threaten, obliquely, to implicate others in the administration.[20] Colby had been in charge of covert activities during a portion of the Vietnam War and may have felt a need to explain some of the Agency's more controversial operations. In any event, a concerned President Ford had had enough of the back and forth in the administration and the resulting outside speculation.

"We have been struggling for two weeks with the consequences of the [New York Times] article," Ford said. "We have come up with three things: I am writing to each intelligence officer to tell them: 'Here is the law and you are expected to obey it.' Second, we will establish a Blue Ribbon Committee to look into these allegations. Third, I will urge Congress to investigate this either by an existing committee or a joint committee."[21]

Deeply concerned about damage from the original leaks, and what he appeared to believe had been Colby's role, particularly in referring matters to the Justice Department, Kissinger was among those suggesting a firmer hand. Kissinger said that Colby should be given guidance as to what to say on Capitol Hill. We thought that would be unwise, and the President should not do that. The President said if anyone thinks he should do it, they should put it in writing. No one did.[22]

I suggested to the President that he needed to get the issue out of his in-box. "Here we are, probably about twenty staff guys in the White House doing nothing except handling this issue for the past couple of weeks," I said. "You've got a country to run. The economy. Energy problems, foreign policy problems. A tough Congress to deal with."

Ford appreciated that, but he wanted to be sure the issue was given the appropriate attention. He recognized the seriousness of the matter. If more covert activities of the U.S. government were exposed to public scrutiny, then our entire intelligence operations would be undermined. I suggested that he put someone he trusted in charge of a presidential-appointed panel—I suggested Vice President Nelson Rockefeller—and leave the day-to-day work on the matter to them.[23]

After considerable discussion among the key figures in the White House and in the Congress, the President's intelligence panel was selected. It consisted of eight distinguished members: former Commerce Secretary John Connor, former Treasury Secretary C. Douglas Dillon, who had served as a member of the Executive Committee of the NSC during the Cuban Missile Crisis, former U.S. Solicitor General Erwin Griswold, labor union leader Lane Kirkland, former Supreme Allied Commander of NATO General Lyman Lemnitzer, and former University of Virginia president Edward Shannon, Jr. This list also included a notable entry in California Governor Ronald Reagan, who was finishing his second term in office and was the topic of widespread rumors about his possible plans to challenge Ford for the Republican nomination for the Presidency.

By early January, the committee of eight members was announced and the newly installed Vice President, Nelson Rockefeller, was named the Chairman. This prevented a potentially awkward moment, since Governor Reagan, a strong conservative, was a vocal opponent of the liberal Rockefeller; indeed, some aides warned Ford that Reagan might bolt the committee if he were not told in advance that Rockefeller would be the chairman.[24] Reagan was so informed, at Ford's direction, and he stayed on the board. On January 4, 1975, Ford issued Executive Order 11828 to establish what became known as the "Rockefeller Commission" on CIA activities. The goal was for the commission to complete its business by March.

Trouble struck not long after, prolonging matters. On January 16, the President met with editors from *The New York Times* for an off-the-record chat. At one point, he said the commission had come across CIA operations that would "make your hair curl." "Like what?" managing editor A. M. Rosenthal asked. "Like assassinations," Ford responded. Despite the conversation's notably unambiguous ground rules, the President's private comment, seeming to indicate new information about the CIA's potential involvement in political assassinations, spread all over Washington.[25] To the administration's disappointment, an unambiguous understanding of the term "off the record" did not still exist in Washington in the months after Watergate. Daniel Schorr, in his CBS news broadcast, reported Ford's remark on February 28, 1975. My assistant Dick Cheney promptly advised Press Secretary Ron Nessen to "refuse all comment," which he did.[26] President Ford also punted in his future interactions with the media. Still, an investigation into alleged past CIA assassination plans was tacked on to the Rockefeller Commission's agenda. Finer parsing of the President's exchange with *The New York Times* suggested something even more disturbing about the management of the executive branch: the White House had, on occasion, likely been out of the loop about activities by one of the government's covert agencies.

I made it a mission to help ensure that the President and the White House would not get caught off-guard again. I advised the President to instruct the heads of all agencies to put their respective employees on notice that they had an obligation to report on anything "that's being done that is illegal or in a gray area." My rationale to the President, as I noted in a memo: "You don't run around telling your four-year-old daughter, 'Don't stick a pencil in your ear,' because you never imagined she would. It may be that they are out there sticking pencils in their ears, and the only way you will know is if you ask them what the hell they are doing."[27]

Meanwhile, there was another major disclosure in the offing, which threatened to further damage the government and U.S. foreign policy in general. Long submerged in the murky waters of the intelligence community, the story of the *Glomar* finally was coming to the surface.

The agreement Colby had brokered with reporters regarding the sunken Soviet submarine ended on February 7, 1975, when the *Los Angeles Times*, unable to resist a news story involving Howard Hughes and the CIA, published its first article on the U.S. clandestine recovery effort.[28] In a race against further revelations hitting the newspaper—and alerting the Soviet Union about American activities surrounding their lost submarine—a second recovery operation was proposed, codenamed MATADOR, to try to retrieve the remainder of the *K-129*. Regrettably, the time for that ran out.

The White House press office immediately began getting peppered with questions that, after the Watergate investigations, had an all-too-familiar ring: What did the President know? And when did he know it?

Like others in government, I had issues with press stories—let alone the media exposés—that relied heavily on anonymous sources. They tended to exaggerate differences and advance personal political agendas, especially when the sources could hide behind labels such as "senior administration official" or "source who asked to remain anonymous." But in the case of the AZORIAN project, it wasn't just egos that were threatened. There was the potential to generate serious problems between the world's two nuclear superpowers, creating tensions not seen since the Cuban Missile Crisis a decade earlier. Leaks about the project also threatened to lead to the exposure of still more delicate matters involving our country's intelligence activities and, in turn, compromise U.S. intelligence operations and possibly the security of U.S. operatives overseas. And, of course, the media speculation had the added drawback of occasionally being true.

The President considered the range of advice he was receiving from his senior aides about the best course of action. One possibility was to simply take full ownership of the AZORIAN project and provide a full accounting of U.S. activities. Phil Buchen, Ford's White House Counsel, favored that approach. Defense Secretary Jim Schlesinger favored it as well.[29] A former CIA Director himself, Jim saw full disclosure as a spur to patriotism, for the *Glomar* was, in his words and in fact, a technical "marvel." Further, the Soviets, he added, did not have clean hands on such matters. It had raised a British submarine back in the 1920s, but also repaired it and used it in the Soviet navy. The truth, Jim argued, was going to emerge eventually anyway, and likely sooner rather than later. At that point, some forty-five hundred government employees were aware of the AZORIAN project, and up to one hundred Members of Congress and staff on Capitol Hill had already been briefed on it.[30] "There are so many people who have to be briefed on covert operations, it is bound to leak," Henry Kissinger reminded President Ford in a January 1975 meeting. "There is no one with guts left. All of yesterday they were making a record to protect themselves about AZORIAN."[31]

A more limited disclosure approach was floated as another option for the President's consideration. This involved briefing additional people on Capitol Hill and friendly foreign governments on the operation, but without giving a full accounting to the press. Careful and selective introduction to AZORIAN, some estimated, might help preclude blindsiding friends, alienating potential allies, and strengthening the opposition of adversaries. No one wanted a repeat of the kind of media backlash Ford received after the "surprise" pardon of Nixon.

The full disclosure route was most in keeping with his nature and instincts. It also fit the ethos of his administration, which had worked to separate itself from the impressions of the secretive patterns of prior administrations.

Yet public admission entailed significant and unusual hazards. Brent Scowcroft, Kissinger's assistant at the NSC, was opposed to acknowledging AZORIAN. Counselor Jack Marsh and Director Bill Colby were as well.[32] Colby warned acknowledgment might re-create the dynamics of the 1960 U-2 spy plane incident with Gary Powers, putting public pressure on the Soviet Union to aggressively respond to this "affront" to its sovereignty.[33] Opening up publicly might also mean laying down diplomatic land mines for the President before his scheduled meeting with Soviet Premier Leonid Brezhnev in several months in Helsinki, Finland.[34] The two leaders were set to sign the Final Act of the Conference on Security and Cooperation in Europe (CSCE), negotiations that had been under way for nearly two years. Full disclosure of the project also risked the ire of the Soviets at a time when the President and particularly Secretary Kissinger were working hard to achieve a nuclear arms limitation agreement between the two superpowers.

Then there was a third approach, which Kissinger and I favored: to "neither confirm nor deny." (It has since been suggested this might have been one of the early uses of that phrase now in the popular lexicon.) We agreed with Bill Colby that it probably wasn't wise to publicly confirm AZORIAN. Doing so could unnecessarily put the Soviets on the spot and conceivably disrupt the evolving U.S.-Soviet relationship. We also believed that endorsing AZORIAN would publicly verify our country's considerable underwater capabilities, which had already yielded important intelligence on the Soviet Union and other nations. Public acknowledgment, we believed, would also further validate leakers—those who had compromised classified information as reliable sources, and possibly incentivize them and others to expose still more secrets in the future. Finally, we were also concerned it would almost certainly raise humanitarian issues about the ninety-eight Soviet crewmen whose remains were still inside *K-129*, which was functionally their underwater coffin.

This, too, had risks, of course. White House silence or unwilling-ness to be forthright with reporters could incite charges that Nixon's secretive presidency had returned. Some would undoubtedly won-der whether the new administration, like its discredited predecessor, was seeking to cover up other activities—possibly even some illegal ones. And then there was the problem of the Soviets. Regardless of how the White House responded, the story was now public enough that the leaders in Moscow certainly hadn't missed it. Might they unmask the project to the world on their own timetable to try to maximize embarrassment to the President and the U.S.?

The President considered the various options carefully, asked probing questions, and made a decision that would have ramifica-tions for years to come. He chose the third approach, proposed by Kissinger—to neither confirm nor deny—while fully aware of the distinct risks associated with nonconfirmation, as the press finally broke the story wide open.

On March 17, Lloyd Shearer, columnist for *Parade* magazine, sent a message to Bill Colby, notifying him that the story was "all over" the National Press Building.[35] Syndicated columnist and commenta-tor Jack Anderson "broke" the *Glomar* story the following day with a report during his syndicated radio program on the Mutual Radio Network. Then *The New York Times* ran a front-page article by Sey-mour Hersh, "CIA Salvage Ship Brought Up Part of Soviet Sub Lost in 1968, Failed to Raise Atom Missiles."[36] Reporters began swarming Long Beach where the *Glomar* was parked.

As the *Glomar* operation came to light, so, too, did other intel-ligence matters long thought to have been put to rest. The inevitable result of the various investigations, especially into the world of covert activities, was that more and more intelligence information began to be available in the media. The Rockefeller Commission, originally charged with looking into allegations about the CIA, was now dip-ping its toes into the work of the Warren Commission. President

Ford, of course, was one of the few surviving who had served as a member. The Warren Commission, assembled by President Lyndon Johnson to investigate the death of John F. Kennedy, had concluded that assassin Lee Harvey Oswald had acted alone. That was a controversial conclusion, one that was still being put to the test.

MEETING WITH THE PRESIDENT
March 20, 1975
2:05 to 3:10 p.m.
Present: Vice President, Marsh, Brent Scowcroft, Buchen and Rumsfeld
The Vice President discussed some of the work of the panel, CIA and a conclusion or two of his, one of which was that he has concluded without any evidence, and because of that anyone would have to deny it as a fact, but he has personally concluded that Castro and the Communists were involved in some way in both Kennedy deaths.[37]

That conclusion by Rockefeller, which he himself admitted was unsubstantiated, threatened to open up a new can of worms—with Ford being drawn in directly. First the *Glomar* episode reawakened questions about the murky relationship between Howard Hughes and Richard Nixon. Now there was a new implication that the Warren Commission might not have told the American people everything they believed about the death of President Kennedy. Not for a minute did I believe President Ford would have willingly withheld information from the public, other than for some truly important national security reasons. His concern was that he might not know all the information either.

Many conspiracy theorists long have believed that either the Soviet Union or the Fidel Castro regime in Cuba, or possibly both, could have been somehow involved in the Kennedy assassination. The fact that Oswald may have been in closer contact with the Cubans than was publicly known, and might have been privy to confidential CIA information about its activities in Cuba, certainly would raise questions. The President in particular was concerned by the possibility that the CIA had kept such information from members of the Warren Commission. If in fact they had, Ford wondered, was it conceivable that they might now be doing something similar to both the Congress and the President?

In February 1976, eight months after the Rockefeller Commission's report had been released to the public and President Ford had made further changes in his Cabinet late the prior year, he announced plans to reorganize the intelligence community. The barrage of leaks, new levels of scrutiny, and congressional investigations being led by Congressman Otis Pike and Senator Frank Church had damaged agency morale, especially in the CIA's Soviet counterintelligence unit, and had promised to affect U.S. handling of covert operations for some time to come.

As for the *Glomar Explorer*, it was kept mothballed for more than a quarter-century before being restored by a U.S. petroleum company for deep-sea oil drilling and exploration. The CIA, while recognizing that the AZORIAN project failed to meet all of its intelligence objectives, still properly considers the project to have been "one of the greatest intelligence coups of the Cold War."[38]

8

The Reagan Shadow

MEETING WITH THE PRESIDENT

March 7, 1975

5:00 to 6:20 p.m.

Oval Office

Rumsfeld (Walker was there for most of it and Cheney for part of it)

We talked about Secretary of Commerce. The President instructed me to give Reagan a call and visit with him personally indicating that he would be excellent—that we don't want to put him [Ford] in an embarrassing position by posing it to him. DR has the action and will do on Monday, March 10.[1]

The Washington Hilton Hotel is a massive building that curves in the middle as it faces our capital city's bustling Connecticut Avenue. Boasting one of the city's largest ballrooms, the Hilton has played host to everything from presidential inaugural parties to the annual White House Correspondents Dinner. It has even hosted charity boxing events. But in early March of 1975, it became the scene of another kind of contest: a proxy battle between two of the most prominent names in the Republican Party. One was the sitting President of the United States.

From practically the start of his presidency, Gerald Ford had received periodic warnings from political advisors and outside observers about Governor Ronald Reagan and his rumored ambitions. When Ford became President, Reagan, tellingly to some, had not offered unqualified support. He said that his support of President Ford in 1976 would be contingent on the outcome of various appointments.[2] One of Ford's first considered appointments, as it happens, was Reagan himself.

"You ought to start thinking of a job for Reagan," advised Dean Burch, then the Chairman of the Republican National Committee. We were seated next to each other at a dinner. It was early October 1974; I hadn't been Chief of Staff for a full two weeks. Burch, a talented and experienced political operative looking forward to the 1976 election and a personal friend, was making the point that it wasn't good for Ford to have the Governor of California, a man who had been a candidate for President before and, rumor had it, still had higher aspirations, "milling around the country."[3]

In the months that followed, taking that advice, members of the Ford administration repeatedly discussed if there might be a way to convince Reagan to take a senior position in the Ford administration. "If they are out, they can make mischief," I said to the President about his potential rivals, "and if they're in, they're in the same rowboat we are."[4] By December 1974, Reagan's name had been floated internally in the White House for Ambassador to Spain, Ambassador to the United Kingdom, Secretary of Agriculture, Secretary of Transportation, Secretary of Housing and Urban Development, and Secretary of Health, Education, and Welfare.[5] Ford recognized the challenge Reagan could pose him, though he didn't acknowledge it publicly. In an effort to make Reagan feel more of an investment in the administration, the President had indirectly and quietly run some potential administration appointees by Reagan, if not for his approval, then to at least see if Reagan had strong opposition to any of them.[6] Now

President Ford had a specific proposal for Reagan. At the President's direction, I was asked to extend the California Governor an offer— that to paraphrase the popular *Godfather* film released the previous year—the President hoped he couldn't refuse.

The energy around a Reagan challenge of President Ford was a symptom of a growing gulf within the Republican Party between a powerful establishment, long dominated by so-called moderate Republicans, and an emerging conservative movement coming into its own. Giving that movement additional oxygen was a President who, at least early on, seemed not to be focused on whether or not he would run for election to the presidency on his own as well as his decision to select the leading liberal, Nelson Rockefeller, as his Vice President.

Having just assumed the presidency, a position he had never sought, it struck Gerald Ford as discordant, even unseemly, for him to immediately start actively planning for the coming presidential election. Since I had assumed the role of Chief of Staff, it fell to me, repeatedly, to field the growing concerns of his many friends and advisors about the urgent need for him to select the key people to develop a campaign organization.

On February 3, 1975, for example, I showed the President an article by the well-known *Washington Post* columnist David Broder speculating on a one-term Ford presidency. There was another article titled, "A Ford Presidency—less than a sure bet," and still another discussing the possible presidential candidacy of Senator Howard Baker, and one speculating that Vice President Rockefeller was aiming for "a major role" in the administration. "Mr. President, these all spell trouble," I told him. "It may be that you're making progress on a presidential campaign structure but you may be making progress slower than the waves leaping around you."

He said, "Well, what do you propose?"

And I said, "Well I'm going to take just a couple of days and just think it through and I'll be back to you."[7]

A few days later, on February 6, I arranged a meeting with the President and Cliff White, the key Republican strategist who had worked for Goldwater's campaign in 1964 and who understood well the conservative support for Reagan. White talked to the President about the frustrations of voters of recent years. "Lack of trust in politicians" was a major problem, White observed. "What moves people is either personality or a banner—an idea or an ideal."

One idea the President mentioned wasn't quite what White had in mind, but it did speak to Ford's determination to build support across the aisle and his consistent focus on his role as President, rather than the task of running for the presidency. He wondered about having all presidential candidates from both major parties meet at Camp David sometime to discuss how to achieve bipartisanship in foreign policy.[8]

A few weeks later, on February 18, 1975, White attended a meeting of conservatives that had been held over the past weekend—noting that attendance had doubled from an expected 250 to about 500. Support for Reagan, or even third-party alternatives, was discussed. I made a note that Cliff White had mentioned to me a Carl [sic] Rove, who was then a young Republican who had defended the party brilliantly.[9]

Around that same time, I met alone with the President in the Oval Office to inform him again that various outsiders were questioning whether Ford really was going to run for election in his own right. "I am going to run," Ford told me. But he said, "Rummy, let's talk a minute. I hate campaign organizations." He said he never formed one when he ran for Congress and added, rather quaintly considering the endless political campaigning and strategizing of the day, "I've always run on the basis of the job I've performed."[10] Ford seemed to be operating in the mind-set of a Republican Congressman accustomed to seeking re-election in a friendly environment. Grand Rapids, Michigan, was a Republican district, and the Democrats there rarely fielded candidates against him who posed much of a challenge. In any event, he added, "I don't want to worry about it. I don't enjoy it, I don't like it."

But then Ford continued on the subject and clarified for me what was troubling him about the push to get him to commit to a presidential campaign: Watergate. "Nixon had that great big organization and they did everything wrong," he said. He noted that Nixon's big landslide in 1972 may have encouraged aides to engage in activities they should better have avoided, including the bugging of the Democratic Party headquarters.

"Well, you could make the reverse case," I countered to the President. "Nixon, with the smallest percentage of people in the Republican Party in history, got the second-biggest landslide in history because he did everything right except a few bad errors involving Watergate and various things in the White House." My point to the President was that in terms of the organization, you could make the case that Nixon's campaign was a very successful effort.

The President was not persuaded. "Well, we are going to have to think about whether or not we can find some outside vehicle to take care of it because I'm going to be spending my time doing my job [as President] and not the other," he replied.[11]

Even many months since the pardon, and even as the shadow of Ronald Reagan began to form over the Ford presidency, another shadow had never completely receded. Invariably, it seemed, there was always something new popping up about Richard Nixon that posed new difficulties for Ford. In October 1974, for example, when Mr. Nixon was admitted to the hospital to deal with a clot in his thigh, there was a discussion as to what the President should do. Some of Ford's advisors recommended against his even making a phone call.

The question of whether flowers should be sent was discussed and left open.[12] A few months later, there was discussion about what the proper etiquette was when Ford visited California, with the President ultimately deciding that his inclination was not to feel he had to go see him each time he went out there.[13] In April 1975, Nixon's new Chief of Staff, Jack Brennan, told me that the former President was having about seven or eight appointments a week, that they were saying they were favorable to what Henry Kissinger and the President were doing. He then raised the question of the movement of some private belongings of Pat's and Tricia's and Julie's to California and was upset by the White House's rebuff of the request. I said, "Well the President [Ford] didn't know about it, and I didn't know about it, but had it been brought to me, I certainly would have said no, in terms of using military aircraft, that I was sure that Jack [Marsh] had made the decision, but it was the correct decision." In my view, there was no reason on earth why the United States taxpayers should pay for the movement of private personal belongings of the Nixon family. "It would just raise sixteen kinds of hell," I said.[14]

Once again the aftereffects of Watergate—and Ford's strongly felt and understandable reluctance to be associated with anything that smacked of an overzealous political organization—quickly resulted in speculation that he might not seek the White House, which in turn encouraged Reagan supporters, who feared the alternative: a run by their liberal nemesis Vice President Nelson Rockefeller.

Some of Ford's top lieutenants openly, and unhelpfully, scoffed at the notion that conservatives could mount a credible challenge to the President. Adding to conservatives' sense of grievance, Bob Hartmann had publicly rejected the idea of Republicans leaving Ford for Reagan or any alternative candidate. "Where can they go?" he said to *The New York Times*, which noted in the article that he "laughed harshly."[15]

Hartmann wasn't the only one who saw Reagan as a less than formidable threat. Later that fall, for example, I received a memo that reported on a conversation someone had had with President Nixon. "RN feels that Ronald Reagan is a lightweight and not someone to be considered seriously or feared in terms of a challenge for the nomination," the memo said. "He (Nixon) further feels that we are building Reagan into a more formidable opponent than would be the case otherwise by responding to him in terms of our trip schedule and how we talk about Reagan's entering the race."[16] I, however, did not dismiss Reagan's possible candidacy as easily. I didn't know him well, but from what little I had heard and seen, his communication skills were second to none.

Ronald Reagan was born in 1911 in Tampico, Illinois, about 110 miles west of Chicago. His family was poor. The Reagans had lived in a number of rural towns in the northern part of the state until they settled in Dixon, Illinois. As a young man, he showed the rare mix of characteristics that can support stellar political careers. He was bright and ambitious, yet easygoing. In high school, he won the student body presidency, acted in drama productions, played football and basketball, and ran track. He worked as a lifeguard for seven summers, during which time he was credited with saving seventy-seven lives. Reagan attended Eureka College, a small liberal arts institution in Illinois and, after graduation in 1932, became a sports announcer on radio. While serving in the U.S. Army, he was discovered by a Warner Brothers agent who offered him a multiyear Hollywood contract. Over the next two decades, he would appear in fifty-three films.

During the peak of the Communist scare in the post–World War II period, Reagan had been elected President of the Screen Actors Guild, the union for actors, a role in which he took leadership in exposing pro-Communist influences in the film industry. In the 1950s, he toured the country as a television host and motivational speaker for the General Electric Company, thoughtfully promoting the relationship between prosperity, capitalism, and classical virtues. Reagan had been a lifelong Democrat, but over time found himself moving toward the right. He admired FDR's rhetorical style and had backed President Harry Truman in 1948, but he campaigned for General Eisenhower in 1952 and in 1956 and for Vice President Nixon in 1960. He officially switched to the Republican Party in 1962 and planted his flag on the national stage two years later with an excellent television address in support of Barry Goldwater, famously titled, "A Time for Choosing." Riding a surge of support from California businessmen and the public, Reagan was elected Governor of the state in 1966.

Reagan, his star steadily rising, was beloved by the Goldwater wing of the Republican Party. The GOP Establishment, largely in the Northeast Corridor, considered him a threat and berated him as uninformed and out of touch. The feeling was mutual. Reagan blasted Washington, D.C., as "the seat of a 'buddy' system" devoted to "the Congress, the bureaucracy, the lobbyists, big business and big labor."[17]

The concern in the Ford camp, of course, was that Reagan was setting his sights on something much higher. Playing the long game, Reagan strategically avoided praising Ford or in any way improving the President's standing. Reagan's case against Ford, which up through the spring of 1975 had remained largely under the radar, was straightforward. Like most if not all conservatives and a great many moderates, he saw Ford's choice of the liberal Nelson Rockefeller as disastrous. And Rockefeller had not helped matters. Within weeks, the new Vice President began actively antagonizing Reagan allies on Capitol Hill. Vice President Rockefeller had gotten into a nasty fight with the post-Watergate Congress about Senate procedure, as well as on the number of Senate votes needed to invoke cloture and end a filibuster. Heightening the controversy, one of Rockefeller's key legislative aides, a twenty-six-year-old lawyer, reportedly refused to even meet with conservatives on Capitol Hill.[18]

But Ford's other sin, in the eyes of Governor Reagan and many of his strongest supporters in the new conservative movement, was his continuation and support of the Nixon-Kissinger policy of détente with the Soviet Union. For some in the anti-Communist conservative movement, who knew well the damage authoritarianism does to all but the elites, détente seemed like an accommodation with totalitarianism. They believed the Soviet Union did not have to be a permanent fixture in the international landscape, and that the free world needed to be more energetic in efforts to resist it.

In March 1975, those two competing visions for the party and for the country were on display at the annual Republican National Leadership Conference. Both President Ford and Governor Reagan were invited to address that year's gathering of party faithful, Ford speaking at the beginning of the conference, on March 7, and Reagan at its conclusion. The tension of this arrangement was lost on no one.

When Ford spoke to the group, he made clear his determination to seek election to the presidency in his own right. "I can tell you without equivocation tonight that I fully intend to seek the nomination of the Republican Party as its candidate for President in 1976," Ford declared. "There is nothing iffy about that statement. I intend to seek the nomination. I intend to win. I intend to run for President. And I intend to win that too."

In keeping with his approach to governance, President Ford made the case for a GOP that broadened its appeal across the nation, to groups that long had not identified with the party, such as African Americans and Latinos. In his remarks, Governor Reagan seemed to challenge that approach. "A political party cannot be all things to all people," Reagan contended in his speech. "It cannot compromise its fundamental beliefs for political expediency, or simply to swell numbers."

The Californian's remarks antagonized party liberals, including Senator Charles Percy of Illinois, who had long sought to reach out to independents and minority groups. "There's nothing like a former Democrat telling a lifelong Republican where he should take his party affiliation," Percy shot at Reagan—who had indeed been a Democrat until the early 1960s.

The press, too, picked up the marked differences in tone between the two approaches. *The New York Times* even called Reagan's remarks a "rebuttal" to President Ford's earlier speech. The scope of the potential challenge Reagan represented to Ford was also becoming clearer. Though Ford was received warmly by the assembled Republican leaders, Reagan received cheers usually reserved for rock stars. The Ford White House could sense a powerful political wind rising. If Ford was going to prevail in 1976, while keeping the Republican Party together, he would have to work quickly.

Ford requested that I make my unpublicized mission to Reagan with a long-shot goal: to persuade him to join the Ford administration, thus short-circuiting Reagan's presidential bid before it even formally began. Offering a senior administration position to a Governor who was being urged to seek the Oval Office was, from the beginning, a tough, if not impossible, sell. But I thought it was wise of Ford to pursue it and that it was at least worth a try. Even if Reagan didn't accept, the hope was that he would at least appreciate the offer.

When I arrived at the Governor's hotel suite, the tall former movie star flashed his famous smile and greeted me warmly. After some pleasantries, I came to the point.

"You know Fred Dent is leaving the Commerce Department to become the new U.S. Trade Rep," I said to the Governor.

Reagan nodded.

"Well, the President was talking about who might be the best bet to replace him in the Cabinet. And a lot of people have suggested that that person should be you."

I outlined the importance of the Commerce Secretary in man-

aging various economic and commercial issues, many of which
Reagan had been discussing so effectively in his lectures for General
Electric. The Cabinet post, I stressed, would involve the important
task of convincing the business community to help improve job
growth and economic activity. The post should also be used to edu-
cate the public about what set us apart from our Communist rivals
in the Soviet Union.

Reagan listened politely, but showed no outward sign of interest.
"Well, Don, please tell the President I'm very honored and flattered,"
he finally responded. "I understand what you are saying completely
about the importance of that assignment."

I sensed a "but" coming. It arrived swiftly.

"But I feel kind of like a guy who is getting ready to get out of the
service."

He explained that after eight years in the governorship, he was
not ready for another job in the public sector. He said he was already
committed to his newly launched radio program and his syndicated
newspaper column, which he said he was writing himself. He was
looking forward, he said, to going out on "the mashed potato circuit"
across the country to deliver speeches and attend dinners. That, of
course, was exactly what a candidate for the presidency would need
to be doing, though neither of us broached that sensitive topic in our
discussion.

"I understand that," I replied. "And the President will, too. Although I must say I'm personally disappointed you won't be tackling
this assignment for the President. I feel you would be an excellent addition to the administration. There are, in fact, a great many people
around the country, and certainly in the Ford administration, who
think highly of you."

He thanked me for the kind words, but didn't soften. Not a bit.
He had delivered a calm, quiet, and firm "no." His rationale—being
ready to leave the political fray—was plausible, as he was just leav-

ing the governorship of an important state. But it was contrary to what many of Ford's closest advisors believed to be Reagan's true aims.

Since I was already there, I thought I would take the opportunity to feel him out about his attitude toward the Ford administration in general. Perhaps I could get a sense of how likely a Reagan challenge to Ford might actually be.

"You know, I was on *Meet the Press* the other day," I told him. "And I was told by the press there was some big conflict between Reagan and the President."

He looked at me carefully, waiting to see where I was going.

"I dismissed that," I added quickly. "And said my impression was that there wasn't."

"You're absolutely right, Don," Reagan said. With *The New York Times* story about his "rebuttal" speech to Ford's at the conference clearly in his mind, he said: "I didn't write my speech in response to the President. I had written it on the plane coming in and it was essentially what I've been giving." He noted that this wasn't the first time the press had sought to push a story line of rivalry between Reagan and more "established" Republican figures. He reminded me that Richard Nixon had come to him with a similar concern years ago. (Reagan had waged a halfhearted challenge to Nixon for the 1968 nomination, and the two men had been widely viewed as rivals by the media ever since.)

Reagan leaned forward in his chair and looked me in the eye. "One of the problems we're going to have is to see that the press doesn't drive a wedge between us," he said.

"Well, I know that the President feels that way," I replied. "I know that he feels a great identification with the views you've been putting forth." I added: "I'll certainly report this to the President."

Reagan thanked me for taking the time to visit. For many months he did not publicly mention our meeting or President Ford's offer of a Cabinet post—that is, not until it would make a memorable impact.

Returning to the White House, I relayed my thoughts on our discussion in a meeting to the President. Considering Reagan a friend, Ford was slow to accept the possibility that Reagan would actually challenge him head-on, despite increasingly clear signs that Reagan might well do so. Ford tended to assume most people were like him: essentially open, up front, and without guile or cunning.

Ford, in fact, was determined to make another personal entreaty to Reagan during a visit to Palm Springs near the end of March. There, he and Betty entertained the Governor and his wife, Nancy, at a private dinner. Though talk of Reagan's potential primary challenge was lurking throughout the polite conversation, it never quite bubbled to the surface.

After the dinner, however, there was news that was unsettling on a number of scores. Two Republican operatives informed the President that Reagan was raising money across the country, as much as $1 million, hardly a sign of a man preparing to leave politics. One of them, Dick Andrews, told us that Reagan's was "a full-fledged operation" and that "there are as many advance men moving around as when Nixon moved around in the 1972 campaign." Reagan, they said, controlled the political machinery in California, and if Ford didn't move quickly, he was going to lose it.

We were also informed that Cliff White, who had helpfully given us advice early in 1975, had been on Reagan's payroll for some months.

"White is smart," one of the operatives commented in the meeting. "He is working hard. Unless we get started now we will have to get ready for a very bitter fight."

President Ford, clearly roused to action by this news, asked for my thoughts.

"They are right," I told him. "We ought to get moving. The key thing to do is to move fast while Reagan is not an announced candidate." That, I suggested, would help flush his true intentions out a bit.

The President was informed that Bob Finch, who served as Lieutenant Governor of California under Reagan, urged President Ford to bring back George H. W. Bush, who had been Chairman of the Republican National Committee under Nixon and was currently serving as envoy to China, to run the campaign and get going.

President Ford still seemed to hold out hope that Reagan really wasn't willing to create a divide in the party by challenging his friend directly. "I have a theory that Reagan doesn't feel that I am a candidate and he wants to position himself so that he can stop Rocky," the President said.

"I don't want to contest your theory, but it doesn't make an awful lot of difference, Mr. President," I replied. I explained to him how a political campaign staff can get going, as in the Rockefeller campaign in 1968, and how it ends up taking on a life of its own. The staff people are working for Rockefeller, they go to a politician in a state and say, "I am for this candidate and he is running." As a result, they have to keep their guy in the race, otherwise they are proven wrong and unreliable to everyone they had talked to to get them to support their man. The thing ends up building muscle around those relationships, and that staff kept pumping up Rockefeller, keeping him in the race long after the thing should have been over.

"Even though your theory might be right on Reagan, which I am not in a position to contest," I said, "the fact of the matter is that at some point he will end up getting shoved by his people."[19]

Ford understood the situation, even though it was clear he really didn't want to. He was about to face the fight of his political life.

It was not long, however, before more pressing matters affecting the country intruded, at least for a period. On the way to Palm Springs, *Air Force One*'s radio operator had handed the President a brown envelope. Inside was a message: The city of Da Nang had fallen to the North Vietnamese. More than 150,000 Communist soldiers were on the march toward the capital of Saigon, and, apparently due to intelligence shortcomings, there was little in their way to stop them. That crisis, and the sad unfortunate fact that the long U.S. role in the Vietnam War was coming to an end, proved to be perhaps the greatest test of Gerald Ford's leadership.

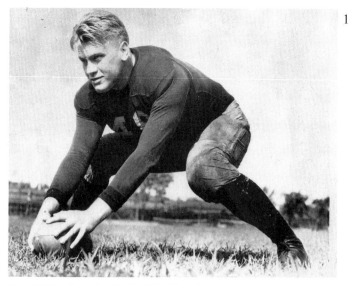

Gerald Ford on the football field at the University of Michigan.

The First Family following the swearing in of Gerald R. Ford as the thirty-eighth President of the United States.

3

President Ford meeting with his transition team.

4

Bryce Harlow (left) was a seasoned advisor to Presidents.

5

President Ford aboard Air Force One with his highly capable personal aide, Terry O'Donnell.

6

Greeting author Ayn Rand and her husband, Frank O'Connor, at the swearing in of Alan Greenspan as Chairman of the President's Council of Economic Advisors.

7

President Ford hosting a breakfast meeting with bipartisan congressional leadership, Senator William Fulbright (D-AR) and Senator Hugh Scott (R-PA).

8

Betty Ford throws a football (a gift from Redskins Coach George Allen) following her breast cancer operation.

Dick Cheney accompanying President Ford on a campaign trip to Indiana.

Secure in his conviction that the pardon of Richard Nixon was necessary on behalf of the American people, Gerald Ford was the first sitting President to testify before a committee of the U.S. Congress since President Abraham Lincoln.

Chicago Mayor Richard J. Daley welcomes President Ford to Illinois.

Ford valued engaging with outside experts and sought out new ideas and a range of perspectives. Dr. Herman Kahn, the prominent intellectual, was a personal friend I introduced to the President.

13

The two top Republican leaders before the presidential primary contest.

14

A "people's President" in his element.

White House staff members watching the anticipated, but still disappointing, mid-term election returns come in.

President Ford meeting with some of our country's finest public servants: Counsel Phil Buchen, Senior Advisor Jack Marsh, and Deputy Attorney General Larry Silberman.

Receiving guidance from the indomitable First Lady, Betty Ford.

President Ford and General Secretary of the U.S.S.R. Leonid Brezhnev at the summit meeting in Vladivostok.

On the train to Vladivostok.

President Ford and Vice
President Rockefeller
with U.S. Senator Mike
Mansfield (D-MT).

20

21

President Ford with
former Governor of
Texas John Connolly.

22

President Ford and
Henry Kissinger with
U.S. Senator Hubert
Humphrey (D-MN).

The President discussing his remarks before an address to be delivered that evening.

President Anwar Sadat of Egypt and President Ford worked well together.

Ford had a natural affinity for great athletes such as Pele, the Brazilian soccer player.

President Ford visiting with Jack Marsh and Henry Kissinger while I provided my thoughts to Vice President Rockefeller.

Ambassador Daniel Patrick Moynihan, whose skill, brainpower, and good humor were rarely matched, prepares for his swearing in as U.S. Representative to the United Nations with President Ford and Justice Byron White.

Here, Ford was being led by Secret Service to the Governor's office in Sacramento, California, immediately after the first assassination attempt, when Lynette "Squeaky" Fromme raised her pistol to assasinate the President.

Aboard Air Force One, after the first attempt made on the President's life, my assistant, Leona Goodell, took notes on his recollections of the attack.

The second assassination attempt on the President. As we walked out of the St. Francis Hotel, the bullet fired by Sarah Jane Moore went just past Ford's head and into the wall of the hotel.

The second assassination attempt, just as Ford heard the gunshot.

Ford was pushed into the back of the presidential limousine, with the Secret Service agent and me on top of him. Two blocks later, in a muffled voice, the President said, "Come on, Rummy, get off! You guys are heavy!"

Gerald Ford, who fought in the Pacific war aboard the aircraft carrier USS *Monterey*, talks with Emperor Hirohito three decades later.

With President Ford at my swearing in ceremony as the thirteenth U.S. Secretary of Defense.

President Ford greatly enjoyed skiing during his visits to Vail, Colorado.

Ford's friendly competitor the legendary Speaker of the U.S. House of Representatives Tip O'Neill (D-MA). Their mutual respect was helpful in restoring Americans' trust in government.

President Ford campaigns in Pittsburgh with movie actor John Wayne.

I must have stopped by Dr. Henry Kissinger's National Security Council office to help him clean up his desk.

Betty Ford with the President, who relied on her counsel and was deeply devoted to her.

$$\text{\large{\Decorative}} \ 9 \ \text{\large{\Decorative}}$$

The Fall of Vietnam

MEETING WITH THE PRESIDENT
March 31, 1975
4:50 to 5:30 p.m.
Wilson House [Palm Springs, California]
The President told Kissinger that the failure of Congress to provide funds for
South Vietnam is the reason it collapsed. I told the President, after the phone
conversation was over, that I didn't believe that, that I just thought there
was a very strong case to the contrary . . . and that we had been providing
money for a hell of a long time and that in my view at some point you have to
take your hand off the bicycle seat and see if they can ride, and it turns out
that they can't. . . .[1]

In his first eight months in office, President Ford faced the issue of
the pardon of Richard Nixon, a growing economic crisis, major
problems in the intelligence community, a huge loss of Republican
congressional seats in the 1974 midterm elections, and predictions
of a serious primary challenge from Governor Ronald Reagan. Yet
Ford seemed to be enjoying his job as President more every day. "I
never wanted to be President, but I'm enjoying it," he told a small

group of us. This was a surprise to some at the time. Many members of the Congress seemed to picture themselves, at least at some point, in the White House. But Gerald Ford never had such ambitions.[2] But this was also, I realized, in some ways a strength. Not having dreamed (or schemed) throughout his congressional career about someday making it to the White House, Ford hadn't compromised any of his ideals or principles, nor had he come to the Oval Office with an outsized view of himself. Not having fashioned any presidential agenda or platform before taking office, Ford had to handle issues as they came to him, even as events were unquestionably now becoming more challenging.

In the spring of 1975, the President was faced with the emergency of emergencies: the perilous collapse of an entire nation—a nation of 20 million souls to which the United States of America had devoted its blood and treasure for nearly two decades. The Republic of Vietnam was falling to the Communists, perhaps the worst defeat for Americans in a military conflict in our nation's history.

While aboard *Air Force One* en route to California, the President received the dire word that Da Nang—the largest city in central Vietnam—had been taken by the Communists. An upheaval was getting underway. What was entirely unclear—and what would soon be debated in the Situation Room in the White House—was how far south the North Vietnamese forces would push and at what pace.

Though there was no technical reason why the President should not leave Washington, D.C., during such a crisis—he and the National Security Council could handle everything that he conceivably would need to do anywhere—some were aware of the disadvantage of being away in California as the TV networks broadcast images of a key Vietnamese city succumbing to the Communists.

Before we left, the President talked about his trip to Palm Springs, a trip Ford looked forward to. "While there is no reason you should not go," I said I felt that he had "lost something" during a recent trip to Vail, when he seemed to be relaxing while portions of the world were in crisis.

It was my job as Chief of Staff to raise such concerns. And it was the President's job to decide how to respond. In this instance, Ford understood keenly a dilemma that faces every President: America's business never ceases. An administration can try to plan for the future as well as is possible, but what might happen the next week, the next day, the next minute—the unknown unknowns, as one might put it—are a mystery. So, for a president, even the briefest vacation, even the shortest absence from the White House, can involve a risk. If at the moment a crisis breaks out our country's senior leader is away and seen as being engaged in some leisure activity, his White House risks being castigated as indifferent or irresponsibly uninformed and unprepared. As with a renowned surgeon sporting a stellar record, it takes but a single slip to lessen or even to lose the confidence of patients and colleagues.

Ford disagreed with that view, and rather emphatically. All human beings need to recharge, even the President of the United States. It's mentally, emotionally, and physically helpful to their day-to-day performance to occasionally get away from the swamps of the Potomac River, to see different scenery, to look at problems from a different perspective, to deal with different people, to breathe fresh air. Yet in this case there was an even more important reason to head to California—it was a very high priority for the President: the health of the First Lady.

Betty Ford had undergone a radical mastectomy and was still a bit frail from the procedure. She had long been suffering from arthritis in her neck. The President believed, indeed he was absolutely convinced, she would benefit from a few days in the Southern California desert sun. He was certain she *needed* it. Betty was a special person and a source of enormous comfort to the President, and of course he had followed closely her struggles with addiction.[3] "She damn near died from alcoholism," he once confided to me, with heartfelt concern.[4] In fact, the situation had been so severe that Betty had been hospitalized for a month. Though she'd made "a beautiful recovery," he didn't want to ever see that happen again.[5]

As his Chief of Staff, I was still concerned, but enormously sympathetic. "I know, Betty needs to go."

"That's right," the President replied. "It's important to get her out of here and into the sun."[6] And so they went.

From the day he had unexpectedly become President, Ford and his national security team had been monitoring the storm that was brewing in Southeast Asia. Back in 1975, dealing with the unraveling taking place halfway around the world in "Indochina" would have been a colossal challenge under any circumstances, not least given the absence of our now readily available twenty-first-century communication tools. The National Security staff, divided between the Atlantic and Pacific coasts as it was, moved quickly to see that the key players were engaged to activate the communication tools and systems.[7]

Though Hanoi's spring offensive struck like a bolt from the blue, the conflict in Vietnam had been a dominant feature of American life for roughly a decade. The war had sharply divided the country, and antiwar protest marches were a staple in Washington, D.C. When I had served in the Nixon administration, at the Office of Economic Opportunity and later at the Economic Stabilization Program as well as in the White House throughout that period, on more than one occasion I had to make my way past antiwar demonstrations near the White House as well as during the President's domestic travels. The smell of tear gas in the air was not uncommon.

As a Navy veteran of World War II, Gerald Ford knew well the costs of war. He also knew it would take time, considerable time, for our nation to heal from Vietnam, where the jungles, beaches, and plains had experienced the sacrifice of more than fifty-eight thousand Americans. He was wrestling with the challenging question about how to deal with the thousands of eligible young men who had made the decision to evade the draft and avoid military service during that increasingly unpopular war.

Speaking to the annual convention of the Veterans of Foreign Wars in Chicago, Illinois, on August 19, 1974, only ten days after taking office, President Ford addressed that subject head-on. He announced that he had requested Attorney General Bill Saxbe and Defense Secretary Jim Schlesinger to report on the status of the fifty thousand Americans who had been accused of violating the Selective Service Act. As both a former member of Congress and Vice President, President Ford had asserted that "blanket amnesty" for those who had evaded or fled military service would be "wrong." Yet in his remarks to the veterans gathered in Chicago, "to bind up the nation's wounds" he stressed the need to offer "young Americans . . . a second chance to contribute their fair share to the rebuilding of peace among ourselves and with all nations."[8] Accordingly, on September 16, 1974, in a speech from the White House Cabinet Room, President Gerald Ford extended amnesty to deserters and draft evaders who would agree to serve two years in public service jobs. "I do not want to delay another day in resolving the dilemmas of the past, so that we may all get going on the pressing problems of the present," Ford said.[9] Three months later, however, there was reason for Americans to worry that those controversial issues were not in the past, and that those old wounds might be reopened.

On December 13, 1974, the North Vietnamese deployed their Fourth Army Corps for the first time and opened a heavy artillery bombardment against Phuoc Luong near the Cambodian border—effectively shredding the U.S. negotiated Paris Peace Accords. After the capitulation of the province on January 6, 1975—the first province captured by the North Vietnamese in fifteen years—South Vietnamese President Nguyen Van Thieu sent a delegation to Washington, D.C., seeking $300 million in military aid, which he argued was the minimum needed to hold off the North Vietnamese. The President, without hesitation, committed himself to meeting that request. The South Vietnamese, he believed, needed and deserved the aid due to their loyalty fighting alongside our troops and holding together what was widely believed to be a vital bulwark against Communism in the region. Loyalty alone, of course, would not have been sufficient justification for many Americans, convinced as they were that their country had already expended too much in the conflict. The President emphasized that an American refusal to help to confront the aggression against our ally would sap our credibility and embolden America's enemies.

The President was fully ready to approach the Congress for the $300 million in military aid. He was convinced the South Vietnamese needed this support for their defense. He was also certain that Americans, though clearly ready, indeed eager, to wash their hands of the Vietnam conflict, would be deeply disappointed if the Communists ended up achieving a total conquest. At a lunch with journalists at *The New York Times*, Ford had said just that. Afterward, I discussed with the President that politically it would be unhelpful to him to send up the request for funds if it was reasonably certain he could not win.

"Don," he said to me, "if South Vietnam goes down the drain, I want a record of having gone up there [to Congress] even if I lose. There's no way to make a record to the public if you haven't gone and instead just say, 'I wish I could but I know I won't get it, so I didn't even try.'"[10] He believed he might have a reasonable chance to prevail. He was a believer in the tradition—not entirely dead in American politics in those days—that the United States should speak with one voice on foreign policy. At one point in early 1975, it was President Ford's suggestion that all potential 1976 presidential candidates should meet at Camp David to discuss ways to forge a bipartisan consensus on foreign policy.[11] The idea likely would have seemed fanciful to some strong partisans in Washington, D.C., and especially so today, some four-plus decades later, but it was fully consistent with Ford's belief in the American people and his sincere interest in healing the partisan divisions.

Over the ensuing months, the President would go "up there" to Capitol Hill and meet with members of both parties in the Congress on a number of occasions. And repeatedly his requests would be rejected by the political opposition and by the pundits for trying to get the funds for what many if not most by then believed had become "a lost cause." Public opinion was sharply against anything that even hinted at expanding American involvement in that increasingly unpopular conflict.

In January, Ford's legislative staff was evaluating whether a military aid request to the Congress would have a better chance as part of an omnibus bill or as a stand-alone supplemental.[12] The President decided on the latter and scheduled a special message to the Congress for January 28, 1975. A day before Ford was to speak, Daniel Patrick Moynihan, the brilliant Harvard sociologist and former aide to President Nixon, who was then serving as U.S. Ambassador to India, ominously cautioned the White House staff that the two previous Presidents—Lyndon Johnson and Richard Nixon—had been consumed and destroyed by Asian foreign policy.[13]

"It is the minimum needed to prevent serious reversals," Ford asserted to the Congress on January 28, referring to the $522 million total (which included $222 million to aid the Cambodian government then being overrun by the Communist Pol Pot regime). North Vietnam, Ford declared, had 289,000 troops in South Vietnam along with tanks, heavy artillery, and antiaircraft weapons "by the hundreds." The U.S. assistance, he continued, was essential to protecting our allies as well as preserving America's credibility and national security.

"All Americans want to end the U.S. role in Vietnam," he said. "So do I. I believe, however, that we must end it in a way that will enhance the chances of world peace and sustain the purposes for which we have sacrificed so much."[14]

Ford, as President, wanted one shot to try to set things right. Taking charge in the Oval Office had infused him with fresh optimism about the possibility of a negotiated peace and a managed U.S. military withdrawal from Vietnam. That bubble was burst with a vengeance. The American people were more than ready to cut our ties to Vietnam. The so-called Watergate Babies of the newly elected Ninety-fourth Congress especially—along with some Republicans—were not willing to accept the President's arguments. Some branded the aid request irresponsible, pointing to inflation. Others labeled it insensitive, pointing to poverty in the urban slums of New York City, Detroit, Chicago, and Los Angeles. Even the South Vietnamese government, Defense Secretary Schlesinger reported, was pessimistic it would get the $300 million from its American ally.[15]

Two days after the President's request to Congress, I visited Richard Heffner, a New Jersey professor of communications and public policy at Rutgers University, the prominent editor of Alexis de Tocqueville's book *Democracy in America*, and a longtime acquaintance, in New Brunswick. He was closely attuned to the public mood. It's true, he said, the current generation of undergraduates had seen most of the war in Vietnam wind down and most of their countrymen return home. They were not, like their predecessors, interested in riots and demonstrations. But their interest was aroused by a sense that President Ford was getting into a fight with the Congress over Vietnam. And unfortunately for the President, the details of the public disagreement, such as his explicit promise to provide no additional U.S. troops, were escaping them. Heffner expected that Ford, not the Congress, would wind up being seen as the villain.[16] The President's still young administration seemed to be moving into a lose-lose situation. The military aid request was ill-fated, yet the President believed he should pursue it. Ford held to his course valiantly and with determination for one reason only: He believed deeply, regardless of the politics, that it was the right thing to do.

After some wrangling, the Congress allowed a bipartisan congressional delegation to travel to Vietnam and Cambodia to make a fresh assessment prior to the vote on Ford's $522 million request.[17] It was his only chance. If the members of the delegation viewed the desperate situation with their own eyes, Ford felt, they might be swayed to support the assistance he was proposing. The White House staff tried to see that at least some potential supporters were appointed, but the delegation of eight ended up with a number of opponents. Included was California Republican Congressman Pete McCloskey (R-CA), who in 1972 had challenged President Nixon for the Republican nomination for President running on an antiwar platform.

The congressional delegation left Washington, D.C., the last week of February 1975, and returned on March 2. Some members made the case that the aid was essential. Newly elected U.S. Representative John Murtha (D-PA), for example, avowed our country's allies should at the very least be given a chance to succeed. Testifying before the Senate Foreign Relations Committee, Murtha wisely predicted a bloodbath in Cambodia if the Khmer Rouge came to power.[18] McCloskey, however, stormed Capitol Hill and delivered a far different message. What the U.S. had "done" to Vietnam, he alleged, "is greater evil than we have done to any country in the world, and wholly without reason."[19] The House Democratic Caucus gathered on March 12 and voted 189–49 against the proposed military assistance for Cambodia. The following day, the Senate Democratic Caucus voted to oppose military aid to Cambodia by 38–5 and against aid to Vietnam by 34–6.

* * *

As the voting in Congress was taking place, the President of South Vietnam, Nguyen Van Thieu, was forced to order the evacuation of the Central Highlands, thereby abandoning the northern two-thirds of the country of South Vietnam. The Communists were shelling and marching south almost unimpeded. The U.S., despite its considerable in-country military and intelligence resources, had been caught off-guard.

The National Security Council—historically has been the executive branch's principal forum for dealing with key international policy issues—was less than effective as a deliberating body providing a full range of views and counsel to the Commander in Chief. At this moment, however, Henry Kissinger was still serving both as the President's National Security Advisor and as the Secretary of State. As a result, the White House lacked a functioning intermediary between State, Defense, the CIA, and other key national security elements. "For all practical purposes," I cautioned the President on April 1, "you don't have a National Security Council staff."[20] The Nixon administration had convened eighty-seven NSC meetings between January 21, 1969, and June 20, 1974.[21] Between August 1974 and March 1975, the Ford administration had convened three or four, and those had been organized by the NSC at the last minute. In fact, March 28, 1975, was the first time Vietnam had appeared on an NSC agenda—almost two months after North Vietnamese General Van Tien Dung had moved into South Vietnam to personally command what became the final offensive.

On February 25, 1975, I learned that the NSC was turning down requests by reporters such as my friend Pierre Salinger (who was then working as a reporter for France's *L'Express*) to conduct interviews with the President. When I asked why they were being denied, I received the response from the lower levels of the NSC, such as, "Henry is in the middle of sensitive negotiations and therefore the President shouldn't mess in foreign affairs." I had no doubt Kissinger's team was acting in the country's best interests but was concerned that the President might have a different view.

Frankly, I said to Ford, I think keeping the President from talking to reporters on such issues is demeaning to the office. There was no reason why Gerald Ford couldn't meet with people from the foreign press. I urged the President not to acquiesce on such questions.

The president replied, "Let's go ahead and do it." Then he added with a laugh, "If I can't handle a conversation with reporters, I can't handle anything."[22]

A few months later, Press Secretary Ron Nessen was sent out to the press in error with inaccurate information from a lower-level aide at the NSC. When Nessen discovered the inaccuracies, he went to Brent Scowcroft, who advised the President's Press Secretary to "let it sit." I told Nessen not to let it sit. The White House had misinformed the press on an issue and we weren't going to let that go just so the NSC could avoid embarrassment. I suggested Nessen call Kissinger and inform him that he was going to put out a statement to correct the misinformation. Kissinger immediately agreed to the statement and the matter was settled.

"If I were Ron," I told Ford, "I would be madder than hell."[23] If the NSC didn't have time to brief the President's Press Secretary on national security matters before he said something that might embarrass the administration, then there was something wrong.

"You have a problem," I told the President. "If you go into Scowcroft's office, there are eight stacks [of paper] . . . on his desk. Each one is red tagged."[24]

The original Nixon appointees to the NSC staff, some of whom represented the best minds on foreign policy—such as Lawrence Eagleburger, Helmut Sonnenfeldt, William Hyland, and Winston Lord—had moved to the Department of State. Those who remained on the NSC staff were carrying a heavy burden with limited staff. Henry's involvement at State sometimes left the rest of the

NSC out of the loop, including Defense Secretary Jim Schlesinger. Schlesinger and the President had an uncomfortable relationship, with Schlesinger sometimes seeming to be lecturing and patronizing in meetings. Kissinger, who also had a strained relationship with the Defense Secretary, at one point apologized to Ford over a disagreement he had had with Schlesinger, and was taken aback by the President's revealing response. "Jim's problem isn't with you; it's with me," Ford told Kissinger. "He thinks I'm a dummy."[25]

None of these were ingredients for an effective National Security Council process. Due to Henry's dual-hatted status and Ford's increasing discomfort with the Defense Secretary, I noted that Henry could "get the instructions he [wanted] at the last minute before he left Washington, D.C., to negotiate on SALT and MBFR [Mutual Balanced Force Reductions]."[26] I was concerned to learn during a meeting with the President that he had instructed Kissinger in person before even talking to Schlesinger on a matter involving a SALT negotiation. I was also concerned when Ford offered to bring Schlesinger up to speed over the phone rather than convening a meeting with him face-to-face to learn the views of the Department of Defense.[27]

Kissinger also had a habit of periodically threatening to resign when he sensed opposition to his views or that Ford might come down on a different side of an issue. White House photographer David Hume Kennerly caught the fallout one evening when he was upstairs in the family residence. "Yes, Henry," David heard the President say to Kissinger over the line. "Oh, sorry about that." Ford hung up and turned to David, "Henry just called about another Evans and Novak thing. He's really mad and says he wants to resign." David responded, "You know what you should do, Mr. President? You should accept his resignation and I bet he never does it again."[28]

Stress on Kissinger and the national security team was understandably high with the Vietnam War coming to an inglorious end.

An open question was where the blame would fall— on the series of Presidents who through Eisenhower, Kennedy, Johnson, and Nixon had steadily committed more American blood and treasure to the conflict,[29] or the Congress for withholding support for the additional military aid Ford had proposed. There was concern that the Congress's obstinacy encouraged North Vietnam "to go all out, in flagrant violation of the Paris Accords," the peace process Kissinger had negotiated under Nixon, which had been designed to bring about a gradual end to the war.

McGeorge Bundy, who had served as the National Security Advisor to both Presidents Kennedy and Johnson and who had counseled the escalation of U.S. ground troops during the war's most intense years, thoughtfully phoned me, concerned about President Ford's reputation and standing with the Congress and the country and believing it was in our country's interest to keep President Ford as "unscarred" by the war as possible. He suggested that he and his former colleagues from the previous two administrations should be the ones to take the heat, not President Ford.[30] It was an enormously thoughtful, gracious, and notably unselfish suggestion, which was appreciated greatly. Gerald Ford, someone who didn't want to spend time casting blame, considered the idea of taking Bundy up on his offer as out of the question. U.S. Senator Stuart Symington, a Democrat from Missouri—and former Secretary of the U.S. Air Force in the late 1940s—pointed his finger at the military. In Hawaii, he had seen the Army Chief of Staff train the Twenty-fifth Infantry Division, which had fought the North Vietnamese in the "Iron Triangle." He claimed that since 1967 he had been telling those involved, including President Johnson, that their approach to combat was "wrong."[31]

Soon even former President Nixon weighed in. From San Clemente, he relayed his advice through his former aide Frank Gannon, who passed it along to White House aide Dick Cheney. Nixon suggested that Ford not blame anyone—not even the North Viet-namese. "[T]hink of the China experience," he said. "Think in terms of history. Do what he believes is right. It will be justified." He ad-vised that Ford's status as a world leader will be enhanced if he takes the difficult course before him and, in the long term, it will be the best politics.[32] President Nixon was close to being right on the mark. In order to move forward, it was best not to assign blame to others, but simply to understand that America had done everything possible for Vietnam. "In my view, at some point," I mentioned to President Ford, "you have to take your hand off the bicycle seat and see if they [the Vietnamese] can ride. And it turns out that they can't."[33] It was a hard truth to face, but one that we had spent more than a decade coming to grips with.

Ultimately, President Ford informed journalists he was "not as-sessing blame on anyone." But he added pointedly that the Congress had not helped matters by reducing the amount of military equip-ment he had said was needed for South Vietnam in fiscal year 1974 and that it had failed to deliver the full amount appropriated for the following year. "I think historians in the future will write who was to blame in this tragic situation," he said during a press conference on April 3. "But the American people ought to know the facts. And the facts are as I have indicated."[34]

The war in Vietnam was coming to an end. The only questions were precisely when and how. White House photographer David Hume Kennerly, who had accompanied General Weyand on his fact-finding trip to Vietnam, had gone on to Cambodia. "Cambodia is gone," he reported back to President Ford when he returned, "and I don't care what the generals tell you."[35]

Over the month of March, Vietnam had evolved from a military con-flict to an increasingly challenging rescue operation. After Da Nang fell on March 29, 1975, U.S. Boeing 727s and 747 cargo planes evacuated many thousands of Vietnamese refugees who had been supporters of the U.S. effort. U.S. military and civilian personnel were evacuated to U.S. Navy ships and contract vessels. Thousands more fled from the South Central Coast on April 2 as North Vietnamese troops moved south. Saigon was bombarded on April 3. The President, seeking to protect the most vulnerable, ordered the evacuation of some orphans the following day. Although the Congress was on its Easter recess, he followed the War Powers Act, which had provisions in the event a President decided to introduce U.S. military forces "into hostilities or into situations where imminent involvement in hostilities is clearly indicated by the circumstances." We were aboard *Air Force One* en route to San Francisco at the time.

To provide the resources urgently needed to carry out the evacuation, the President had to notify the Speaker of the U.S. House of Representatives, Carl Albert (D-OK), who, as it happened, was at the time in the People's Republic of China, the country that was supplying the arms for the North Vietnamese forces. "It's either like [Kafka] or Allen Drury; I'm not sure which," I noted in a memo.[36] The President and the White House staff went to considerable lengths to contact members of the Congress since few were in Washington, D.C. It was a race against the clock to save lives, yet Ford wasn't going to risk accusations that he was ignoring his former colleagues in the legislative branch or that he was violating the War Powers Act. My memo on April 1st read:

MEETING WITH THE PRESIDENT

April 1, 1975

8:02 to 9:08 a.m.

He [the President] then gave me a report on his phone call with [Secretary of Defense] Schlesinger. He said that Schlesinger was concerned about the evacuation that there are still 300 Americans in Natrang. [U.S. Ambassador] Graham Martin is inclined to hold out till the very end, and that the President and Jim kind of felt that they shouldn't hold out till the very end. . . . He told Jim to call Brent Scowcroft and tell him if the margin is close they want to go ahead and start moving US people out. Schlesinger is pessimistic. He says the regime can hold out for at most 60 to 90 days; he is afraid of a panic. . . .[37]

What became known as "Operation Babylift" started on April 4, but began with a tragedy. The very first flight, which was carrying 314 passengers, crashed shortly after takeoff. The locks on the rear cargo door of the C-5A Galaxy had failed, blowing off parts of the plane and damaging the flight controls on the tail section. One hundred thirty-eight died. In total, between April 3 and September 3, 1975 Operation "New Life" evacuated more than 110,000 refugees from South Vietnam.

The task was to get our fellow citizens safely out. In mid-April, the estimate was that there were about six thousand Americans still in and around Saigon. Secretary Schlesinger was in favor of launching an evacuation. His estimate that the South Vietnamese government would not last more than sixty or ninety more days was considered by some to be a pessimistic forecast. Ambassador Martin argued to hold out longer. Everyone was aware that initiation of an evacuation effort could well trigger a panic and jeopardize additional lives. The President carefully weighed the views of Ambassador Martin and of Secretaries Kissinger and Schlesinger. The challenge would be to present the right message and move at exactly the right pace— quickly enough to save lives, but not so quickly as to create panic and damage the critical extraction efforts. There were concerns by a few that some embittered South Vietnamese soldiers might even turn on the departing Americans. "If you want out and said the situation was hopeless and we were pulling Americans out, that would trigger it," the President advised at a Joint Congressional Leadership Meeting. "If they think we have given up, that will set them off."[38]

As the evacuation of Americans began, U.S. Senator Henry

"Scoop" Jackson, a senior and respected Democrat from the state of Washington, threw the White House for a loop on April 8, 1975. On the floor of the U.S. Senate, Senator Jackson alleged that the Nixon administration had worked out "secret agreements" with South Vietnam that promised future military assistance, and surprisingly suggested that the administration could be leaving Americans in Saigon as hostages to squeeze the Congress for military aid and to effectively reignite the war as part of the secret agreement. Jackson, almost always a solid, thoughtful Senator, didn't name a source or provide any details of his imagined theory. But the charge, as inaccurate as it was, was serious coming from the man who was then leading in the Gallup poll for the 1976 Democratic presidential nomination.[39] The Ford White House and NSC was completely in the dark as to what Senator Jackson might be referring to, as were the American people. "The issue was 'were there secret commitments made?'" White House Press Secretary Ron Nessen asked the question in a memo, adding, "I know of none. The President knows of none. The Secretary of State, who was intimately involved, asserts knowledgeably that there was none. What more can one ask?"[40]

The situation in South Vietnam continued to deteriorate. President Ford, wishing to speed up the evacuation, set an address before a joint session of the Congress for April 10, 1975. Some twenty divisions, virtually the entire North Vietnamese army, had by then moved into South Vietnam. In January, Ford had asked the Congress for the $522 million in military aid. This round he wanted to request $722 million—an amount that had been recommended by General Weyand—plus $250 million for economic and humanitarian assistance. Kissinger didn't think the Congress would agree. Ford was pessimistic as well, but believed, or at least hoped, that by having the U.S. display steadiness of purpose, the situation might stabilize at least temporarily and ease the risks of the ongoing evacuations. That was the best case. His entreaties for more military and humanitarian aid were so unpopular that he was advised that he might be booed on the floor of the U.S. House of Representatives—something previously unthinkable during a presidential address to the Congress on foreign policy. He said, characteristically, he would work through any boos.[41]

"Fundamental decency," the President said to the joint session of the Congress that evening, "requires that we do everything in our power to ease the misery and the pain of the monumental human crisis which has befallen the people of South Vietnam." His address encountered even more resistance than expected. Beyond some boos, two freshman Democrats, U.S. Representatives Toby Moffett of Connecticut and George Miller of California, stood up, turned around, and walked out of the chamber, in a notable breach of decorum. The opposition continued in the days after, when, in an unusual step, the members of the Senate Foreign Relations Committee requested a face-to-face meeting with the President. "I will give you large sums for evacuation, but not one nickel for military aid," said New York Republican Senator Jacob Javits.[42] The President explained it wasn't that simple. "It's a two-way street," he said, reiterating that American lives would be endangered without the aid.[43]

The Senate Foreign Relations Committee in turn proposed a $200 million "emergency fund" with inflexible language and some notably unhelpful caveats. "My judgment is that amount is as bad as nothing," the President said in a Cabinet meeting. "If the Congress sticks to its indicated attitude, it could lead to dire circumstances. We must be consistent. We asked for the right program. I hope the Congress comes through."[44] Adding to the tensions, the Communist insurgent forces in Cambodia, known as the Khmer Rouge, stormed into Phnom Penh and seized control of the country on April 17, 1975. In a daring feat, eighty-two Americans were evacuated, most by helicopters, to the carrier USS *Hancock* and the assault ship USS *Okinawa*.

On April 21, President Nguyen Van Thieu resigned his post after ten years and fled South Vietnam. "The Americans have asked us to do an impossible thing," he said in his final public appearance. "You have asked us to do something you failed to do, with half a million powerful troops and skilled commanders." He added as a parting shot: "Are U.S. commitments still valid?"[45] With perhaps an answer to Thieu's haunting question, the U.S. Senate rejected President Ford's appeal for $722 million and appropriated $200 million to be used strictly for evacuation and humanitarian purposes. The almost unfailingly even-tempered and understanding Gerald Ford was as angry as I had ever seen him over the decade-plus we had worked together. He exclaimed, "Those bastards." He added that "just a relatively small American commitment" could have met "any military challenges."[46]

The President accepted that our country's only remaining mission in that conflict was the evacuation of Americans and of the South Vietnamese who had assisted us and to whom the U.S. had "a moral commitment."[47] This message was clearly set forth in the President's speech at Tulane University on April 23. "Today, America can regain the sense of pride that existed before Vietnam," Ford said to the more than forty-five hundred people gathered at the campus field house. "But it cannot be achieved by refighting a war that is finished as far as America is concerned. As I see it, the time has come to look forward to an agenda for the future, to unify, to bind up the nation's wounds, and to restore its health and its optimistic self-confidence."[48] The speech had its intended effect: persuading the American people that the discussion over their country's involvement in Vietnam was over. His remarks were greeted with, as *The New York Times* reported, "prolonged and enthusiastic applause."[49]

But even that small success was tainted by controversy. Returning from New Orleans aboard *Air Force One*, the President went to the back of the plane and spoke with the traveling press pool. He was asked if Henry Kissinger had been involved in the preparation of the President's speech. Ford replied that he had not. Contrary to standard practice, the President's speech on foreign policy had not been properly staffed out. It had been crafted virtually overnight from an earlier draft by speechwriter Milton Friedman, which had not even mentioned Vietnam. Contrary to the standard White House policy, apparently no one other than President Ford had seen anything other than the original draft, which had been significantly revised personally by the President. The President's response created a stir in the press and led some to conclude quite inaccurately that Kissinger's influence in the administration was waning.[50]

Even comedy writers would have been hard pressed to conceive what happened next. When Kissinger had been asked in parallel about his hand in the Tulane speech, he responded that he had played a role and had discussed it at great length with the President. And, of course, Henry was absolutely correct in saying that. He had most certainly discussed all of the subjects in the speech extensively with the President in a great many meetings over many weeks. But in this instance Henry had apparently assumed the journalists were asking about a different speech, which the President gave the same day to the Navy League at the Fairmont Hotel in New Orleans.[51]

The confusion from these two seemingly conflicting interviews led to a discussion over how to untangle the misunderstanding. Needless to say, the President was notably unhappy with the speech-writing team for their failure to fully coordinate the speech with Kissinger. Henry pushed for Nessen to indicate he had in fact played a major role in the development of the Tulane speech, which in a sense he had, given Henry's numerous discussions with and advice to the President. But in another sense, he hadn't actually seen the speech itself. In an attempt to untangle the mess without being dishonest with the press corps, the President asked Nessen to approach the press and "emphasize that Kissinger and the President are in agreement with respect to Southeast Asia and that Kissinger supports the President's policies."[52]

Four days later, General Duong Van Minh was sworn in as the new president of South Vietnam. He lasted only two days. With North Vietnamese rockets and artillery shells pounding the runways at Tan Son Nhut, the Saigon airfield, helicopter evacuation was the only remaining option. And that led to yet one last uncomfortable moment in a conflict that had had so many.

MEETING WITH THE PRESIDENT
April 30, 1975

I told [the President] that there had been a bit of a flap last night that I thought he ought to be aware of. I showed him the full report pointing out that they were still evacuating Marines some 2 hrs. after the Secretary of State had said that all Americans had been removed. Therefore it was clear we had to do something.[53]

On April 29, 1975, Henry Kissinger had issued a statement announcing that all Americans in Vietnam had been evacuated, finally bringing U.S. involvement in the conflict to an end. The problem was that late that evening, Jim Schlesinger called saying, "You shouldn't really have put that statement out—it's not accurate." I was surprised and asked him in what respects. He said, "Well, in the first sentence it says that it was based on reports that all Americans were out. There were no such reports."

He said that elements of the U.S. military advised Secretary Kissinger that Ambassador Martin was airborne. According to Schlesinger, Kissinger had been told that Martin would be the last one out. But, according to Schlesinger, he wasn't. I said to the President that I really didn't know what the facts were but it was an awkward situation. Kissinger felt that he knew what his end of the phone conversation was and felt that the mistake had been at Defense. Schlesinger felt that Defense knew what their side of the phone conversation had been and that the mistake was made at State. I said there was no paper that passed anywhere so there is no way to prove anything.

Considering his respective relationships with his Secretaries of State and Defense, it came as no surprise that the President was inclined to accept Kissinger's view of events. And in a stressful situation such as this one, it was also not a surprise that we saw a flash of the President's rare temper. "I was damn mad about it," Ford told me. "All I know is that Kissinger was told the evacuation was over and it was verified that it was over."

"No, sir," I replied, "you don't know that. All you know is that Kissinger told you he was told it was over, and he may very sincerely believe that but it may or may not be a fact."[54]

While a few of those considering the situation wanted the administration not to issue a correction to the press, I disagreed. "This war has been marked by so many lies and evasions," I said, "that it is not right to have the war end with one last lie."[55] The President ultimately agreed with that position, and a correction was made.

In any event, at 5:00 a.m. the next day, the last U.S. helicopter left, taking off from the roof of the U.S. Embassy on Thong Nhat Boulevard in Saigon, and the government of South Vietnam surrendered.

MEETING WITH THE PRESIDENT
April 30, 1975
10:00 to 10:25 a.m. Cabinet Rm.
Meeting with the Egyptian Parliamentarians
It was a very warm meeting. I left early. During the course of the meeting Kissinger came over to me and said, "Don, I want you to know that I believe you handled the matter last night just right. Had you not checked with Schlesinger and had we put that story out we would have ended up in a peeing

match within the government and we don't need it. He said I owed you that and wanted you to know it. . . .[56]

President Ford believed that America's commitment to South Vietnam extended beyond the successful evacuation. It was a notably unpopular position. "There is no political support for it in this country," U.S. Senate Majority Whip Robert Byrd, a Democrat from West Virginia, warned.[57] Meeting with a group of influential Senators, Ford repeatedly tried to sway them with what he believed deeply was our country's moral responsibility to help refugees fleeing persecution. Repeatedly, a number of Senate Democrats dissented, including the young outspoken Senator Joe Biden (D-DE). In the heat of the discussion, I detected a difference in the attitudes of some members of Congress toward the Vietnamese.[58]

MEETING WITH THE PRESIDENT
April 14, 1975
Senator Biden of Delaware then spoke up and got back again on the delays in getting Americans out. He also expressed hostility towards the idea of bringing out any South Vietnamese. [Senator] Claiborne Pell [D-RI] then made a pitch for Borneo. He said ten years ago he and [Senator] Javits introduced a resolution recommending that we get a truce in Vietnam and evacuate all those who do not want to live under communism and then let the north have it. He said Borneo is only 400 miles away and he wants it considered as a site for relocation of Vietnamese refugees.[59]

In the face of this attitude toward refugees, the President was at his most eloquent and persuasive. These were not just any refugees; they were allies of the United States government who faced severe repression and persecution if they stayed under the Communist regime. He reminded the members of Congress that when the Soviet military invaded Hungary in 1956, the Eisenhower administration, with the support of Congress, gave asylum to thousands of Hungarians fleeing Communist persecution. Ford said we had an obligation to treat the Vietnamese the same way. He made a strong statement that they deserved exactly the same treatment anyone else did and that it was in the best American tradition to handle it that way.[60]

Opposition in the Congress to the resettlement of Vietnamese refugees mounted through April. Some from Texas and California especially were increasingly vocal against permitting the Vietnamese into the country. Recommendations starting flowing in that refugees should be resettled in the Trust Territory of the Pacific Islands, or elsewhere outside the continental U.S.[61] The President forcefully dismissed them. America owed the South Vietnamese a special obligation for having determinedly fought for decades against Communism. On April 30, Ford asked the Congress to approve a bill that would provide $507 million for the transportation and care of South Vietnamese refugees. The House rejected his request on May 1. "Unbelievable!" Ford wrote in his memoir. "To ignore the refugees in their hour of need would be to repudiate the values we cherish as a nation of immigrants, and I was not about to let Congress do that." Undeterred, the President went around government, and with the help of citizens and volunteer organizations, some 120,000 Vietnamese—about half of whom were children—found a new life in America.[62]

By the time the Vietnam War had ended, the United States had lost fifty-eight thousand Americans. More than one hundred thousand others had suffered injuries. The war had cost well over $100 billion. And America was without a well-thought-out post-Vietnam foreign policy. I discussed this with the President in the Oval Office on May 1.

"What about the last part of the foreign policy address to the Congress?" Ford said, referring to the April 10 address before the joint session. "That laid it out."

"No, sir—it didn't," I suggested. "It was a laundry list."

I posed a scenario. If trouble broke out in the next thirty days—for example, in Korea—the American people could claim, and not entirely without justification, that their country's adversaries had been emboldened.[63] As it happened, trouble broke out eleven days later, not in Korea, but just off the coast of Cambodia.

⊫ 10 ⊫

Ford at the Helm:
The SS *Mayaguez* Crisis

MEETING WITH THE PRESIDENT

May 12, 1975

12:04 to 12:52 p.m.

National Security Council Meeting in the Cabinet Room

While the President was waiting for Kissinger, . . . the President talked about the Defense cuts. SecDef said he didn't like them, that the House Floor is the danger, it is coming up Wednesday.

We talked about the seizure of a US merchant ship by a Cambodian gunboat. Apparently we were notified at 3:15 a.m. that it happened about sixty miles southwest of Kompong Som and about eight miles from an island claimed by both Cambodia and Saigon. Schlesinger said the ship was probably in port by now.[1]

Deputy NSC Advisor Brent Scowcroft entered the Oval Office at 7:40 a.m. on Monday, May 12, 1975. He was carrying a maritime distress signal from an aging, 480-foot-long U.S.-flagged container ship: the SS *Mayaguez*. The ship had been transporting food, paints, and chemicals from Hong Kong to Sattahip, a port in southern Thailand, when a Cambodian P-128 gunboat had approached and fired shots across its bow. Members of the gunboat then boarded the *Mayaguez* and took its thirty-nine-member civilian crew hostage. The provocation occurred in international waters near Poulo Wai, an island roughly sixty miles off the coast of Cambodia claimed by both the Cambodians and the Vietnamese. At that moment, there were reports that the *Mayaguez* was being towed toward Kompong Som, a coastal city in the southwestern part of mainland Cambodia. It was not yet clear what would happen to the American crew, or even if they were all still alive. This posed a new challenge for the President only weeks after having turned the page on our country's long, unsuccessful experience in Southeast Asia.

The Vietnam War was technically over. U.S. combat troops had returned home. The most formidable power in the world had been nearly fifteen years in the jungles of Southeast Asia only to emerge with a defeat. As much as the U.S. had tried to leave the conflict on the far side of the Pacific Ocean, it seemed to be refusing to leave us. As the U.S. would discover over a week in May 1975, our country's Communist foes in the region, as anticipated, seemed to be emboldened by America's departure and were apparently ready or even eager to test the outer limits of U.S. resolve.

In the wake of the U.S. retreat from South Vietnam, President Ford was determined to re-establish our country's credibility—to calm our allies and to caution our adversaries. "As long as I was President," he later wrote in his memoir, "I decided, the U.S. would not abandon its commitments overseas. We would not permit our setbacks to become a license for others to fish in troubled waters."[2] Better coordination and clear, readily understandable strategic thinking by those in government were needed.[3] It was next to impossible, the Ford administration was finding, to advance an agenda without a conceptual framework that united the key components of the bureaucracy and the various elements of the country.[4] Two weeks after the fall of Saigon, the Gulf of Siam became the scene of another challenge for the U.S.

Looking at what had become the new map of Southeast Asia, our friends were few and far between. We had no diplomatic relations with the communist Khmer Rouge, which had toppled the Lon Nol pro-U.S. regime in Cambodia the previous month. Our ally in South Vietnam had been toppled by the Communist regime in the North. The generally pro-U.S. Thailand was understandably deeply concerned and bitter about the unfavorable upheavals in their immediate neighborhood in Southeast Asia.

The President convened the National Security Council for an initial meeting on the SS *Mayaguez* in the Cabinet Room at 12:04 p.m. EST.[5] The NSC meeting, the first of several that would take place over the next few days about the *Mayaguez*, was a bit bumpy, reflecting the bureaucratic fissures that had long existed. There was no substantive analysis of the dynamics animating the Khmer Rouge to risk such a provocation.[6] The one constant in the unstructured opening discussion was the President working to draw out and assemble the facts, asking probing questions, and carrying an indisputable aura of command and confidence in the midst of the crisis.

With still only limited details about the situation available, options were posed cautiously: seize Cambodian assets, assemble a force in the Gulf of Siam, issue warnings to Cambodia through their interlocutors in China, establish a blockade, or seize Koh Tang, another island close to where the *Mayaguez* was and about thirty-four miles from the mainland.[7] The objectives of the Cambodians were not yet clear. Perhaps this was part of the ongoing fracas between Phnom Penh and the Vietnamese? The Cambodians had recently seized a Panamanian boat and a Filipino boat in the area and later released both.[8] Early on, as with many early intelligence reports, there were questions such as whether the attackers were Khmer Rouge—though it was soon confirmed that they were.

There was broad agreement in the meeting that there were two related problems and few satisfactory courses of action. The first problem was how to get the *Mayaguez* back and rescue the crew. A second was how to do so without doing damage to U.S. standing. One thought was to seize something of the Cambodians' and demand release of *Mayaguez* and its crew. However, Defense reports were that it could be two and a half to three days before we could move appropriate U.S. warships to the area. Another thought was that the U.S. could mine the harbor, use air power to bomb relevant targets, or we could send a ground force in to free the crew of the *Mayaguez*.[9]

Secretary Kissinger urged "tough talk" and a demand to free *Mayaguez*. "At some point," he thoughtfully said in his deep German voice while leaning over the table, "the United States must draw the line. This is not our idea of the best such situation. It is not our choice. But we must act upon it now, and act firmly."[10]

The President agreed. He directed that the U.S. issue strong warnings through the Chinese, undertake continual photo reconnaissance, get several U.S. warships organized in Subic Bay in the Philippines—then one of the largest U.S. overseas bases—and order to the area the USS *Coral Sea*, a Midway-class aircraft carrier.[11]

Vice President Rockefeller spoke up, tying the situation to a previous maritime crisis that still haunted America. Back in January 1968, North Korean forces had captured the USS *Pueblo*, a U.S. Navy intelligence vessel disguised as an oceanographic research ship. The U.S. government had not responded quickly enough. As a result, the American crew was subjected to mental and physical torture in North Korean prison camps for nearly a year. Wanting to avoid another such tragedy, the Vice President argued for an immediate, robust military response. He mentioned bombing and a set of escalating steps.[12]

Defense Secretary Jim Schlesinger then pointed out that *Mayaguez* was likely already in port on the Cambodian mainland. I asked, "When did we first find out about the incident?"[13] At "7:15 a.m.," Kissinger replied. It was "3:15 a.m.," CIA Director Bill Colby quickly revealed. It then became clear for the first time that neither Secretary of State Kissinger nor the White House and NSC had been alerted about the capture of the SS *Mayaguez* and its crew for four hours after it had happened. That period might have afforded the President a considerably larger range of options, in that the ship would not yet have been moved to a Cambodian port.[14]

I suggested that the NSC staff prepare a clear set of options and we were cautioned to keep the information and options confidential until we gathered more information and the President had decided upon the course of action. The suggestion was made to put out an announcement, acknowledging that the incident occurred, that the NSC had met, and that the U.S. government was communicating with the appropriate governments and taking steps to secure the release of the crew of the *Mayaguez*.

That was Kissinger's view, but in addition he suggested that a public demand for the release of the *Mayaguez* and its crew be added. The President agreed,[15] and the U.S. statement declared that the capture of *Mayaguez* was an "act of piracy" and warned of "the most serious consequences" absent the release of the vessel and its crew.[16]

The President signed off on sending the aircraft carrier USS *Coral Sea* and several destroyers, including USS *Holt*, to the area at flank speed. He ordered that the area be put under continual surveillance by available carrier aircraft. He gave Secretary Schlesinger authority to use antiriot measures against the enemy if the *Mayaguez* crew were moved toward the mainland. At Schlesinger's recommendation, the President authorized a battalion landing team of eleven hundred Marines airlifted from Okinawa to U-Tapao in Thailand and for two Marine platoons from the Philippines be available if needed.

Just after 6:00 p.m., Brent Scowcroft met with the President. Brent reported that as of 2:30 p.m., reports from U.S. P-3 overflights indicated that the *Mayaguez* might still be at sea. Within the span of the exchange, which lasted about seven minutes, a note was brought in saying the sighting was doubtful.[17] At that point reports were first that the SS *Mayaguez* was supposedly steaming toward Kompong Som, next that it was anchored off Koh Tang island, and then later that it was heading toward the mainland again. This sequence lived up to the old adage that in crises first reports are often wrong and to the truth about "the fog of war."

I met with the President in the Oval Office the following morning. At 7:15 a.m., Brent Scowcroft had relayed that the *Mayaguez* was thirty miles off the coast of a second island. An intercept followed that there was an unknown ship near *Mayaguez*, and that the Americans in the crew had been removed from the *Mayaguez* and put on the island in Khmer Rouge captivity.[18]

Word streaked like lightning across Washington, D.C. Ron Nessen stepped into the Oval Office minutes after the meeting with a report of a leak, reportedly out of the Pentagon. A wire service was reporting the U.S. was sending Marines from Okinawa to Thailand as part of a response to the Cambodian seizure of *Mayaguez*. The President was not pleased. He had asked that there be no comment on the matter. By then it was nighttime in Cambodia, and daylight there would not be until about 6:00 p.m. EST.

The President decided to notify the appropriate members of Congress, on an "advisory basis," rather than on a "consultation basis." That decision was based on his conclusion that the War Powers Act did not apply in this particular instance.[19] Also, it was reported that Thai Premier Kukrit Pramoj had been quoted in a separate wire story claiming the U.S. would not be allowed to use U-Tapao to get to the *Mayaguez*. The assumption in the meeting was that his comment was for domestic consumption and likely not an actual threat. Regardless, the President was prepared to take whatever steps were needed to rescue the crew, our countrymen, whether or not the Thais approved.[20]

Another NSC meeting began in the Cabinet Room at 10:22 a.m. on Tuesday, May 13. CIA Director Bill Colby reported that the *Mayaguez* was then at Koh Tang island. The Vice President, annoyed by the changing intel reports, challenged Secretary Schlesinger on his account at the previous NSC meeting that the *Mayaguez* was in port on the mainland. The President stepped in to defuse the tension by outlining what he saw as the contingency options.[21]

First, the U.S. would use our military aircraft to prevent any boats leaving Koh Tang—there were several in the cove—if it was determined the *Mayaguez's* crew might be aboard. To avoid friendly casualties, the U.S. military aircraft would be directed to fire in front of the boats and use searchlights and flares. As a last resort they would be authorized to hit the rudders and the tugboat that had been spotted.[22]

Second, the U.S. would stop all boats heading to Koh Tang. That was an easier decision, in that there was confidence that there wouldn't be any Americans aboard other vessels. The U.S. aircraft could use force to prevent the evacuation of the American crew if the Khmer forces tried to remove them from Koh Tang. And last, if required, U.S. Marines would board the *Mayaguez* or if necessary land on the island.[23] Another NSC meeting was set for 10:30 p.m. EST that day.

I met briefly with the President after the morning meeting. He concluded it was appropriate that U.S. actions send a signal of strength there and throughout the world.[24] At the same time, it was desirable that U.S. actions be measured and not be seen as an overreaction.

At 6:12 p.m. on Tuesday, Secretary Schlesinger called and reported that the *Mayaguez* had been fired upon by a gunboat. He discussed destroying the gunboat, and concluded that he would reopen the question once USS *Holt* arrived on scene in the morning. The order stood for our forces to look carefully to see if friendly personnel had been loaded onto any boats.[25] The Chinese had rebuffed the message the U.S. had asked them to relay to the Cambodians, effectively ending any possibility of the PRC helping to solve the crisis diplomatically. Secretary Schlesinger then reported, "There's bad news."

Indeed there was very bad news. A U.S. CH-53 transport helicopter en route to U-Tapao had crashed, killing all twenty-three Americans on board. It wasn't yet clear whether it might have been attacked.[26]

When the meeting was over, the President said that the NSC process was not working as well as he wanted. He was concerned that some of his orders might not have gone out. It struck me that while there are always likely to be glitches, it was important for the President to use the *Mayaguez* incident to take steps to iron out any kinks he might see out of the system, a complicated system that stretched from the White House over to Foggy Bottom at the Department of State, across the Potomac River to the Defense Department, and out to the various intelligence and national security elements. He mentioned that the relationships among Kissinger, Schlesinger, and Colby seemed frayed, which didn't help to assure that the national security process would run smoothly.[27]

A third NSC meeting started at 10:40 p.m. on May 13. The President directed that U.S. Marines be placed on standby to seize the *Mayaguez* and sweep Koh Tang.[28] That message was hand delivered to the Cabinet Room from the Situation Room as further steps were being discussed. A U.S. Air Force A-7 aircraft was reported to be considering destroying a vessel leaving Koh Tang for Kompong Som when our pilot reported over his radio that he thought he had spotted "Caucasians" on the ship's deck. "Get a message to that pilot to shoot across the bow but do not sink the boat," the President advised the Secretary of Defense.[29] The President was then notified that several other patrol craft had been destroyed after they had ignored U.S. signals to stop. "Suppose those vessels had carried crew members from *Mayaguez* below their decks?" he recalled thinking. "There was no way to tell, and that possibility was not pleasant to contemplate."[30]

I met with the President in the Oval Office the next morning. He was sensitive to the reality that U.S. foreign policy ultimately had to have the support of the American people. He discussed the importance of getting the crew back, and doing so in a way that didn't encourage future acts of piracy. That suggested engaging diplomatically with the Thais, boarding the *Mayaguez*, and preventing any boats from moving to or from the island. That also could mean attacking Koh Tang and the mainland and then disengaging as soon as possible. The President discussed having U.S. Navy jet aircraft from the USS *Coral Sea* provide surgical strikes to reduce possible civilian casualties. Vice President Rockefeller favored using the B-52s from Guam. Because using the large four-engine bombers, which had become so closely associated with the Vietnam War, could have been seen as overkill and unhelpful optically, the President decided against using the B-52s.[31]

The members of the NSC gathered again at 3:52 p.m. on Wednesday for a fourth and final meeting on the subject of the SS *Mayaguez*. There was no new information as to the whereabouts of the crew and Cambodia had not responded for over three days. The USS *Holt* was still twelve miles away and out of sight. The USS *Hancock*, the Essex-class carrier that the President had asked the Secretary of Defense to send to the area, would not arrive until noon two days later. But the USS *Coral Sea* was on station.

At 4:34 p.m., President Ford authorized the Secretary of Defense to initiate a three-pronged attack: a Marine helicopter assault on Koh Tang, strikes on military installations near Kompong Som by attack aircraft from the USS *Coral Sea*, and a naval interdiction operation to capture the *Mayaguez*. Kissinger advised that any prisoners should be taken with us and the President agreed. There was discussion about issuing an ultimatum through a diplomatic initiative. Kissinger advised that he had already done it.

The President and Kissinger differed with Schlesinger. "Henry and I felt that we had to do more," the President noted. "We wanted them to know that we meant business."[32] Then at 5:00 p.m., the President decided to go with aircraft from the USS *Coral Sea* in waves against Koh Tang and the mainland. The first wave would begin at 8:45 p.m.[33]

The intelligence available, as is often the case in a crisis, was less than perfect. There was only one map of Koh Tang immediately available, and the reported two dozen ragtag Cambodians turned out to be between two hundred and three hundred reasonably well-armed, battle-hardened Khmer Rouge troops in embedded positions.[34] Of concern, the *Mayaguez*'s crew didn't seem to be on the island. Further, the USS *Holt* had pulled alongside the targeted ship, but the small force of Marines found no signs of the *Mayaguez* crew there either. At 8:15 p.m., with U.S. aircraft in the air and the first wave of airstrikes due to start in thirty minutes, Cambodians broadcasted over a local Phnom Penh radio station their willingness to return the *Mayaguez*. They said nothing about the crew. Unable to rely upon such an imprecise message, the President moved forward with the air strikes.[35]

The President returned to the Oval Office at 11:00 p.m., after a working dinner with Dutch Prime Minister Johannes den Uyl. Secretary Schlesinger called from the Pentagon to inform the President that the third wave of attack had commenced. Some of the U.S. Marines were unaccounted for and the fighting on Koh Tang was heavier than expected. As of 11:20 p.m. one Marine was known to have been killed in action and eight others were wounded.[36]

A meeting with the President and Kissinger started twenty minutes later. I was there along with Brent Scowcroft, Ron Nessen, Bob Hartmann, Jack Marsh, and Max Friedersdorf. Schlesinger telephoned to report that a reconnaissance plane had spotted a Thai fishing vessel with what appeared to be Caucasians on the deck, and they were waving white flags. The Secretary of Defense called again minutes later. The vessel had approached the destroyer USS *Wilson* and the individuals on board were in fact the crew of the SS *Mayaguez*. "They're all safe," the President reported to cheers of relief. "We got them all out. Thank God."[37] The Khmer Rouge had apparently released the crew out of fear of still more reprisals. Having switched into a business suit, President Ford went on television and announced that U.S. forces had successfully rescued the *Mayaguez* crew.[38]

Only a very few in the media and the Congress contended that the President had evaded the War Powers Act by "informing" lawmakers of his actions rather than "consulting" with them before responding in the time-sensitive crisis. But the ranking member of the Senate Foreign Relations Committee praised the President and added his approval of the President's dealing with the Congress. "I've always felt that we were fully advised as to what was taking place," Senator John Sparkman, Democrat from Alabama, told reporters just steps away from the White House. Tom Brokaw of NBC News reported that the public's response was "overwhelmingly favorable," with calls and letters running about ten to one in support of the President. The international community seemed persuaded that the U.S. was on its way back.

Things were a bit less encouraging inside the administration. On May 16, the day after the *Mayaguez* crew was rescued, Secretary Schlesinger called. He believed that the State Department was circulating stories that they had been leaning forward while the Defense Department had opposed the use of force.[39]

Mel Laird suggested that everyone ought to be low key about Cambodia. The message was passed to Scowcroft that no one should be gloating. The experience clearly called for taking steps to smooth out the NSC process.[40]

The rescue of the *Mayaguez* crew had not come without sacrifice. The 3 Marines the U.S. lost on Koh Tang were the last three names included on the Vietnam Veterans Memorial Wall in Washington, D.C.[41]

In the week after the *Mayaguez* crisis, Secretary Schlesinger usefully raised the need for better coordination. He suggested the possibility of closed-circuit television connecting the Defense Department, the State Department, the CIA, and the White House. Whether on the phone or in person at an NSC meeting, he said, key people had to be working off the same information.[42]

Cabinet-level officials need to make many of the decisions. The President need not be engaging in less than presidential-level details of military or diplomatic matters. The President asked that in the future his orders be written down and shown to him for confirmation. Then if an order ended up not being followed, he wanted to know the reason.[43]

In some ways, the *Mayaguez* episode proved to be a turning point for Ford, who had had to demonstrate his command at a time of international crisis. He had performed well. Aided by a recovering economy, President Ford's approval rating rose from 40 percent to 51 percent. It was one of the largest "rallies" yet in measured presidential approval.[44] As I watched the President handle a meeting with Republican leaders shortly after the episode, I made a note to myself. My old friend, Jerry Ford, I wrote, "has done most of what he must learn to do and he's learned more every day. He's brought in some good people and is now thinking about 1976 and the campaign. It won't be smooth sailing, but he's on the way, and he's done well and is learning continuously. He's starting to refine and tune-up, yet throughout it he has kept his balance and what makes him what he is. He knows who he is and what he is, and he may just be exactly the right person for today." The President had handled the unexpected extraordinarily well—but there were other unanticipated tests still to come.

11

Commander in Chief

MEETING WITH THE PRESIDENT
May 9, 1975
8:32 to 9:09 a.m.
We believe freedom is a God-given right of man and that it's a natural state and, therefore, it is worth preserving.[1]

Nearing the end of the first full year of his presidency, Gerald Ford was earning respectable marks from the press for his efforts on the world stage, and had received a significant bump up for his successful handling of the *Mayaguez* incident. But throughout his tenure, he found himself squeezed between two foreign policy impulses, impulses picked over by professors of international relations, but given real-world weight by the sprawling policy infrastructure inside the D.C. Beltway. One was traditional. The other, while it certainly reflected ideals and experiences of the American tradition, represented something distinctly contemporary.

The traditional impulse was the classical realism of Richard Nixon and Henry Kissinger, which held that stability in the international realm was best assured by balancing the power of different states. The challenging view, championed prominently on the right by Ronald Reagan—and soon after by writers and scholars who became known as "neoconservatives"—argued that a more aggressive posture, paired with concern for human liberty, was preferred. "Peace through strength," Reagan would avow as an echo of Eisenhower and Washington before him when challenging Jimmy Carter for the Presidency in 1980.

Looking back, it's interesting that all five of the presidents preceding Ford and six of the seven following him were considered by historians and journalists to have a foreign policy "doctrine." With the shortest time as President, it is not surprising that President Ford's set of beliefs about America's responsibilities and duties remain less definable. With all the challenges he was facing as one who had never run for the office, President Ford was too preoccupied with the problems of the present to set forth a "long view." In other words, one of the more significant disadvantages of his instant presidency was that he was never afforded an opportunity to map out his own distinct vision for America's role.

That is not to say Ford didn't have strong views when it came to foreign policy. He had a streak of idealism when it came to overseas actors and their motivations. He was concerned by the never-ending strife in the Middle East. He knew war. "War is devastating—destructive—and kills the faith and hope of all mankind," he lamented to Kissinger in a letter in January 1975. Yet there was no doubt he was in his core an optimist. In that letter, he proposed the creation of a "Middle East Common Market" between Arabs and Israelis that might "give all their peoples a life of peace and tranquility."[2]

Because he was President such a short time, he never enunciated a Ford Doctrine. What Ford did do was balance the policies of the inherited Nixon presidency with the growing movement for a stronger tone from the Republican right. But even in his short tenure, Ford made a series of decisions that arguably helped set the stage for America's Cold War victory. For the better part of his first year in office, President Ford achieved an admirable record on human rights, a record that, to his credit, he built of his own volition—and even more to his credit because more often than not it was forged against the admonitions of some in the State Department. Working closely with Kissinger, whom he respected greatly, he ushered Park Chung-hee aside during his trip to Asia to make known his concern about the South Korean President's repressive policies. He vocally supported anti-Soviet dissidents in Ukraine, earning him the gratitude of the Ukrainian Congress Committee of America.[3] In January 1975, he signed the controversial Jackson-Vanik amendment into law, a critical reform to trade with nonmarket economies that ultimately allowed more than half a million Soviet refugees to resettle in the U.S. and an estimated one million Jews from behind the Iron Curtain to resettle in Israel.

Much of this, however, was overshadowed by a decision that became among the more memorable moments of the Ford foreign policy and that also demonstrated Ford's delicate balancing act.

Aleksandr Solzhenitsyn, an acclaimed Russian writer who had been pivotal in raising awareness about the Soviet Union's extensive forced labor system—perhaps most with his monumental 1973 book, *The Gulag Archipelago*—visited the U.S. in the summer of 1975. Human rights activists sought a meeting with the President, a request communicated to Ford via a letter from North Carolina Republican Senator Jesse Helms. This raised alarm bells in the Ford White House— Helms was one of the leaders of the Republican right, a hard-liner toward the Soviets, and a periodic critic of the Ford administration, and of Henry Kissinger in particular.

All of this of course was set against the backdrop of Washington, D.C.'s relationship with the Kremlin, and particularly our efforts to reach a SALT II arms control agreement, building on the progress that had been made by Nixon and Kissinger and the progress in Vladivostok the previous summer by Ford and Kissinger with General Secretary Brezhnev. There had been a shimmer of hope for improved relations. That July, Apollo and Soyuz spacecraft docked in orbit. This link-up, the first ever between U.S. and Soviet spacecraft, was hailed as the end of the space race that had begun in 1957 with Sputnik. "It was the most spectacular event in U.S.-Soviet relations since their troops linked-up at the River Elbe 30 years ago," wrote Richard Lewis in a July issue of the *New Scientist*. Scientists from the two countries, he continued, "shook hands; inspected and admired each other's space vehicles; ate each other's food; and exchanged gold medals, flags and even (for the sake of science) personal microbes."[4]

Unfortunately, the good feelings engendered by that historic event eroded. The White House learned that the Soviets were violating at least the spirit of the first SALT Agreement by concealing missile silos and other military infrastructure.[5] Four days later, *The Christian Science Monitor* ran an article positing that the Ford administration hadn't been candid about Soviet violations, citing sources at the Pentagon.[6] Then another article appeared, this one in *The Washington Post* and citing sources at the State Department.[7]

The Solzhenitsyn invitation was the last thing some in the administration felt it needed. Jack Marsh reported that the National Security Council, under Kissinger, was advising against a meeting.[8] Bob Hartmann was seen as opposed as well.[9] The NSC had logical reasons for their position. The President was scheduled to meet with General Secretary Brezhnev at the end of July, and the NSC staff was convinced that keeping détente intact required not ticking off the Kremlin unnecessarily with what Moscow would undoubtedly see as a provocative act.

Dick Cheney, on the other hand, believed the President should meet with Solzhenitsyn. By this point, the President had come to value Dick as an aide and advisor. This relationship had been built up by design. Early on in the administration, I went to the President and said I thought we needed to institute a deputy system where there was someone in each of the key four or five offices that was number two whom the President would be willing to work with interchangeably. I said that he would have to get comfortable with that or mistakes would get made. It was not possible for the Chief of Staff to go on every trip and keep things moving along at the White House. Balls get dropped. I insisted the President agree, which he did, to work interchangeably between me and Dick Cheney, as well as between two or three other key people he counted on like White House Counsel Phil Buchen and his deputy, Phil Areda.

Ford was impressed by Cheney's professional, thoughtful demeanor and nearly total unflappability. But the President on occasion liked to test that, for example when he teased Cheney for being quoted in an article in *Newsweek*. Ford told me, with a laugh, "Every time I mention that article to Dick he turns red."

"I've worked with him for years and never knew he blushed!" I replied.[10]

In any event, Dick felt so strongly on the Solzhenitsyn matter that he produced a lengthy memorandum outlining the case. One of several arguments he made was that a decision *not* to see the Soviet dissident would be "totally out of character for the President."

"More than any President in recent memory," Dick wrote, implicitly citing Ford's spokes-of-the-wheel style of management of the White House, "he's the man who's willing to see anyone, talk to anyone and listen to anyone's views, no matter how much they differ from his own." Cheney also reasoned that rebuffing Solzhenitsyn would lead to "a misreading of détente," for it would send the wrong signal to the world "that all of a sudden our relationship with the Soviets is all sweetness and light," and that political concerns triumphed over human ones.[11]

The President was in a predicament. He was dealing with the great counterweight of a long history of decisions and actions by the Nixon administration to avoid antagonizing the Soviet Union. This was at the heart of the approach known as "détente." Ford had assumed office assuring Americans he would continue those policies, which had won Nixon and Kissinger great popularity and acclaim.

Kissinger raised a more sinister specter with the President—the threat of resuming a more hostile, even dangerous, relationship with the Soviet Union. As Kissinger would later remark to the press, he believed Solzhenitsyn wanted the United States to "pursue an aggressive policy to overthrow the Soviet Union." "Now I believe that Solzhenitsyn is a man whose suffering entitles him to be heard and who has stood with great anguish for his views," Kissinger said. "But I do believe that if his views became the national policy of the United States, we would be in a period—we would be confronting a considerable threat of military conflict."[12]

Not without difficulty, the President sided with Kissinger and Scowcroft. Ford also decided not to attend an AFL-CIO dinner that was convened in Solzhenitsyn's honor. The situation was further exacerbated by miscommunications to the press, which quickly caught wind of Ford's "snub." The White House press office first seemed to indicate that Ford couldn't meet with Solzhenitsyn due to time constraints and later that the President would prefer "substantive" meetings over "symbolic" ones.[13] *The New York Times* wryly noted that when Press Secretary Ron Nessen made such a statement, President Ford had taken the time "to greet the 1974 National Farm Family of the Year, Mr. and Mrs. James Ottoman and their daughter, Dana, of Malin, Oregon. The Ottomans gave Mr. Ford two books, one of which was 'The Complete Potato Cookbook.'"[14]

Once the Ford "snub"—as it would be characterized—made its way into the media, as the President himself later stated in his memoir, "the furor began."[15] The furor went on and on, stoked by the media, by Solzhenitsyn, and, understandably, by anti-Communist hard-liners in the United States. It also annoyed some of the President's closest friends. "My God!" Mel Laird exclaimed. "The President meets with all kinds of athletes who have all kinds of political philosophies in the world—why the hell can't he meet with Solzhenitsyn?"[16] A bipartisan group of Senators sought to introduce a congressional resolution urging that the Russian dissident be invited to speak before a joint session of Congress. Democrat Senator Ernest Hollings bluntly labeled the administration's decision "an embarrassment."[17]

For weeks, the White House staff internally debated whether to eat crow and solicit Solzhenitsyn, who had very publically castigated Ford's approach to the Soviet Union. The writer had accused Ford of the "betrayal" of Eastern Europe by planning to attend a conference in Helsinki, Finland, to discuss human rights, which some Soviet critics saw as an action that would have the result of giving Communist puppet governments in the Iron Curtain legitimacy.

Initially, in response to Solzhenitsyn's sharp elbows in the media, the President concluded that it was too late to approach him with hat in hand.[18] He then reversed position, feeling that perhaps it wasn't too late, and told confidants that he would be glad to see Solzhenitsyn when he had returned from the Helsinki meetings in August. The staff prepared talking points for the President. He would admit that he had botched the situation and praise Solzhenitsyn as a distinguished person and writer.[19]

I suggested that the President simply, without any further horsing around, say he would be happy to meet with Solzhenitsyn and move on.[20] The President agreed, but several more days passed without action.

Kissinger was undoubtedly concerned about the spectacle and characterized Solzhenitsyn as an unacceptable threat to détente. The White House struggled to answer a series of questions involving détente. Why was the U.S. still engaging with dictatorships that trampled human freedoms? Why was America dealing with the Soviet Union and aligning with Saudi Arabia, even though both nations discriminated against minorities?[21]

America had a wide array of relationships with countries around the world. Given that, and the fact that our country was founded on principles in which we deeply believed, including the preservation of freedom, then weren't we as a people obligated to be against injustice? To be against injustice meant we should be supportive of our principles through persuasion. At the same time, it would be harmful for us to sever our relationships with every country in the world whose views didn't align perfectly with our own. Doing so would severely harm our national interest.[22]

An editor from *Time* magazine stepped forward, offering to be an intermediary between the President and Solzhenitsyn, but by then it seemed that the Soviet dissident was not willing to meet with Ford under any conditions. Solzhenitsyn knew well he was a symbol of opposition to détente and had likely decided that meeting with President Ford would have undermined his cachet. When the President became aware of Solzhenitsyn's position, he felt the dissident had gone too far.[23] Still, the "open" invitation stood, but President Ford was fully aware there was little chance of having a meeting. He also believed—and wrongly in the opinion of some—that the more Solzhenitsyn spoke out against the White House, the more he was discrediting himself.[24]

In the end, a meeting did not take place. Solzhenitsyn claimed he was too busy to visit Washington, D.C. Regardless, much of the American public—or at least many of those who paid attention to these types of things—judged the President's "snub" negatively.[25] For years it would be referenced by close allies of Ford's political rival, Ronald Reagan, as spurring the former California Governor on in his uphill battle against the President.

The Ford White House struggled to make up ground after the Solzhenitsyn affair. On August 1, 1975, during a second round of meetings in Europe, the President signed the Final Act of the Conference on Security and Cooperation in Europe, otherwise known as the Helsinki Accords. Joined by leaders of thirty-four countries, including Soviet leader Brezhnev and UN Secretary General Kurt Waldheim, this was said to be the largest gathering of European heads of state since the Congress of Vienna in 1815. The CSCE agreement was momentous, at least in the eyes of the Europeans and some administration figures.

"Ford, Brezhnev, and the other leaders," Ron Nessen recollected, "pledged to cooperate with each other; respect the sovereignty, borders, and internal affairs of other countries; refrain from using force to settle disputes, and not violate human rights."[26] Privately, Kissinger and many others, including me, noted that the agreement was not binding and recognized that while it could turn out to be a grandstand play to the left, nonetheless, it made sense to go along with it.

What was expected of the President at Helsinki was affirmation of U.S. support for those behind the Iron Curtain. Yet, as historian Daniel Sargent noted, the President's address in Finland's capital showed the "paradox" of the agreement. "Even as it articulated a role for human rights, the CSCE presumed a stable international order of nation-states, divided into Cold War blocs."[27] There wasn't much proof that the U.S. was eager to actively alter East-West geopolitical dynamics.

Ford himself believed differently, perhaps even presciently, that the Helsinki Accords put the Soviet Union, unwittingly, in a box. As Ford assured the American people, "The Helsinki documents involve political and moral commitments aimed at lessening tensions and opening further the lines of communication between peoples of East and West." Responding to those Americans and others who believed the agreements were a concession to the Soviet Union, Ford said, "If it all fails, Europe will be no worse off than it is now. If even a part of it succeeds, the lot the people in Eastern Europe will be that much better, and the cause of freedom will advance at least that far." At least one well-recognized Cold War historian, John Lewis Gaddis, agreed. Helsinki, Gaddis noted, "gradually became a manifesto of the dissident and liberal movement." What the Soviet Union and its Eastern European puppet regimes had agreed to in effect was "that the people who lived under these systems—at least the more courageous—could claim official permission to say what they thought."

Looking back today, Helsinki in some ways could be said to have marked the birth of the modern human rights movement. It listed individual rights and liberties and the responsibilities of governments to protect them. It recognized universal human rights, including freedoms of thought, conscience, and belief. And it sent an unequivocal message to dissident groups like Solidarity in Poland and Charter 77 in Czechoslovakia that individual citizens can monitor and report on the human rights records of their governments.[28] Civic groups sprouted up across the Soviet Union in the wake of the Helsinki Accords. What the Helsinki Accords lacked in legally binding terms, Ford could and would argue, it made up by terms that it could be argued were morally binding.

In the meantime, Ford was determined to pursue a historic arms control agreement with the Soviets before his term was over. A sticking point was that military technology was evolving faster than SALT, which had been penned in 1972. When President Ford came into office in August 1974, cruise missiles—aerodynamically guided missiles designed to hit distant targets with high precision—hadn't yet been demonstrated to be an operational success. Soon after Vladivostok, they became a factor, and the need to distinguish them from more traditional ballistic missiles—missiles with a trajectory that sent them into outer space and that are guided only during brief periods of flight—proved to be a new problem.

Defense Secretary Jim Schlesinger had accepted a proposal that placed constraints on new cruise missiles, but avoided certain limitations on the Soviet Union's recently released Tupolev Tu-22M "Backfire," a supersonic, long-range strategic and maritime strike bomber.[29] The proposal, in effect, accepted the Kremlin's demand that the Backfire bomber, which boasted a nuclear weapons delivery capability and could fly from the Soviet Union to Cuba without refueling, be defined as a "nonstrategic weapon."[30]

Kissinger was bothered by what he perceived as President Ford's post-hoc concerns, believing the U.S. had to work with the Soviets on the grounds already established.[31]

He was more at ease with some ambiguity about the new military technologies, while those at the Department of Defense were less so. The Soviets had not been forthcoming about the level of their defense expenditures and infrastructure investments, and, therefore, it was an enormous risk not to clearly classify cruise missiles and the Backfire as well as the Soviet's newly introduced RSD-10 intermediate-range ballistic missile which, with some tweaking, could become a missile capable of being launched from one continent and hitting another.[32]

The President was unhappy, and I understood why, given all the internal debates taking place. Kissinger had been successfully working the negotiation for some time and was right insofar as there was a logic to marching forward with the Soviets within the bounds of the original understanding. I believed that the cruise missile was good leverage—the leverage needed—for getting a grip on the Backfire bomber, the full capabilities of which were far from fully understood at that time.[33]

The President became quite explicit that he wanted a SALT agreement, and that it was one of the most important efforts of his Presidency. He believed strongly that strategic arms limitations were in the best interest of the U.S., and he argued we would not get an agreement in 1976 if we didn't act constructively.[34]

The President knew he needed to build support in the country for whatever ended up in an agreement. He was advised to give addresses and have speeches made by surrogates, including foreign policy leaders such as Zbigniew Brzezinski, with whom he planned to consult prior to or immediately after signing an agreement.[35] Without making the case, he understood he would not get the needed support and flexibility from Congress or buy-in from the American people.

The challenges of détente and the existing threats from the Soviet Union were difficult to fully appreciate and, as a result, the details were less than fully understood by the public. Issues surrounded by mystique or silence, can be exploited by one side not least because others don't force proponents to provide substantive arguments because they themselves may not be sufficiently conversant with important facts.[36] Détente had been widely discussed. Some had framed it as a success when in fact it was a continuing evolving process in which the U.S. was trying to ease tensions. It was fair to make a case that, even though America had its own beliefs and the Soviets had notably different beliefs of their own, it could still be to our advantage to try to find ways to relax tensions. But that was true only as long as we were persuaded that doing so was in the interest of preserving peace, while facing allegations that the policy of détente had the unintended effect of seeming to be turning a blind eye to human suffering at the hands of Soviet totalitarianism.[37]

Secretary Kissinger planned a trip to Moscow for late January 1976 to further discuss limitations on strategic arms with General Secretary Brezhnev and Foreign Minister Gromyko. The timing was complicated by a proxy conflict in the southern African nation of Angola. Three months earlier, Cuba had launched a large-scale military intervention in support of the leftist People's Movement for the Liberation of Angola, which had been supported and supplied by the Soviet Union.

"To my knowledge," said Brent Scowcroft, "the U.S. government has no direct support there, and we're not hiring mercenaries."

Well, I replied, that answer leaves open the possibility that we might be paying for other mercenaries, possibly indirectly or that something could be occurring beyond our knowledge. I asked, "Is that what you mean?" He said he would get an answer, and get it over to the Pentagon so we could get everyone on the same set of facts.[38]

What we soon learned was that Angola was a nuisance for the Soviets as well. Anatoly Dobrynin, the Soviet Union's Ambassador to the U.S., relayed that his country was willing to break its back to get a SALT II agreement, but they didn't know how to get the Cubans out.[39] Henry's trip to the Soviet Union had the potential to be a public relations problem.

"I have always said that these are separable parts," the President said, "that if you can get a plus out of SALT, even though you get a minus out of Angola, that doesn't mean you don't take the plus out of SALT."

I said that the effect could be that Henry goes over there to meet with Brezhnev in the middle of this Angola flap, and the guy sitting here drinking a beer could say, 'What in the hell is going on?'"

I worried the American people were going to see the U.S. doing eight or nine things favorable to the Soviet Union, such as selling them grain and seeming to be making defense concessions, then hear about Kissinger's cordial meeting with Soviet leadership, and that that could make it extremely difficult to avoid a hostile atmosphere at home. What exactly—the person from Kansas, Michigan, or California might ask—is the U.S. getting out of all this?

"I am not saying he shouldn't go, not saying we shouldn't work for SALT," I told the President, "I am saying we have got one hell of a problem because we have got a policy that the American people either don't understand or do understand and can't accept."[40]

The President said he would never forgive himself if we missed an opportunity to get a decent SALT II agreement. Henry ended up going over, and he and Brent Scowcroft came to terms on a proposal for the Soviets. Newspaper articles being put out in the Soviet Union claimed a secret deal could be in the works.[41]

Back at the White House, the President continued to stress that he wanted a good, substantive agreement for the country, pointing out that no agreement would be the worst outcome. We discussed that he meant an agreement within the parameters of the differences we've been debating. It would be more desirable to get that agreement than no agreement. But obviously the *worst* thing would be to get a bad agreement. The President agreed with that sentiment, of course.[42]

I was worried that the President might be leaving an impression to some around him that he wanted an agreement, period, but I knew that was certainly not his position.[43]

As it happened, the SALT agreement, much like every other issue, was about to become front and center in a divisive political campaign that threatened to further divide the Republican Party.

⇥ 12 ⇤

Assassins' Target

MEETING WITH THE PRESIDENT
August 26, 1975
6:40 to 7:18 p.m.
Alone

I told him that there were complaints about the Secret Service and that I personally thought they were out of line in Chicago and Milwaukee. The President said there was some rumors of threats—maybe that had something to do with it.

DICK, if there were rumors of threats, you or I should have been told and we weren't. WHAT WENT ON. We should make sure that [Special Agent in Charge Richard] Keiser doesn't tell the President rumors like that without telling you or me.

The President said I want to bend over backwards to have those people to not be offensive. I said I was going to talk to Keiser. He said fine.[1]

In any presidency there is an inherent tension between the requirement to do everything reasonable to protect a President's safety and a President's understandable desire to meet and shake hands with fellow Americans. In September 1975, one year into the Ford presidency, two events brought that tension front and center in dramatic fashion.

Only a few weeks earlier, David Packard, a senior advisor who had been a founder of the Hewlett-Packard company and had served as the Deputy Secretary of Defense in the Nixon administration under Secretary of Defense Mel Laird, had come to the White House to discuss with the President a challenging but important issue. Given the unique circumstances resulting from the resignation of both a Vice President and a President in recent years, the issue he wanted to discuss was what would take place in the event President Ford did not survive his presidency. This was a critically important and a historically unique question. In our lifetimes, President John F. Kennedy had been assassinated, and there had been concerns about President Nixon's health during the long Watergate crisis. David Packard and I agreed it was important to raise these issues with the President: questions of command and control of America's nuclear arsenal and what actions might have to be taken in the event of still another assassination or the incapacity of the President and the Vice President. Ford asked for a briefing on the matter and I had suggested that the Vice President have a separate briefing as well.[2]

But these thoughts were not at the front of our minds, at least not then. The summer of 1975 had been filled with other issues and concerns. Betty Ford, for example, had appeared on *60 Minutes*, talking openly about things most other First Ladies had avoided—such as her outspoken support for an Equal Rights Amendment to the Constitution. She also got quite personal, telling interviewer Morley Safer she would probably try marijuana if she were a teenager, that she'd seen a psychiatrist, and that "I wouldn't be surprised" if her daughter told her she had had an affair. The unusually forthcoming First Lady sparked a sensation across the country and led a fair number of Ford aides to raise questions about her effect on the Republican Party's conservative base. I, for one, believed you'd be howling into the wind by trying to tell Betty Ford what she could or could not say. Over time, as it became clear Americans across the spectrum admired Betty's outspokenness and general zest for life, the worries eased.[3]

The summer of 1975 also featured a continuation of some hardly unprecedented differences between various officials—Bob Hartmann was suspected of leaking stories to the media against Henry Kissinger, which Kissinger, understandably, was not happy about. He was determined to identify the leaker. "He may have a legitimate gripe," I advised the President in August, "but you do not want to have your administration get like Nixon's did about that problem of leaks."[4] Vice President Rockefeller was trying to persuade people into backing various policy proposals he'd developed, which concerned key Presidential aides, including Alan Greenspan. Based on feedback I'd received from a number of quarters, I raised a caution flag to the President. The Vice President is enthusiastic and many key staff members were reluctant to disagree with the positions he takes, I said. "That is not a criticism of the Vice President, it is a criticism of the circumstance that you deal with as President because those people are afraid to deal with him—they are afraid to speak up when he is present, they are afraid to speak up even when he is not present and you just ought to be aware of it."[5]

There were lingering discussions and differing views concerning America's intelligence-gathering activities, further reports of Governor Reagan's political activities, and the advent of new crises. Added to those immediate tasks were: a looming financial crisis in New York City and a search for a new Supreme Court Justice to replace the retiring William O. Douglas. The President outlined his criteria for the post: quality, confirmability, age—so that the nominee could be there for a while—breadth on the Court so the Court did not have eight people of any one category, some diversity, and finally that the individual should be moderate to moderate conservative.[6] (Ultimately, he nominated John Paul Stevens.)

These controversies and issues—important, to be sure—were promptly put on pause when we were quite suddenly faced with a considerably more pressing concern: President Ford's mortality.

On Friday, September 5, 1975, President Ford was in the historic Senator Hotel in Sacramento, across from the California State Capitol building where he was scheduled to meet with the state's new Governor, Jerry Brown. At approximately 10:00 a.m., he left the hotel with his Secret Service detail. He moved toward a sizable gathering of people, several rows deep, who had come out to greet the President. They were lined along the side of a path through the large park in front of the state Capitol. As Ford crossed L Street onto the Capitol grounds, he deviated from the plan—but in a way that hardly surprised anyone who worked with him. He moved immediately toward the many well-wishers who had gathered to see him and started shaking hands left and right.

The President was pulling—as he had on his trip to Japan—what is often called an unscheduled "grip and grin" session. This understandably raised the pulse of the Secret Service agents—as well as the concern of those whose task it was to keep the President on schedule—but it was certainly not a surprise. Gerald Ford was a man of the people. He had concluded it was worth the risks given the challenges the country and he had faced together—and overcome—to meet and engage personally with his fellow Americans. Further, very simply, he liked people and, given his midwestern friendliness, he truly appreciated their coming out to meet him.

As the President approached a stand of trees on the left, a woman in the second row of the crowd caught his eye. She was wearing, Ford later recalled, "an unusual red or orange dress." The woman, he recounted, "had gray-brown hair and a weathered complexion." Ford assumed she was going to shake his hand, but he hesitated to greet her. His sensitivity and awareness was understandable. As a member of the Warren Commission, which had been assigned the responsibility to investigate the assassination of President John F. Kennedy, Ford was fully aware of the dangers that lurked for prominent public figures surrounded by crowds. While he felt it was important to greet as many people as he could, he was still sensitive to the reality of the potential threats a President faces. Apparently something about this woman—perhaps her "unusual" brightly colored dress—stood out for him. Suddenly, when he was just a few feet away from her, he noticed she was gripping an object. It was a .45 caliber pistol, which she began to raise in the direction of the President.

The threat that September morning in California was thwarted quickly. An alert Secret Service agent beside the President had also seen the pistol. True to his training, he did not hesitate before pouncing on the would-be assassin. The quick-thinking team of agents then grabbed the President by his shoulders and moved him down and out of the possible line of fire. As he was being rapidly moved away toward the state Capitol building to safety, Ford turned and looked back just long enough to see a flash of red as several officers wrestled to the ground the armed woman who had set out that morning to assassinate the President of the United States.

The would-be assassin turned out to be a woman named Lynette Alice "Squeaky" Fromme, a twenty-six-year-old follower of the notorious mass murderer Charles Manson. The so-called Manson Family had been responsible for the brutal murders of five people, including actress Sharon Tate, in August 1969. Fromme was a fanatic, but reportedly had not taken part in the murders herself. She had, however, done her part as a loyal "Family" member to support Manson and his followers when they were on trial. She had carved an "X" into her forehead after Manson had done the same. She had also served a jail sentence for trying to tamper with a witness in the Manson trial by lacing her hamburger with LSD.

Rudderless with her cult leader behind bars, Fromme contended she believed that smog from automobiles was going to cause California's redwoods to collapse. She asserted that by killing President Ford she would draw more attention to the plight of the trees.

"It didn't go off," she kept saying after her attempt at assassinating the President was thwarted by Secret Service agents. "It didn't go off. Can you believe it?" That was the result of her inexperience or Providence, or both. Her pistol had four bullets in its magazine, but the slide had not been properly pulled to move one of the bullets into the firing chamber.[7] The assassination attempt happened so quickly, and the President's schedule was so busy, that he may not have had time to fully absorb the shock of what had happened and that the President of the United States might well have been shot dead in that instant. He went on with the business of the day.

What I remember most vividly about the episode in Sacramento was President Ford's demeanor, his seemingly natural manner in keeping everything moving along as if nothing extraordinary had occurred. As White House Chief of Staff, I was focused on seeing that he was safe. The President, however, must have felt that even a minor alteration in his tone or any change in his routine might be the wrong signal to send to the American people. His approach was commendable, even downright brave.

Only minutes after the President's close call with "Squeaky" Fromme, we were at the East Entrance of the California State Capitol building, and very shortly he was sitting down in his scheduled meeting with Governor Jerry Brown. Having nearly lost his life, one might have imagined the President mentioning the threat to the Governor. But his meeting with the Governor went on for some time before the assassination attempt came up. President Ford stayed focused on the business at hand.

Speaking to reporters shortly after his meeting with Governor Brown and his address to the California state legislature, the President expressed his appreciation to the Secret Service. He added, "This incident under no circumstances will prevent me or preclude me from contacting the American people as I travel from one state to another and one community to another."[8]

At the airport later that day, the President again wanted to shake hands with the people waiting for him. In this case, the Secret Service objected, and the President reluctantly relented.

Eventually, when the events of the day were over, the President did pause to reflect on the attempted shooting. In the cabin of *Air Force One*, perhaps in reaction to the concerned faces of staff members around him, including mine, the President grew quiet. Referring to the attempt on his life, he said, "Rummy, this is one of those things where you say a prayer and the good Lord takes care of you."[9]

On November 19, 1975, after an occasionally farcical court trial during which she threw an apple at the judge,[10] Lynette "Squeaky" Fromme was sentenced to life in prison for attempting to assassinate the President of the United States. In August 2009, at the age of sixty, she was released on parole after serving nearly thirty-four years of that sentence.

MEETING WITH THE PRESIDENT
September 11, 1975
9:01 to 9:14 a.m.
In the Cabin [of Air Force One]
The President called [Bob] Hartmann and me up to the Cabin and showed us the bullet-proof vest that the secret service had advised he wear. We talked about the extra weight and the fact that it would tire him and the fact that it might dehydrate him if it were warm up there and decided that the handling of it would be the only possible answer is, namely that we don't discuss security matters[11]

On September 22, the President traveled to San Francisco to address a conference of the AFL-CIO. In light of the earlier assassination attempt in California, the Secret Service team was particularly attentive. San Francisco, Ron Nessen noted, was "well known for its population of liberal anti–Vietnam War, anti-establishment hippies."[12] Still, Gerald Ford was not one to shy away from a commitment. Though our experience with "Squeaky" Fromme's attempt to kill him was a sobering reminder of his and indeed every President's mortality, he was determined to continue as before and in the manner he believed was appropriate for the President of the United States. That meant continuing his scheduled public appearances unabated. His speech to the AFL-CIO Union went ahead as planned and was carried off without incident. But shortly thereafter another near-catastrophe occurred.

MEETING WITH THE PRESIDENT
September 22, 1975
10:15 to 11:45 a.m.
Arrival in San Francisco.
Went to the AFL-CIO meeting. The President gave the energy speech [based on a plan by Nelson Rockefeller]. It was sad. I think it was a mistake. Ranks behind three or four major personnel errors in seriousness but very high. As we left to go up in the freight elevator, I walked out about two feet in front of the President. The President walked out next to Bob Georgine. And the elevator door fell down on the President's head and stunned him badly. The minute it hit his head it bounced back up. It had, apparently, an automatic safety device, but it broke the skin. I then rode in the car with the President and [White House Dr.] Lukash over to the suite and in the St. Francis Lukash put some cold packs on the head.

NOTE: About 11:45 I went down to the street and mixed around with the demonstrators that were out there and they were a pretty scruffy bunch. . . . That city gives you a weird feeling. I went back upstairs and was fully convinced that the President shouldn't work that crowd, which is why I stayed close to him as we went downstairs . . . which is exactly what the Secret Service concluded, Kennerly had concluded, and Terry [O'Donnell] and Red [Cavaney] had concluded. I guess it didn't take a genius to figure it out.[13]

In an attempt to avoid giving the press much of a view of the injury to the President's head—and given an emerging false narrative that Ford was something of a stumbler—I was determined to try to move the President past the large crowds waiting to see him in the lobby of the hotel and also gathered outside. We advised him to move quickly into the limousine parked at the curb on Post Street, directly in front of the hotel entrance waiting with the right back door open. The President heeded our advice and avoided shaking hands with the large group that had gathered in the lobby. Instead, waving with both hands, smiling, and saying hello, he headed quickly out of the front door of the hotel. As we exited and were walking the few steps toward the open back door of the waiting limousine, Ford began waving to the large crowd that had gathered outside on both sides of the street. At that moment, we heard the loud crack of a gunshot fired at the President.

We learned later that Oliver Sipple, a thirty-three-year-old former Marine, had been on his way to San Francisco's Fisherman's Wharf and happened by the St. Francis hotel, where the President had been speaking. He saw the large crowd waiting to greet President Ford and decided to wait with them. The ex-Marine had waited on the sidewalk across from the hotel for almost three hours. His patience may well have saved President Ford's life and, since I was standing beside him, possibly mine as well.

During Sipple's wait, he had noticed a middle-aged woman milling about. When the President finally emerged from the front entrance of the hotel, Sipple waved and started to clap for the President along with the others in the crowd. It was then that Sipple noticed a chrome-plated gun in the woman's hand, which she had raised and was aiming toward the President.[14]

"Gun!" Sipple, the former Marine, yelled loudly, grabbing the woman's arm just as her pistol fired. The Vietnam veteran later recounted that the moment was "probably the scariest thing that ever happened in my whole life."[15]

Hearing that outburst and the gunshot, the President ducked, as did I. The bullet whizzed past his head and hit the front wall of the hotel just behind us. Secret Service agents Ron Pontius and Jack Merchant pushed the President forward through the open door and down onto the floor of the backseat of the thirteen-thousand-pound armored Lincoln Continental limousine. The three of us moved into the car on top of the President.

For the first several blocks after leaving the hotel, we stayed flat on top of President Ford. As the motorcade sped from the scene, we heard the President's muffled voice from below us. "C'mon, Rummy, you guys get off," he said. "You're heavy!" The President's motorcade raced to the airport.

Betty Ford, who had been featured at a separate event in Pebble Beach, arrived at the San Francisco International Airport a few minutes after the President had boarded *Air Force One*. She walked the few steps down the aisle on *Air Force One* toward the President's table, sat down across from him, and asked cheerfully, "How did they treat you?" referring to his meeting with the union members. She had not been told of what had happened. The President didn't say anything. She showed interest but no emotion as I described our eventful morning to her. As always, Betty Ford was a steady hand.

The individual who fired the pistol at the President was soon identified as a woman named Sara Jane Moore, a Marxist radical who had been picked up by the local police a day earlier on an illegal handgun charge but had been promptly released.[16] She had been standing across the street, about forty feet from the President, when she fired. "I do regret I didn't succeed, and allow the winds of change to start," Moore said immediately after the shooting. "I wish I had killed him. I did it to create chaos." Needless to say, emotions were running high given the tension involved with the President coming back to California only seventeen days after the earlier assassination attempt in Sacramento.

Ron Nessen, who had leaped into the second car in the President's motorcade, lashed out as he sped away. "Goddamn California!" he yelled, pounding the door and front seat with his fist. "Why . . . did we ever come back here! I hope we never come back to this . . . state."[17] As it happened, Ron had jumped into the wire service car, which also included the White House UPI reporter Helen Thomas.

During the flight back to Washington, D.C., the President remarked that the Secret Service agents and state and local law enforcement had performed their duties in an outstanding manner, and he asked that his thanks be expressed to them all.

The President relaxed and requested that the Navy steward bring him a libation. With black humor flowing, the mood on board *Air Force One*, Nessen recalled, was "a mixture of relief and hysteria." After we touched down in Washington, D.C., around midnight, the President told reporters, "I don't think any person as President ought to cower in the face of a limited number of people who want to take the law into their own hands." That was not, however, a statement without controversy.

With the President having been targeted for assassination twice in less than three weeks, the concern in the country as well as in the White House was high. A U.S. Senate committee held hearings on the Secret Service and the President's safety, with former presidential nominees in both parties—Senator Barry Goldwater (R-AZ), former

Vice President Hubert H. Humphrey (D-MN), and Senator George McGovern (D-SD), among them—all urging their friend President Ford to minimize any activities that could risk possible exposure to still another assassination attempt. Bill Simon, the Secretary of the Treasury Department, which had as one of his responsibilities overseeing the Secret Service, testified that the number of threats to President Ford had tripled since the two recent assassination attempts in California.

Senator Goldwater phoned me with a message for the President. "For Christ's sake, the President should stay home. He doesn't need to chase his tail all over the country. He's got the presidency sewn up if he can stay alive."[18] Congressman John Rhodes, another Arizona Republican, was less colorful but offered the same advice. "Thank God they missed him," but tone down the travel. Yet another member of Congress, Dr. Tim Carter of Kentucky, called saying that the President's determination to travel and defy threats to his life could amount to an invitation to crazy people.[19]

Other revelations from that widely watched Senate hearing, as reported by *The New York Times*, included:

Federal agents were seeking a member of the American Indian Movement armed with automatic weapons who had indicated to undercover agents that he had been interested in the President's movements.

An alcoholic in Belleville, Ill., who is a former mental patient and had offered an undercover agent $25,000 early this month to kill Mr. Ford, has been arrested, and is now in a mental institution.

The last six persons involved in political assassinations or attempted shootings of prominent Americans were not on the Secret Service "trip list" of suspected assassins. The six are Miss Moore, Lynette

Alice Fromme, Arthur H. Bremer, Sirhan B. Sirhan, James Earl Ray and Lee Harvey Oswald.[20]

I was deeply concerned that President Ford stood a chance of being shot and killed or wounded during his presidency. If someone—anyone—was determined to kill a president, and was willing to accept that they would likely be killed or captured in the process, the Secret Service would have an extremely difficult time preventing it, particularly with Presidents determined to mix with the American people.

What might come after the successful assassination of the President—or more specifically who might come—was also of interest. Nelson Rockefeller's personality, as noted, was not a good match for the responsibilities of the presidency. And Rockefeller continued to offer new reasons for concern.

On one occasion, a senior White House staff member came to me and said that Vice President Rockefeller had told him that Secretary of Treasury John Connally, whom Rockefeller viewed as a political rival, had come back from the Middle East with gems of some sort. The unspoken implication, without any evidence, was that there might have been something improper about it. When I received that report, as Chief of Staff I felt an obligation to meet with the Vice President and to ask him about it. If it were true and if the Vice President knew something possibly illegal had occurred, I told him that either he or I as White House officials had an obligation to talk to White House Legal Counsel and/or the U.S. Attorney General. The Vice President, while not denying what I had been told he had told the senior staff member, backed away from what had been reported to me and indicated that he had no information that required us to initiate an investigation. It was all in all a bizarre episode.

To this day, I believe that the assassination of still another President would have proven to be a serious jolt to the social bonds of our democracy, especially at that moment in our history when tensions over Watergate were still raw. A steady leader would be needed at the helm to steady the ship of state. To our nation's good fortune, Gerald R. Ford survived to complete his term in office.

Once again, the task was to calm a distressed nation. President Ford was certain that he should just carry on. Any situation in which our political leaders are forced into isolation away from their constituents because of a few dangerous malcontents should not be tolerated. An unimpeded exchange of ideas, he added, was fundamental to our system of government. "The American people are good people—Democrats, Independents, Republicans, and others," the President said. "Under no circumstances will I, and I hope no others, capitulate to those that want to undercut what's all good in America."[21]

I believed that implementing new security arrangements was necessary from a different standpoint—despite the reality that any new arrangement would not and could not assure perfect safety. I concluded that to do nothing would be "reckless." Given the President's attitude, I knew I was the one who needed to inject the proper degree of caution into the President's schedule, since it was clear he would not. We agreed, at least at first, to have the White House press office tell the public: "We're fully aware of the risks and aware of the circumstances. The President's travel activities will be announced as they have been in the past. An appropriate security process is in place."[22]

At one point NBC News anchor John Chancellor called, explaining he had researched assassination attempts and spoken with a psychiatrist who cautioned that the President was likely doing exactly the wrong thing. By acting as if nothing had happened, he was broadcasting a message to all the psychopaths out there: "You can't stop me!" What John Chancellor related from the psychiatrist he had talked to was a concern that the public position of the White House could unintentionally have the effect of goading possible assassins into thinking, "Oh yeah!?" and then perhaps making an attempt against the President. Finding the best words to reassure the American people without creating an added risk to the life of the President was not an easy task. There was at least a possibility that we would know if we had failed only once it was too late.[23]

A few more days went by before we arrived at several specific security changes. We would announce the President's schedule closer to the day, making his appearances a bit more spontaneous, thereby reducing the time available to a would-be assassin to plan an assault. At the appropriate time, I would carefully let it leak out that we were including the use of "plainclothes" Secret Service agents, officers who would be considerably more difficult to detect, in order to try to deter attacks or at least make it more difficult for them to succeed.[24]

I was clear with the President. Our republic had already been through a great deal. Worst-case scenarios had been weighing on our minds and we needed to address them. And we had to do all we could to get his potential successor up to speed.

"Mr. President," I said, "there's a reasonable likelihood you could be killed or wounded. I'm going to develop some arrangements for the Vice President to be briefed and to know what the hell is going on in the government."

"Fine," he replied.

"I just don't want you involved in it," I responded.

"Fine," he answered a second time.[25]

I couldn't fault him for his curtness. No normal person likes to dwell on his or her possible demise. And no U.S. President would want to think about abandoning the country at a time when steady leadership was so badly needed.

* * *

There was a metaphor for the broader problems the still new administration was experiencing, one that perhaps unconsciously underscored in the President's mind the risks of a less than professional operation. An opportunity to address it occurred out of the blue, in the most unlikely of places—the quiet state capital of Connecticut.

After speaking at a dinner at the Hartford Civic Center, the President, along with members of his traveling team, boarded his motorcade and headed down the main thoroughfare to the airport. Usually local police assist the Secret Service team by temporarily closing off every intersection briefly before and until a President's motorcade has passed. However, that evening, for whatever reason, one intersection was missed by the local police and not properly blocked. As a result, just as the President's motorcade was passing, a 1967 yellow Buick, driven by nineteen-year-old James Salamites and containing several of his teenage friends, drove through the one unblocked intersection and, to everyone's surprise, crashed directly into the back left side of President Ford's limousine.

Recognizing that this could be yet another attempt on the President's life, the Secret Service swarmed the scene. Salamites's car was wrecked, while the President, the Connecticut Republican Chairman, and I, who had been sitting in the rear seat, had been abruptly thrown to the floor as the car smashed into the President's limousine. We were relatively unscathed. "Well, the cat has nine lives," the President said that evening as we proceeded toward the airport to avoid any further mishaps.[26]

Though publicly and privately the President resisted blaming anyone for that accident, the event was an embarrassment for both the Hartford police and the U.S. Secret Service. It could well have led to a far more tragic result, for the President as well as for the teenagers who, because the intersection had not been blocked, had made history by crashing into the limousine of the President of the United States of America. This was, in my mind, and admittedly unfairly, an example of a too loose White House operation, one that needed to be tightened up.

The (So-Called) Halloween Massacre

MEMORANDUM FOR THE PRESIDENT

From: Donald Rumsfeld and Richard Cheney

October 24, 1975

". . . Because of our deep sense of these problems, the only way to conclusively make the case and demonstrate the importance we attach to the kinds of changes recommended, is to assure that there will be absolutely no question in your mind that anything said below would affect us in any way or be to our advantage.

You must be free to decide, with absolutely no question on your mind about the motives of those making the recommendations. We are convinced that the job you need done cannot be done unless these major changes take place. You must be free to decide quite apart from any personal relationships including us. Therefore, our resignations are attached."[1]

You know, there are funny things you think of just before you go to sleep," President Ford mused to me in a meeting on October 22, 1975. "This will shock you," he continued. "I am not proposing it. I'm just saying I thought of it, and it should not be repeated—

Schlesinger's handling of the Defense Department is a disaster and, well, I'm tempted to send Rocky over there and bring George Bush back from China as Vice President, right now."[2]

We had been meeting that morning in the Oval Office in a continuation of his periodic discussions about the administration's state of affairs.[3] The poorly coordinated speech shop, irritating press leaks, and often out-of-sync National Security Council team, and the President's poor relationship with the Secretary of Defense continued to pose problems with solutions not yet in sight. The challenges of the unexpected presidency of Gerald Ford were sizable, but there were also some unnecessary self-inflicted wounds that hampered operations.

This was one of the drawbacks that President Ford faced in having never run a presidential campaign prior to his move to the White House. A tough campaign requires a candidate to make difficult and occasionally distasteful decisions, often about personnel. Dealing with unpleasant personnel situations did not come easily to Ford, who was as kind a man as I suspect ever occupied the Oval Office. That is, until he decided he had no choice.

Having grown into his role as the only never nominated and never elected President of the United States in history, making the decision he wanted to seek the nomination and hold the office, and coming to grips with all that was on the line for the country, President Ford decided to make some staffing and organizational changes. These major decisions, apparently made without consultation with anyone, were a surprise to me, to his team, and in Washington, D.C., and went beyond what anyone might have expected. His announcements were mischaracterized in the media as "the Halloween Massacre," even though they in no way amounted to a "massacre"—Gerald Ford would never treat his associates in such a way—and they weren't designed or announced on Halloween. Though questioned by a few at the time, the moves revealed that the President had come into his own and decided to put in place a Ford administration in every sense of the word. To the best of my knowledge, this is how it happened.

The new Ford administration had encountered and weathered some of the standard challenges faced in many if not most new administrations. One of my many meeting memos, dated June 1975, commented on this issue.

MEETING WITH THE PRESIDENT
June 11, 1975
8:31 to 9:04 a.m.
. . . The President said he was very concerned about the [Fred] Barnes article saying that there was staff conflict. I said it was a terrible article and that in reviewing the thing, if I were to blame anyone, I would blame me for assigning coordinating responsibility to the Counsel's office, and then I would blame the Counsel's office for not coordinating . . . effectively, and finally, I suppose, blame the President for setting up a staff system that has the "spokes of the wheel" coming up where you have different people doing different things, everyone thinking that they are dealing directly with the President, and assuming that everything is going to work out all right, and at some point where you have to mesh more than one spoke of the wheel, it doesn't get done unless the President does it. . . .

Furthermore, the fact that Hartmann and the Speech Shop, and the political operation, are separated from the White House—he doesn't come to the staff meetings, the fact that the Domestic Council and Rockefeller are separated from the White House, and he doesn't come to the staff meetings, the fact that Kissinger and the NSC are separated from the White House and he doesn't come to the staff meetings leaves the situation where people don't have a daily rubbing of shoulders and that instinctive desire to protect each other.

The three big pieces—each one goes straight in to the President, no

one else in the building knows what's going on there, and they are never
around . . . the effect of that on the White House is very, very damaging,
and it is because of the design of the organization that he imposed. I said to
him that you simply cannot have each person operating in a way that the
rest of the people feel that he is doing his own thing and to hell with the
rest of them.[4]

Over several months, the President was beginning to indicate a
readiness to consider suggestions from his friends to begin to fix his
problems. I suggested that there were two ways to move forward,
with the goal of gaining control and boosting morale. First, whenever
someone came through the wrong channel, he or she needed to be
put back into the staff system. Some of the major policy mechanisms,
such as the Domestic Council and the NSC, were not functioning as
smoothly as they must, with the result that people were understandably moving outside the normal channels to get their jobs done.

Second, I suggested management by example. The President
might best deal with less-than-professional staff work, leaks, and
public disagreements by consciously deciding to reward good performance and punish poor performance. Whenever one of his senior
staff members did something inside the line of acceptable conduct—
whether controversial or not—the President should make a point to
support and defend them. Conversely, when someone did something
that was over the line, the President needed to crack them.[5] That
meant, for instance, that inferior drafts of speeches had to be sent
back, deadlines had to be set and met, and people not performing
had to be corrected by him as well as by me and, when necessary, replaced. More broadly, the President needed to be respected as a leader
who was fair, but who could, when necessary, be tough.

During a meeting with his close staff about half way through the
month, the President asked why his approval rating had leveled off
despite the economy's turnaround and his foreign policy successes.

Bryce Harlow, the seasoned and highly respected pro who served as an unofficial advisor for the President, warned that "public divisions" within the administration were creating an impression that the President was not fully in command. As one example, Bryce directly pointed to the deepening public rift between Kissinger and Schlesinger.[6] Because of his close relationship with the President, Kissinger was in a position to and did in fact wield outsized power and influence. Conversely, Schlesinger's views, and therefore the views of the Department of Defense, were considerably less influential due to Jim's notably prickly relationship with the President.[7] This problem was further compounded by the fact that in every NSC meeting, Vice President Rockefeller was a consistent vocal supporter of any position or view Kissinger put forward.

Unlike his relationship with Schlesinger, Ford's relationship with Vice President Nelson Rockefeller had developed into a warm one. As a result, Ford had a difficult time wrestling with his decision as to whether or not to replace him on the GOP ticket. The Vice President, from the time he was confirmed, had been the prime target of conservative opposition as a result of his history, his outspoken liberal policy views, and the growing public perception of his influence in shaping Ford administration policies, given his long personal relationship with Henry Kissinger as well as his assigned role in domestic policy. But even beyond those factors, the Vice President seemed to not mind and on occasion even relish being the target of conservatives. I supposed this aided him politically in a state like New York, which tended to lean to the liberal side. But this issue was clearly unhelpful to President Ford in his efforts to secure the Republican nomination for President.

Nothing during the intervening months had lessened Rockefeller's conviction that he had been empowered by the President with sweeping authority for the administration's domestic, economic, and energy affairs. The result was a breakdown in the President's chain of command on those issues. Also, perhaps inevitably, I along with my deputy Dick Cheney became the VP's nemeses as we worked to achieve reasonable order in the White House on behalf of the President.[8]

A familiar pattern had begun to emerge. Rockefeller would periodically offer up an idea or policy initiative, present it in one of his private meetings with the President, and do so with little if any coordination with the President's relevant senior policy personnel. Because President Ford was a gracious person who wanted Rockefeller to feel part of the team, he would often give Rockefeller some kind and supportive words, which Rockefeller would not unreasonably take as an endorsement. Then Ford would hand the proposal to me—or to Dick—and ask, "What . . . do we do with this?" I'd reply, having not seen the VP's proposal, "Well, we will staff it out," which meant sending it through the White House staff system for consideration and comment by the President's senior relevant policy officials in the Cabinet and on the White House staff. The result was, on many occasions, a range of policy comments, concerns, objections, and resistance, which we would then have to report to the President. Unsurprisingly, the reactions of the President's policy officials would often displease Rockefeller. He seemed to see the staff's comments not as policy differences, which was what they largely were, but as an infringement on what he saw as his responsibilities as the "head of domestic policy," as assigned by President Ford, and those who differed were throwing sand in his gears. The Vice President was not used to having staff people take policy positions different from his views.

One notorious example came about when the Vice President presented an energy proposal to the President apparently crafted by his personal connections and resources outside of the administration. He did not have it briefed in a meeting with the President's senior policy experts on energy, but gave it to the President personally. I was not in the meeting, but Rockefeller must have left with an impression Ford was interested and did not oppose the VP's proposal. Later that day the President handed the VP's proposal to me to "handle." I advised him I would send it out, as I did with every proposal, to the appropriate federal departments and agencies with relevant statutory responsibilities and to the relevant senior White House policy officials for their review and comment. The feedback from the policy experts overall was not positive. It became clear later that the President may well have had an impression from Rockefeller that the key White House policy officials had provided their input and either were in support or at least were not opposed. It became my task to explain to the President what had actually taken place. After learning what had actually occurred in the case of the energy proposal, he took a deep breath and reluctantly told me that, nonetheless, he felt he should keep his agreement to send the VP's proposal up to the Congress as an administrative proposal. I said that I believed that would be a mistake. Nonetheless, he insisted on keeping what he saw as his commitment. As a result, the Vice President's proposal then was sent up to Capitol Hill for consideration by the Congress as the President's proposal. As the President's energy staff experts had anticipated, the proposal dropped like a rock in midocean. Later that year even a greatly reduced and modified version of the Rockefeller energy proposal was defeated in a vote in the U.S. House of Representatives, a totally avoidable embarrassment for the President and his administration.

In March 1975, I observed the Vice President's unusual performance at a breakfast gathering at which the President was present. "The Vice President spent all his time at [the] breakfast walking around and shaking hands," I noted. "He was still doing that when the President started talking." During the President's remarks and the remarks of others, Rockefeller, in the audience, would say, "Hear, hear," in response to assertions he favored, which, while supportive of the President, was a distraction.[9]

The Vice President began inviting some Ford White House staff members to fly in his private aircraft to his home in New York. But given the legal maelstrom from which the White House was still recuperating, I discouraged that practice.

In August, Rockefeller decided to redesign the seal of the Vice President of the United States that had been established during the Truman years, which in my view could lead to unnecessary controversy in the media.[10] In short, while he was an enthusiastic "hail fellow well met," and certainly a strong friend and supporter of President Ford, his positive attributes came with some downsides, which I suppose is true of most of us.

President Ford, for his part, may well have given Rockefeller ambiguous signals as to his intentions about keeping him on the ticket in 1976. This would not have been because Ford would ever have intended to be duplicitous. Instead, it was likely due to the fact that Ford was of two minds on the subject. At some points, such as during a meeting on February 1, 1975, he left the strong impression that Rockefeller would be his running mate though, at the time, some of Ford's political advisors were concerned and suggested the possibility that he leave his options open on the VP question.[11] On April 28, 1975, Ford told me he had advised the Vice President that he would be on the ticket. Later that day, however, Ford held a meeting with the Governor of North Carolina, who warned him that there might well be an "open revolt" against Rockefeller at the GOP convention.[12] By late May, the President's thinking on the Vice President had evolved. Hearing the concerns within the GOP, he began to take steps to try to keep conservatives from defecting to Reagan.

On July 10, Bo Callaway, whom President Ford had selected as his presidential campaign manager, came into the Oval Office with an unorthodox suggestion. "This is absolutely confidential and does not go out of this room," Callaway began. He explained that someone he considered "very shrewd" had suggested to him that the President arrange for Rockefeller to become Secretary of State and for John Connally to become Vice President.[13] I had no idea who this "very shrewd" person was, but I was reminded of someone who had always been chief among John Connally's admirers—Richard Nixon.

Eventually Ford reluctantly acquiesced to the concerns expressed by a number of his political advisors, saying that while he favored Rockefeller for VP, he would support an open convention that would allow delegates to choose the party's vice presidential nominee. This approach seemed to satisfy the President, but it was unlikely to have satisfied Rockefeller. In an open convention, it was close to a certainty that the more conservative Republican delegates would vote to nominate someone else.

By the fall of 1975, while personally respecting Rockefeller as a friend, Ford had reluctantly concluded that he was a political liability, particularly if it contributed to a decision by Governor Ronald Reagan to challenge Ford for the Republican nomination. When the President mentioned this, in late-October, Dick Cheney suggested to Ford that Rockefeller might step forward and "take a Sherman"— a reference to General William Tecumseh Sherman, who had made unmistakably clear that he would not pursue or accept the nomination for President in the election of 1884. Cheney went on to suggest that Rockefeller could also then call on Reagan, for the sake of the GOP's prospects, to similarly step aside in a statesmanlike manner.[14]

Less than a week after this conversation, President Ford apparently met with the Vice President. I was not briefed on exactly what transpired: Either Ford asked Rockefeller to step aside or possibly the Vice President offered to do so. In any event, the result was that Rockefeller advised the President that he would announce that he would not be a candidate for public office in 1976. Ford recounted the conversation to me, quoting Rockefeller as saying, "I would be happy to do anything that you want. I came down here to help, and I will help in any way humanly possible." This was a classy and admirable response by Vice President Rockefeller, one that I sensed was greatly appreciated by the President.

Resolving the issue of the vice presidential nomination was helpful but hardly a solution to all of the administration's challenges. It was just one, albeit an important one, in a series of issues Ford needed to handle before he entered the decisive election year of 1976.

On Saturday, October 25, shortly after 11:00 a.m., Cheney and I met with the President in the Oval Office. We were there to discuss a memo that I had drafted and hand delivered to the President. The memo, dated October 24, 1975, outlined a series of challenges facing the Ford administration. The memo included some suggested "do's" and "don't's" for the months ahead, and concluded with some suggestions. I opened my cover letter to the President by outlining his successes, from having ended U.S. military involvement in Southeast Asia to dealing with what was likely the most difficult economic situation since the end of World War II. "Perhaps most important of all," I wrote, "you have successfully healed the wounds of a nation deeply divided, a nation grown weary of scandal and mistrustful of its leadership. . . ."

At the end of the memo, to underscore my seriousness and to make clear I had no agenda but the interest of the country and the President's success, I attached my resignation letter. I asked Dick Cheney to review the memo. He did so, agreed with the recommendations and asked to join in signing it. He then attached his own letter of resignation as well.

Dick and I were serious about the memo. For whatever reason, I had failed to successfully get the President to take the management actions that I was convinced were required for him to succeed. I felt that I had told him what I believed needed to be done for him to succeed, but I had up to that point been unsuccessful.

When President Ford read the memo and our letters of resignation, it focused him on the concerns. The President paused, regained his composure, and then proceeded to reread the entire memo. Toward the end of it, I had advised that many of the actions suggested in the memo should best be announced and if possible carried out prior to a formal candidacy announcement for President by Governor Reagan. Finally, I urged at the end of the memo that he decide that he was determined to win in 1976 and that he would do everything possible to achieve it.

A few hours later, Kissinger and I were called in to meet with the President. Ford calmly and methodically explained that he was going to make some personnel changes shortly. First, Rockefeller would withdraw his name from consideration as his running mate, and Henry's seasoned deputy, Brent Scowcroft, would become the National Security Advisor.

To deal with the nearly yearlong controversy over America's intelligence activities, Ford told us that he decided to nominate someone outside the ranks of the intelligence community to replace the experienced but under-fire CIA Director Bill Colby. Ford seemed to have lost his patience with the criticisms of Colby and the CIA and the implications that the Agency was stonewalling investigations into its activities. At one heated meeting in September 1975, Ford told Colby directly: "I want you to know that we are not going to classify anything to cover it up, whether it is a mistake, an error of judgment, no matter how bad it is. I won't do it."[15] In our meeting, Ford said that his choice as Colby's replacement would be George H. W. Bush, then the U.S. envoy to China.

The President also said he intended to replace Schlesinger as Secretary of Defense, and that he had been considering doing so for some time. What might well have been the last straw for the President was a recent press conference in which Schlesinger had criticized the Chairman of the House Appropriations Committee, Democrat George Mahon. Mahon was a close friend and colleague of the President. Neither Ford nor Mahon appreciated Schlesinger's critical comments of the chairman.

To succeed Jim Schlesinger at the Department of Defense, Ford apparently considered John Connally, and also our friend and former colleague in the Congress from Kansas, the experienced Bob Ellsworth, who was a former U.S. Ambassador to NATO and had been an Assistant to the President under Nixon. Ford wanted to avoid angering conservatives even further.[16] He then said that he intended to nominate me for the post. Ford knew that I had a great deal of personal respect for Jim Schlesinger and that I shared many of the same views—which was perhaps a consideration for Ford in nominating me. Dick Cheney, the President added, would succeed me as White House Chief of Staff. The series of decisions by the President came to Henry and certainly to me as a complete surprise.

Ford knew I had a great deal of respect for Henry Kissinger's impressive intellect and accomplishments and his stated intention was that Henry and I could end the public debates between the Departments. I hoped, as did Ford, that we would be able to work together in ways that the Departments of State and Defense hadn't. I was determined to do all I could to help make this work.

The President also opened up about his own future. He noted he had the option of not running for election as President in his own right. However, he said with confidence that he was convinced he had been a good President and that a Democratic win in 1976 would take the country in the wrong direction. With a passion I had not seen before, he boomed, "I'm running. It will be a tough race, but I'm not going to pull a [Lyndon] Johnson and bow out. It will be bloody right down to the last gong if Reagan runs." Only a few weeks later, Governor Ronald Reagan announced that he intended to do just that.

14

Rumble from the Right

MEETING WITH THE PRESIDENT

April 6, 1976

10:10 to 10:25 a.m.

Present: Rumsfeld alone

At the end of the previous meeting I told the President I wanted to stay and see him alone. I told him that he looked down, that I could tell he was concerned about something, and that I wanted him to know that I was available to help. . . .The President said he felt there was a fifty/fifty chance that Kissinger would quit, and he didn't believe that he could say anything more on Kissinger's behalf. . . . He [Kissinger] said he took very personally Ronald Reagan's comments.[1]

It was winter in New Hampshire, but the cold weather did not stop the energy from crackling among the group of journalists gathered in Manchester. The man who took the podium was dressed in a simple suit, an understated brown plaid that helped bring out his Hollywood tan and shining dark hair. Nobody knew just what he was going to say, but by then, there was a real chance he was about to change the face of the American political landscape. On February 20,

1976, four days before the New Hampshire primary, Ronald Reagan, the insurgent candidate for the Republican nomination, had called a press conference.

Since the former California Governor had formally announced his bid to challenge President Ford for the presidential nomination in November 1975, confirming the long-held fears of Ford's advisors, the Governor had moved swiftly to draw the lines of battle between President Ford's vision—at least as Reagan characterized it—and his own. Reagan portrayed himself as a stronger, more forceful leader out to rescue an America in decline, in terms of both conditions at home and prestige abroad. Ford, for his part, presented a more pragmatic governing approach that had served him well as a leader in the Congress and in bringing stability to the nation as President.

Reagan had been far from clear about his future for many months. Periodically before Reagan announced, a well-regarded Republican strategist named John Sears visited the White House to give the President his views on Reagan's thinking. (Sears left the impression he might be helpful to the Ford effort but eventually he became Reagan's campaign manager.)

MEETING WITH THE PRESIDENT
May 21, 1975
8:36 to 9:10 a.m.

I gave the President a report on what John Sears had told me and [that] I felt it probably represented Reagan's view. . . . I get the feeling that they feel that the President is sincere and is restoring trust, but that that isn't enough, that the country has not had a positive leader since Kennedy, and that there was a need for a man who had the presence and ability to communicate and lead and that they think Reagan's that guy and maybe the President isn't and that they want to be ready if he isn't—that there seems to be not a proper use of words and ideas and concepts in leadership. . . .[2]

Still apparently finding it hard to believe that a loyal Republican would challenge a sitting President of his own party, Ford wanted me to make crystal clear to Reagan that the President was in the race to stay. So at the President's request, I met with Reagan on June 17, 1975. As with my earlier meeting with Reagan that March, when I had relayed President Ford's offer of a Cabinet post, I told the Governor that I had come at the President's request. I acknowledged that there had been a number of rumors about Ford's intentions as well as about the Governor's. "The President wants no ambiguity between the two of you," I told Reagan. "He will definitely be running and will be announcing very soon." I also added that I was personally disappointed that Governor Reagan hadn't decided to join the Ford administration and that I thought he would have been "a very valuable addition."

Governor Reagan thanked me for the information. "My plans are unclear," he said, or words to that effect. He indicated his position was unchanged—he hadn't yet decided what he would do, but that a good many people felt he had an obligation to run.[3]

On the eve of Reagan's formal entry into the race, on November 20, 1975, campaign pollsters reported that "while the President leads his potential opponent in almost every state, [Ford's] support is soft."[4] So, in the run-up to the crucial first primary in New Hampshire, Ford campaign supporters went on the attack, characterizing Reagan as a spokesman of the archconservative wing of the party and not well prepared for governing at the national level. At a news conference at the White House on February 18, 1976, President Ford had discussed what he saw as the policy differences between Reagan and himself, and, considering himself a pragmatic midwesterner, declared: "I believe that anybody to the right of me, Democratic or Republican, can't win a national election."[5]

Discussing the press conference with him the next day, I urged the President to stop talking about Governor Reagan altogether. I suggested he consider staying above it, leaving the campaigning to his campaign team.[6] As it turned out, Reagan was just about to strike back against that strategy.

Two days after Ford's remarks, on February 20, Reagan returned to New Hampshire after spending a week back in California to prepare for his campaign tour through the "first in the nation" primary state. When Reagan came before reporters in Manchester that day, Jon Nordheimer of *The New York Times* noted that he "appeared well rested and tanned" from his week away from the campaign trail.[7] The Governor's team told reporters they had convened the press conference to address the Ford campaign's accusations that he was too far-right to win the presidency. As he often did, Reagan had a twinkle in his eye and a trick up his sleeve.

"I am a little surprised about his statement about my so-called extremism," Reagan said casually, referencing the President. "It does come rather strange because he tried on two different occasions to persuade me to accept any of several Cabinet positions in his administration."

A reporter asked the obvious question: Did the Governor think the President made the offers to prevent just this sort of primary challenge? Reagan cracked a coy smile and said: "No, I just thought he recognized my administrative abilities."[8]

His comment about the Ford administration's overtures to Reagan, through me, were of course completely accurate but had not previously been disclosed to the press either by Reagan or by the White House, adding to the drama of Reagan's moment.

The New York Times noted, "A conclusion that seemed inescapable was that Mr. Reagan had carefully withheld any mention of Mr. Ford's [by then] year-old attempts to bring him into the Administration until he could drop it when it would have an optimum impact." The *Times* story—front page, above the fold—was headlined "Reagan Discloses Ford Cabinet Bid: Countering Rival's Attack on Him as Extremist, He Cites 2 Offers of Posts."

As he intended, Reagan's revelation severely undercut the Ford campaign's narrative and left them flat-footed. If the President thought Reagan to be too far to the right, one would fairly ask, why then was President Ford so keen to have him serve in his Cabinet?

The news surprised the media, which increased its impact, leading to front-page headlines across the country—undoubtedly as the Reagan campaign team had intended. The White House, for its part, had to confirm the overtures, suggesting the offers had been made "to unify the Republican Party and bring to the Administration a wide range of views," which had the benefit of being true.[9]

Reagan's skillful move not only caught the White House by surprise, but signaled early on that he wasn't going to play by any established rules. It was a shot across the bow from a skillful sharpshooter, delivered by one who had a well-developed flair for the dramatic. If there had been any doubt within the Ford campaign team, it had become clear: This was the beginning of a long, hard slog for the presidency.

On the same day *The New York Times* had reported Reagan's dramatic disclosure, the paper carried another story—also front page, above the fold—with a headline the Ford campaign also would have preferred to avoid: "Nixon Trip Revives Issue Vexing to Ford in Primary." Despite the former President's suggestion to Ford that he planned to keep a low profile during the campaign, Nixon had chosen that moment, while his successor and the man who had pardoned him at great political cost was facing a significant political challenge in a critical primary, to make a return visit to the People's Republic of China. This untimely reminder of what *The New York Times* called the "Nixon connection" proved awkward, forcing Ford to have to revisit his widely unpopular pardon of Richard Nixon as he campaigned across New Hampshire.[10]

Responding to questions from students at Keene High School, for example, Ford said that Nixon was among some ten thousand other Americans who went to China every year. Nixon, he said, was now a private citizen who could do what he wanted, just like anyone else. If that were true, a young man asked Ford, why wasn't he facing "criminal charges in the same way as any other American would, instead of pardoning him?" An awkward silence followed, until Ford replied, "As far as penalty is concerned, the former President obviously resigned in disgrace. That is a pretty severe penalty. One out of thirty-seven Presidents had that happen to him."

That wasn't the only difficult moment Nixon caused Ford. Since Nixon's trip involved his postpresidential dealings with the Chinese, it also played into what was emerging as a, if not the, dominant issue of the Republican primary campaign: America's foreign policy. While Ford's pollster, Bob Teeter, had reported in late 1975 that Ford then held a lead over Reagan in perception of handling foreign affairs, he had identified an issue that was continuing to rub not the entire country, but specifically Republican primary voters the wrong way: détente. Teeter flagged as problems both the word *détente* and the policy the term identified, with some conservative voters equating seeking accommodation with a Communist country with weakness. "Détente is a particularly unpopular idea with most Republican primary voters and the word is worse," Teeter wrote in a memo. "We ought to stop using the word whenever possible."[11]

Reagan of course was fully aware of détente's unpopularity among the GOP base and made attacking the policy a key theme in his campaign. He argued that détente did not demand enough from the Soviets. "Through détente we have sought peace with our adversaries," Reagan asserted when he announced his campaign. "We should continue to do so, but must make it plain that we expect a stronger indication that they also seek a lasting peace with us."[12] Coming under particularly heavy fire were two of détente's chief proponents in the administration: Secretary of State Kissinger and Vice President Rockefeller. Reagan zeroed in on Kissinger particularly, painting him as the embodiment of a worldview that was too accommodating to the Communists, disadvantaging America and making our nation appear feckless, thereby lessening our respect on the world stage.

President Ford wasn't going to let anyone depict him as weak. He had, after all, faced the dangers of combat with courage in World War II, the war that ended with the first-ever use of nuclear weapons. As one who both understood war from firsthand experience and understood the increased capacity for destruction since the days of Hiroshima, he was not eager to see America again on belligerent footing. Further, there was no one in his administration for whom he had greater respect than Henry Kissinger, and he was determined to strongly defend both the policy of détente as well as his Secretary of State, advisor, and friend Henry Kissinger.

In August 1975, Ford attempted to distinguish the Nixon détente policy from a Ford détente policy—taking issue with the term itself—during his speech to the American Legion convention in Minneapolis. "First of all, the word itself is confusing," Ford argued. "Its meaning is not clear to everybody." He allowed that "French is a beautiful language, the classic language of diplomacy," and while he wished there was "one simple English word" to use instead, "relations between the world's two strongest nuclear powers can't be summed up in a catchphrase." Then he defined the word as it related to the policy of his administration: "Détente literally means 'easing' or 'relaxing,' but definitely not—and I emphasize 'not'—the relaxing of diligence or ceasing of effort. Rather, it means movement away from the constant crisis and dangerous confrontations that have characterized relations with the Soviet Union."[13]

Then the President became more personal, carefully describing the French word *détente* as he intended it. Tackling the issue directly, he said, "To me, détente means a fervent desire for peace—but not peace at any price. It means the preservation of fundamental American principles—not their sacrifice. It means maintaining the strength to command respect from our adversaries and provide leadership to our friends—not letting down our guard or dismantling our defenses or neglecting our allies. It means peaceful rivalry between political and economic systems—not the curbing of our competitive efforts."[14]

He cited a number of accomplishments he felt had been brought about by the Nixon-Kissinger policy of détente, including an easing of tensions over Berlin, the ABM and SALT treaties, and troop reductions in Europe. But he went on to vow that "détente must be a two-way street, because tensions cannot be eased with safety and security by one side alone."[15]

Yet President Ford's heartfelt defense of his policy did not always translate clearly to all segments of the American public. In December 1975, *The New York Times* reported that "interviews with dozens of members of Congress and officials, plus the results of public opinion surveys, indicate that there is broad support for détente among the American people," but added the significant caveat that "the support is shallow, accompanied by deep suspicion of Moscow's motives and widespread sentiment that the Russians have had the better of the deal."[16] A Republican staffer on Capitol Hill quoted by *The New York Times* summed up the GOP conservative wing's reasoning: "The conservatives never liked the way Kissinger was conducting détente, but as long as Nixon was around they figured Henry wouldn't be able to give away the store to the Communists. But Ford—they never felt he could control Henry."[17] Even if that were not true, and from my firsthand observation it was not true, that public perception was engendering some concern among the conservative Republican base and contributing to Governor Reagan's growing momentum.

President Ford opened 1976 with yet another defense of détente in a television interview with NBC News. When reporter Tom Brokaw asked if the President had concerns about his policy in view of the Soviets' neglect of the Helsinki Accords on human rights, Ford responded: "I think it would be very unwise for a President—me or anyone else—to abandon détente. I think détente is in the best interest of this country. It is in the best interest of world stability, world peace."[18] Brokaw followed up by asking the President the more immediate question: "Won't you be under a lot of domestic political pressure in this election year to change your attitude about détente?" Ford answered that "it would be just the reverse," since détente had already led to such positive developments as SALT I and the Berlin agreement. "And if the American people take a good, calculated look at the benefits from détente, I think they will support it rather than oppose it," Ford argued. Then he made a prediction: "Politically, I think any candidate who says 'abandon détente' will be the loser in the long run."

The New Hampshire primary would put that sentiment, and the strength of Ford's campaign, to the test. I spoke with the President by phone around seven-thirty on the evening of the election.[19] At that point, the returns were still coming in, and as the President was finishing his dinner he was still four points behind Reagan in the returns.[20] If he lost in the first primary in the nation, Ford knew the race might well be over as soon as it began. Reagan not only would have gained crucial momentum, but would benefit from increased campaign donations and supporters. Fortunately, there were still ballots to count in New Hampshire's north country and in the end President Ford pulled out a victory, albeit a slim one—49.43 percent to 47.97 percent. Still, a win was a win. Ford later joked in his memoirs that "it proved I could win an election outside the Fifth Congressional District of Michigan," but what was also made clear was that, in Reagan, "we were up against a very tough competitor."[21]

While the President only narrowly escaped a defeat in New Hampshire, Reagan's momentum stalled. Ford's victories in the next few primaries were reassuring. In the first half of March, Ford won Massachusetts, Vermont, and Illinois, all by more significant margins. Only the Florida primary, held on March 9, was close—52.8 percent to 47.2 percent—but it was still more comfortable than New Hampshire.

Though I was fully occupied with the challenges at the Department of Defense, including the ongoing Strategic Arms Limitation Talks (SALT) deliberations and was not involved in the presidential campaign, I still found myself confronted with issues that, if not handled carefully, could have made the President's campaign more difficult. In late February, for instance, shortly after the New Hampshire primary, Deputy Secretary of Defense Bill Clements advised me that he had been informed that neither President Ford nor Secretary Kissinger had used an American interpreter during some of their meetings with Brezhnev and the Soviets. If Clements heard this, I reasoned, others were hearing it, so I raised it with the President.[22] I said to President Ford that someone might ask the question, Do you think this country ought to run in such a way that when the President of the United States meets with Brezhnev in Vladivostok and Helsinki the only interpreter there is Viktor, Brezhnev's personal interpreter? "Well," the President countered, "Stoessel was there," referring to U.S. Ambassador to the USSR Walter Stoessel, who was a Russian speaker.

I mentioned to the President that I had been told that "Stoessel's competence in the Russian language [may be excellent but] when he meets with Russians, he takes an interpreter for himself. . . ."

Quite apart from that, I said, politically it can be made to sound unwise. I sensed the President would be certain to see that the State Department regularly provided interpreters in the future.[23]

Another concern was a perception that the timing of the election might be having some effect on our SALT negotiations with the Soviets. As noted, there had been a few newspaper stories in which State Department officials were quoted saying that SALT depended on the outcome of the election, and also suggesting that the U.S. may have made some decisions about U.S. China policy because of the election.[24] Most of the professionals at the State Department and on the National Security Council staff tended to be seasoned political observers. And while their jobs were to observe the goings-on in other countries, understandably they would naturally do the same here at home. "They spend their lives looking at people around the world, countries, politics, and reporting on them," I mentioned to the President, "and it is inevitable that they are going to watch you." We would prefer that some junior diplomat in the State Department entourage not sense something that could give him reason to say: "Aha! The President is making a decision . . . based on a political timetable!"

Kissinger, for his part, became concerned with what the President and he both considered to be the Department of Defense's intransigence on the arms control agreement. At one point earlier in the year, he told me he may slow down from pushing for SALT.[25]

By mid-March 1976, the GOP primary campaign began to turn rougher. There seemed to be a shift in Reagan's strategy shortly before the Florida primary, which he might have hoped to win by taking a tougher tone. A few days before the Florida vote, Reagan's team previewed a speech in Orlando by promising that it "should be the strongest thing he's ever said about the President," using "language that the Governor has wrestled with in his own mind since the campaign started, and which he has now decided needs to be said."[26] President Ford and Dick Cheney, who as White House Chief of Staff was taking on a growing role in the campaign, informed me of the planned Reagan attack that afternoon.

The President was disturbed that the race had already begun to degenerate into more personal attacks. "That certainly settles one thing that won't happen," he grumbled. He didn't elaborate, but I suspected he meant that Reagan's attack might preclude him from being considered for the vice presidency on a Ford ticket if and when the President secured the nomination.[27]

Meanwhile, a key issue in the primary campaign surfaced again on March 5, when the President spoke at a forum in Peoria, Illinois. Someone from the audience pointed out the criticism leveled at détente by Governor Reagan, Governor Carter, and others, and Ford's response was characterized as Ford shifting his stance.

"Well, let me say very specifically that we are going to forget the use of the word *détente*," he said, adding that "the word is inconsequential." He emphasized that the United States had been and would continue to be tough negotiators with the Soviets—"good Yankee traders," in his phrase—but he made clear the French word was now being phased out.[28] It was a clear concession to the fire the Reagan campaign had lit underneath that word and the policy it represented.

After losses in places like Florida and Illinois, the Reagan campaign began to view the upcoming March 23 North Carolina primary as possibly his last stand. If they were going to go down, they were going to go down fighting. One of the supporters of that strategy was North Carolina Republican Senator Jesse Helms, a dedicated conservative and an early and important Reagan backer. He believed he could help deliver his home state for Ford's more conservative challenger, and he intended to do so.

A wily campaigner who knew his North Carolina voter base well, Helms huddled with his political operatives and decided they would blanket the state's airwaves with a blistering thirty-minute speech by Reagan. The program was aired on all but two North Carolina television stations.[29]

Reagan's speech was a barn burner, strongly articulating his differences with President Ford, and most notably Kissinger. Quoting Winston Spencer Churchill—a grandson of the famous former U.K.

wartime Prime Minister—Reagan described America's foreign policy as "wandering without aim." Ford's shift on the use of the word *détente* also had not escaped Reagan's notice: "Mr. Ford"—not President Ford—"who a few weeks ago said no one can forsake détente and get elected, now tells us he will abandon the word but retain the policy." Reagan asserted that "it's the policy that made the word unpopular," adding that "no words from Washington can hide the fact that we no longer deal from strength."

Reagan said it was "difficult" for him to trust America's Secretary of State. "Henry Kissinger's recent stewardship of U.S. foreign policy," he argued, "has coincided precisely with a loss of U.S. military supremacy." He went on to say that while President Ford displayed "evident decency, honor and patriotism, he has shown neither the vision nor the leadership necessary to halt and reverse the diplomatic and military decline of the United States."

As Secretary of Defense, my annual testimony to Congress on the Defense Department budget also received Reagan's notice. "The new Secretary of Defense," he noted, "former Congressman Donald Rumsfeld, tells us our strength is, quote, 'roughly equivalent,' unquote, to that of the Soviet Union." That much was accurate. But when Reagan went on to say, "It *is* suitable if you mean to say we're second, period"—that was certainly not accurate. The U.S. was certainly not second to the Soviets.

But the heart of Reagan's campaign speech focused on an obscure issue that was seemingly tailor-made to win the Republican base: namely, control of the Panama Canal. Several preceding presidential administrations had been working to find a way to move the Canal, construction of which had been famously begun during the administration of Teddy Roosevelt, from U.S. to Panamanian control. Kissinger had advised President Ford back in 1975 that returning a piece of Panamanian territory to the Panamanians was important to our international standing and regional stability, arguing, "If these negotiations fail, we will be beaten to death in every international forum and there will be riots all over Latin America."[30] Ford accepted his Secretary of State's arguments and held to the previously established U.S. position, even as he received a number of warnings from conservatives in the Congress, such as Senator Strom Thurmond, who suggested that it was just the sort of nationalist issue to rile up his opponents.[31] Thurmond warned that Ford was "going to catch unmitigated hell" from conservatives.[32] Still, Ford believed it was the right policy.

Reagan referred to the U.S. talks with Panama—which was then under the control of General Omar Torrijos, who had seized power in a 1968 coup—as "quiet, almost secret negotiations" that made the talks sound like a sinister plot. "Everyone seems to know the negotiations are going on," he said, "except the rightful owners of the Canal Zone, the American people."

"The Panama Canal Zone is sovereign United States territory," Reagan thundered to North Carolinians, "just as much as Alaska is, as well as the states carved from the Louisiana Purchase." Then he delivered his powerful and memorable closing thrust reference to the canal: "We bought it, we paid for it, and General Torrijos should be told we're going to keep it."

The tone and the nationalist assertions were a dramatic departure for Reagan. Where President Ford had sought to engage with allies and enemies alike and to respect our international commitments—including those that had been made to the Panamanians for years by successive U.S. Presidents—Reagan promised a new order. He offered in effect an "America First" vision.

North Carolina's Republican voters, at least, signed on to the Reagan approach. On March 23, they delivered Ronald Reagan his first presidential primary victory. He defeated Ford by more than six percentage points. This was the win the Reagan campaign desperately needed to roar back to life. As the Governor's son, Michael Reagan, remembered: "Had Dad not won North Carolina, he would have had to have dropped out of the race. It would have been over."[33]

President Ford took the defeat hard. The tough business of governing continued, but in a National Security Council meeting on the SALT negotiations the day after the North Carolina vote, I could see how the loss had affected him. My friend was as tired and as down as I'd ever seen him.

The next morning, I said to the President that I had recently heard him make a remark that included the phrase "regardless of who is President next year." That kind of thinking and statement from the top wasn't good for any organization. "You've been a good President," I assured him. "You shouldn't get down after a primary, and you ought not to refer to the possibility that you won't be President. You ought to just carry right on." There was no doubt that much of the credit for Reagan's primary victory in North Carolina was due to his half-hour broadside attacking Henry Kissinger as well as Ford, which understandably ticked off both men something fierce.

A few days later, a spirited discussion took place in the Oval Office. President Ford, Kissinger, and Scowcroft were discussing an upcoming presidential speech. Kissinger was determined that the President remove text in the draft referring to how well the Soviets were doing in their military buildup. "The impression that we are slipping is creating a bad impression around the world," Henry argued. He was not incorrect, and not only did it look bad, it was giving Reagan fodder for his campaign. The problem was that as Secretary of Defense, I knew that what the President's draft speech said about the Soviet buildup was accurate.

Kissinger responded: "Then we have to define our goals. It is inevitable that our margin since '60 has slipped. Are we trying to maintain the same margin as we had in 1960 or to maintain adequate forces?"

To me, the answer was clear. We had to take the steps and make the investments to assure that the Soviets did not overtake the U.S.

"We have been slipping since the sixties from superiority to equivalence," I argued, "and if we don't stop, we'll be behind."

At this point, President Ford stepped in. "I don't think the President should say we are slipping," he said. "I can say we need to redouble our efforts. I don't want to say we are getting behind, I'll say we have a challenge, we have rough equivalence and we've got to keep up."[34] He had listened to both of our views, saw that the difference of emphasis each of us had argued were accurate, and prudently chose a middle course.

Kissinger then addressed the elephant in the room—the increasingly ugly GOP primary battle and how the administration should respond. "I think the posture to take," he observed, "is that Reagan doesn't know what he's talking about."

I could well understand Henry wanting to dismiss Reagan's arguments. Perhaps anticipating the blistering attacks that were coming and likely not wanting to cause a problem for the President, Kissinger had offered to resign as Secretary of State the previous December, only to be talked into staying by the President.[35] While I didn't think Reagan had represented the reality of "rough equivalence" accurately, Reagan and I certainly agreed completely that if the U.S. was not to slip below "rough equivalence" to an imbalance of force tilted in the Soviets' favor, then we needed to significantly increase U.S. defense investment. I also knew that both the President and Kissinger agreed with that position and each had been strong supporters of the needed increase in defense investment.

It was a reality that if the USSR was steadily increasing its capabilities and the U.S. was lagging in our defense investment, we would, over time, fall behind. That was why I was determined to make sure the President was accurate about what the Soviets were up to. Henry Kissinger had a valid point given his role—but the President was right to say that we needed to increase our efforts in the face of a challenge.

These important issues weren't going away anytime soon. On March 31, they were flashed across television screens when Governor Reagan broadcast another half-hour address, similar to the speech he'd used to such positive effect in North Carolina. This time, he was taking his persuasive message coast to coast.

The President didn't watch the Reagan TV speech, but I did, and I discussed it with him in the Oval Office the next morning. The first half of his speech was slow, I felt, and I wouldn't have been surprised if some of his viewers had switched off their sets or changed their channels. But those who stayed for the second half of his remarks were in for a superb speech. Reagan started flying, ripping both the President and Kissinger on everything from Vietnam to the Panama Canal. He attacked one thing after another, and I sensed that listeners might conclude there was so much smoke that there must be some fire. As a piece of political theater, it was impressive.[36]

Of course, some of the smoke was of dubious origin. That very day, the State Department took exception to a quotation Reagan had attributed to Secretary of State Kissinger: "My job as Secretary of State is to negotiate the most acceptable second-best position available" for the United States. Lawrence Eagleburger, a skilled State Department official and one of Kissinger's closest associates, told the press that his boss "did not say that," and added: "It is pure invention and totally irresponsible."[37] It certainly didn't sound to me like anything Henry would think or say, unless it was a joke.

Still, as with the North Carolina speech, Governor Reagan's television broadcast was something to be reckoned with. President Ford had read about it in the morning newspapers and was particularly bothered by what Governor Reagan had said about the economy. "It's just factually untrue," Ford said, "and damn harmful to the economy to go around undermining confidence, which in fact can itself harm the economy." I said I agreed that leaders can damage confidence in the economy, but I felt that it would only further hurt if President

Ford responded or highlighted what Reagan had said. I argued that he ought to not attribute to Reagan the power to affect the economy.[38]

Reagan's political attacks clearly were of concern to him. After a meeting in the Oval Office with Cheney and Scowcroft, I stayed behind to speak with the President alone. "You look down," I told him. "I can tell you're concerned about something."[39] Yes, this was the President of the United States, and the boss, but at bottom he was a friend. And I could see he was hurting.

He said he was going to win the nomination, but if Reagan happened to win it, Reagan would need to apologize before Ford would support him. "I personally believe what Reagan is doing and saying is terribly damaging to the country," he said.

I told the President I understood how he felt—it's never pleasant to be attacked, especially when you think it's done unfairly—but that he simply couldn't spend so much time focusing on Reagan.

"You have a hell of a responsibility," I said, "to win that nomination and win the election and govern this country. You have to accept your personal feelings and set them aside." Reagan, I suggested, should be approached not as a personal matter but as a problem to be managed. Focusing on personal feelings, I reminded the President, was about the worst thing he could do.[40]

"I agree," President Ford finally said, "and I'll certainly try and do that."

I happened to have a meeting with him on the day of the Wisconsin primary, the first primary since Ford's loss in North Carolina, which may have attributed to his gloomy mood. Cheney told me that the internal polling had been all over the place. In one week, the polls had apparently jumped from Ford winning 60–30 to a 49–40 race. Dick thought the President might lose in Wisconsin, and even if he won, it could be close enough to keep Reagan in play. As it happened, the President won Wisconsin with 55 percent of the vote. Three weeks later, Ford defeated Reagan in Pennsylvania with 93 percent of the delegates (due to the state's unusual voting system). Then in May the trouble started. Between May 1 and 11, Reagan ran the table, winning the Republican presidential primaries in Texas, Georgia, Indiana, and Nebraska. His campaign roared to life once again. Next on the horizon was the May 18 primary in the President's home state of Michigan. Losing Michigan, which Dick and others thought could be a possibility, would be a serious blow to Ford, politically and especially personally.

Fortunately, Michiganders came out to support their favorite son. The President won by a comfortable margin, and again slowed Reagan's momentum. But the heated primary duel between President Ford and Governor Reagan continued like a seesaw, as they alternated winning primary victories through the spring and summer. As the contests went on, the count of Republican delegates pledged to each of the candidates increasingly became the focus of both campaigns. Since it was becoming clear there was not going to be a runaway victory for either candidate, it became a possibility that a few dozen of the party faithful might be able to determine the winner of the Republican nomination for President.

That meant the real showdown—where a sitting President would have to face off against a challenger from his own party—would be on the floor at the Republican National Convention, scheduled to open on August 16, 1976, in Kansas City, Missouri.

15

Last Campaign

MEETING WITH THE PRESIDENT

September 8, 1976

10:35 a.m. to (President left meeting about 11:32) and meeting continued there-after . . .

PRESENT: The Ford Campaign people

The President opened the Cabinet meeting and a lot of people were introduced.

Doug Bailey said the people vote on personal qualities, not on the issues—four qualities are important: vision, compassion, confidence, integrity—together they comprise leadership. . . . Talked a bit about Carter. . . . He is now being measured as to the four qualities mentioned above.

Then he said they have the following eight objectives with respect to the Presidential campaign (1) show the President's personal history (2) show his common sense and his personal conduct of the Presidency (3) the compassion dimension (4) the record of accomplishment in the past two years in the context of the difficult national condition when the President took office which too many people in the country seem to have forgotten, and which is a tribute to his leadership (5) the future goals of the Administration (6) they want to cut Jimmy Carter down to size (7) want to provide some momentum to the campaign when we need it in the last three weeks and reflect movement to the President (8) want to paint a comparison between Carter and the President, experience versus inexperience, explicitness versus studied vagueness, open policy versus manipulative, President versus candidate for President. . . .

Kissinger spoke at the meeting and gave his . . . assessment on the issues saying that we are making an error if we run on only two years of foreign policy, we should run on eight years he said. Second, he said we should [be] the Party of Peace against the Party of War, not by their desire, but by their approach, and the fact that people then have to overcompensate for the vacuum of power and deal with the convulsive maneuver which ends up in war. The Republican Party has ended those wars and not gotten us into wars.[1]

In the summer of 1976, Kansas City, Missouri, was ground zero of what became a lively, hotly contested intraparty contest, which reflected one of the largest splits in the Republican Party since Teddy Roosevelt and William Howard Taft had competed in 1912. It is also fair to say that the 1976 convention offered some of the most unusual moments in recent political history. The tension between the Ford and Reagan delegations was intense and, in at least a few cases, long lasting. Two friends from Mississippi who wound up as delegates on opposite sides of the Ford-Reagan battle would not speak to each other again for at least forty years.[2] Then there was the unusual introduction of First Lady Betty Ford to the convention by the actor Cary Grant. The legendary film star, who was by then up in years, intended to salute Mrs. Ford's outspoken support for women's rights issues by suggesting with a smile that "women had been one of his causes, too." The famous actor's reference to "pillow talk" raised some eyebrows.[3]

Perhaps as telling, however, was the tale of a gigantic inflatable elephant. Originally conceived by a downtown Kansas City community group to welcome President Ford, Governor Reagan, and the thousands of Republican delegates and supporters to their city, the mammoth balloon weighed 1,700 pounds, loomed 40 feet tall, and stretched 55 feet from end to end. The plan, on which Missourians had invested $2,300, was to float the polyethylene GOP mascot high above Kemper Arena, where the convention was being held.[4] Unfortunately, it never rose to its intended height. This particular elephant, apparently, was not able to fly. In fact, it seemed not even able to stand upright. The *Pittsburgh Post-Gazette* reported that when workers initially tried to inflate it the Sunday shortly before the convention kicked off, "They couldn't get enough air in the balloon, so it looked more like a flattened-out blimp." Whatever the exact circumstances, the slow and public demise of such a potent symbol of one of the two great political parties was hard to miss. The *Post-Gazette* wryly noted that "it may have been a bad omen for things to come" and quoted a "local wit" as saying, in a reference to the Democratic Party's nominee, Jimmy Carter, "It's an ill wind that blows from Georgia."[5]

As far as the Ford campaign team was concerned, however, that "wind" was blowing not from Georgia, but from the West. A certain former Governor from California was threatening to make life difficult for the incumbent President, if not actually seize the nomination from him altogether.

Through the summer of 1976, the media carried stories of Reagan's momentum and the prospect of a floor fight at the convention. While Ford long had resisted responding to Reagan's periodic comments against his administration, the President's rhetoric toward Reagan had become sharper by the close of the primary season. "Governor Reagan and I do have one thing in common," Ford would say on the campaign trail. "We both played football. I played for Michigan. He played for Warner Brothers." Ford, as an incumbent President, was in a far stronger position than his challenger. The President was the clear choice of Republicans nationwide, leading Reagan in Gallup polling by double digits all through the spring and into the summer.[6] The delegate count, too, was in the President's favor, if narrowly. But neither candidate had amassed the 1,130 delegates required to clinch the presidential nomination outright.[7]

There were enough uncommitted delegates remaining who could conceivably tip the balance in favor of Reagan during the formal balloting. The Ford team believed that the best way the California Governor could win would be if he mounted an aggressive floor fight in Kansas City over delegate counts and credentials.

Reagan's team began to believe that their man needed to do something more dramatic to turn the edge away from the incumbent President. As Reagan advisor Ed Meese put it later: "We had kind of run out the string of things to do in terms of what would generate news and keep the campaign in the news."[8] On July 26, they had made an unorthodox move. Without having won his party's nomination, and before the convention had even opened, Reagan called a press conference to announce he had selected his running mate: Richard Schweiker, a liberal Senator from Pennsylvania. This was clearly a play for Pennsylvania's important bloc of delegates as well as an effort to appeal to moderates skeptical or even fearful of the Californian. The announcement was a shock.

Ford, for one, thought Reagan's selection was a joke when he first heard it, since Schweiker had already come out for Ford.[9] Once he was persuaded it was true, Ford believed that the choice was a costly misstep. Schweiker might even have been to the left of the widely disliked Rockefeller and the selection would likely infuriate what many called "the True Believers," the conservative delegates.[10] The Schweiker move seemed to buttress the Ford team's effort to portray Reagan as more political and calculated than his reputation as a conviction-driven conservative suggested. As Ford and his senior campaign advisor Stu Spencer noted, "Reagan had taken in more taxes and spent more money than any governor in California history."[11]

Perhaps the charges leveled by the Ford campaign team during the heated primary to the effect that Reagan might be too far right to beat the Democratic nominee in the fall had gotten to Reagan and his team, leading them to an attempt to balance out his ticket. But if that was the case, picking one of the most liberal Republicans in the U.S. Senate was an overcorrection. As Ford had predicted, reaction from conservative Republicans was swift and almost universally negative. "Privately," the *Chicago Tribune*'s Washington bureau chief noted, "many old Reagan loyalists were complaining that their standard-bearer had forsaken principle for political expediency—thereby sacrificing the one quality they had always believed distinguished him from other conservatives like Gerald Ford."[12]

John Connally had throughout the campaign season been playing both sides. But he knew when to move to a winning side. The former Texas Governor and Nixon favorite called Ford after Reagan's selection of Schweiker to say that Reagan's decision showed that Ford was "unmistakably" the better choice. Ending his very public neutrality, Connally offered to endorse Ford publicly. Ford suggested that he do just that.[13]

Reagan's selection of Schweiker increased pressure on President Ford to accelerate his own plans for announcing his preference for the GOP nominee for Vice President. Reeling from the reaction to their gambit, the Reagan team pointed to the announcement of the Schweiker choice as demonstrating Reagan's transparency. Why, they asked, was Ford keeping his choice of a running mate a secret from convention delegates? But Ford held off. His plan apparently was to name his vice presidential candidate in what was then the traditional manner: only after his nomination for President was assured. To do otherwise, Ford believed, was presumptuous and, as Reagan had shown, a sizable gamble.

The President had asked me, among a number of others, to suggest a short list of potential vice presidential nominees. My initial list consisted of three Senators who I thought would garner respect from most segments of the party and would help the President govern. They included Howard Baker of Tennessee, Jim Buckley of New York, and Pete Domenici of New Mexico. I also suggested former Secretary of Defense Melvin Laird, and George H. W. Bush. To gain confirmation as CIA Director, Bush had pointedly removed himself from consideration for Vice President, but I believed Ford could make a case for him anyway had he decided to do so. Later I wondered if I should have added a "wild card"—a Democrat and a towering intellect who had served earlier as an advisor to President Nixon, my friend and former colleague Senator Pat Moynihan of New York. Pat was a sizable talent with a wonderful sense of humor who was outstanding at everything he did. But although Moynihan was respected by many Republicans, adding a Democrat to the ticket would have been too great a risk, so I left his name off.[14]

The convention officially came to order at 10:30 a.m. Central Time on Monday, August 16.[15] From the outset, the Ford and Reagan delegates tried to outdo each other at every turn, most notably with cacophonous chanting duels. They even competed to see who could give a more rousing cheer to their candidate's wife, when First Lady Betty Ford and Nancy Reagan made their official entrances on Tuesday.

One pro-Ford delegate stumbled and broke her leg shortly before a key procedural vote. But since the alternate who would have taken her place was apparently a Reagan delegate, the injured delegate stayed on the floor to take part in the vote instead of being rushed to the emergency room in the nearby hospital. Tom Korologos remembered that a doctor was found among one of the delegations, and he "put a splint on her leg made out of convention programs . . . and she stayed there for an extra hour until after the vote." Only then was she taken to the hospital for assistance.[16]

Politics can sometimes be a contact sport. Vice President Nelson

Rockefeller demonstrated that when he engaged in a personal alter-
cation with a delegate from North Carolina. Rockefeller had been
trading barbs with nearby North Carolina Reagan delegates from his
seat among the New York delegates, and reportedly grabbed the sign
from a North Carolina man named Jack Bailey. According to the
Associated Press, Bailey "asked Rockefeller to return it, but the Vice
President refused."[17] [18] A Utah delegate reportedly tried to intervene,
ripped a telephone off the wall in anger and had to be taken off by
security before things calmed down.[19]

Anticipating that Reagan forces would likely try to put forward a number of platform planks to create issues with Ford, Stu
Spencer had a standing instruction for Ford delegates to give the
Reagan team almost anything they wanted.[20] One such gambit in
particular, however, concerned the President and, particularly, his
Secretary of State. Called the "Morality in Foreign Policy" proposal,
the Reaganites commended Soviet dissident Aleksandr Solzhenitsyn, reminding delegates of the Ford "snub," attacked détente, and
criticized so called "secret agreements" in foreign policy. All of these
were seen as criticisms of Henry Kissinger, Ford's Secretary of State,
and his foreign policy positions and were intended to get under
Ford's skin.

"They are trying to humiliate us publicly," Kissinger said to the
President, urging a battle with the Reagan forces on the matter. Brent
Scowcroft agreed, and said the Reagan delegates should not be allowed to get away with this obvious repudiation of the Ford administration's foreign policy.[21]

In a meeting with Ford, Cheney, Spencer, advisor Tom Korologos, and others, Kissinger reportedly dug his heels in, refusing to accept a change to the party platform that would reflect badly on him
and his policies—the policies he had helped to fashion and imple-
ment in both the Nixon and Ford administrations. He threatened to
resign over it.

At one point, Tom Korologos, ever quick with a humorous quip, spoke up. "Hey, Henry, will you resign now?" he asked. "We need the votes."[22]

Though strongly sympathetic to Kissinger's concerns and an advocate for the policies that were being criticized, Ford was persuaded by his political advisors not to hand the Reagan forces a fight they not only would likely win, but one that might conceivably reinvigorate their chances for the nomination. As a result, what was seen as a antidétente plank was eventually added to the platform by the Reagan delegates. Depriving Reaganites of badly needed oxygen, Ford was easily nominated on the first ballot, with a margin of 117 votes.[23] With feelings between the Reagan and Ford forces strained, there was apparently not any serious consideration given to inviting Governor Reagan to join the ticket. Though Reagan appeared to have changed his stance at the last minute, the Ford and Reagan camps had apparently previously agreed that whoever won the nomination, the VP question would be off the table.[24] Instead, Ford chose Kansas Senator Bob Dole, a well-liked, sharp-witted conservative, and a friend of Ford's and mine from our days in the Congress.

The President's acceptance speech had been a subject of considerable discussion by his campaign team. His remarks after securing the nomination would have to unite Republicans, most importantly those who had supported Reagan, but also set his general election campaign on a strong footing to compete with his Democratic challenger, Jimmy Carter of Georgia.

Overall, the speech Ford delivered in Kansas City largely related his long-standing themes. Ford spoke forcefully despite the late hour and the stress of the previous, tension-filled days. Early on, he acknowledged the unusual circumstances that had brought him to this point: "I have been called an unelected President, an accidental President," he said. "Having become Vice President and President without expecting or seeking either, I have a special feeling toward these high offices. To me, the Presidency and the Vice-Presidency were not prizes to be won, but a duty to be done."[25] That was vintage Ford.

He reminded the audience of the words he had spoken two years before, proclaiming that "our long national nightmare is over." "It was an hour in our history that troubled our minds and tore at our hearts," he recalled. But we were able to right the ship and now we were set on a better course.

As he closed his remarks, he did something that was unusual, wise, and gracious. He invited Governor Reagan to come up to the stage with his wife, Nancy, to address the convention. In doing so, Ford made another act of healing—this time for his party. He decided to put his personal feelings aside and reach out to a man who was not only a skillful orator, but one who had repeatedly raised questions about Ford's ability and judgment. "We are all a part of this great Republican family," Ford proclaimed to the audience. "I would be honored, on your behalf, to ask my good friend Governor Reagan to say a few words at this time." Reagan was undoubtedly taken by surprise, but with Nancy beside him, he graciously came up to the stage.

Reagan thanked President Ford warmly, and gave a thoughtful nod to his political team's successes in securing many, if not most, of their positions on the party platform, calling the final version adopted "a banner of bold, unmistakable colors with no pale pastel shades." Despite not having prepared remarks, he launched into the soaring rhetoric that set him apart from the more plainspoken Ford. He said to the delegates he had been asked to write a letter for a time capsule in Los Angeles, and had thought about the people who would read it in a hundred years' time: "Will they look back with appreciation and say, 'Thank God for those people in 1976 who headed off that loss of freedom? Who kept us now a hundred years later free? . . . This is our challenge and this is why we're here in this hall tonight."[26] At the end of his elevating remarks, he did not offer a specific full-throated endorsement of President Ford, as might have been expected. Instead, he said that Republicans "must go forth from here united" and quoting a "great general," admonished that "there is no substitute for victory."[27]

Even then, as he conceded defeat, Reagan's presence filled the convention hall. It was clear to many observers that his days in public life were far from over. But moving toward the general election of 1976, it was clearly Ford's turn. He had emerged bruised from the tough contest, but stronger and more seasoned. He had been nominated for the Presidency by his party in his own right. Now he was determined to do everything he could to win the general election against what proved to be another formidable rival.

If many in Washington, D.C., thought Governor Jimmy Carter offered the attributes the country desperately needed in a national leader, then they kept it a closely guarded secret. The relatively obscure one-term Georgia Governor appeared on the national scene almost out of nowhere. Many Ford supporters were slow to take him seriously as a candidate for the presidency. The Ford campaign team considered him uninformed on how the federal government worked, which he was, and a bit arrogant. He appeared to them to be something of a political chameleon, running for Governor as a candidate somewhat to the right of his party, and then moving to the left.

In a July 15, 1976, memo to White House aide David Gergen, Bob Mead, a campaign advisor, pointed to Carter's appeal to religious voters. A Southern Baptist, Carter had made a point of discussing his faith, and his nominating speeches at the Democratic convention had reflected that. "I realized during the nominating speeches that an air of the Gospel was flowing from my television set," the advisor wrote. "Speeches were more like testimonials or confessionals. Phrases used i.e. 'when you come to know him the way I do' (used by Jesus's disciples) and '. . . he can lay that burden down . . .' (in obvious reference to the plight of racism) are typical of how the campaign has been going."[28]

When it came to potential opponents, Ford had a preference of his own—the veteran Democratic Senator and former Vice President Hubert H. Humphrey. Humphrey and Ford hardly saw eye to eye on policy matters, but the two men had a mutual respect for each other and a warm friendship. Ford also saw in Humphrey what he did not see at the time in Carter—a worthy opponent for the presidency. Whenever Humphrey came to the White House, Ford encouraged him to linger. Then he'd put his arm on Humphrey's shoulder and say, "Hubert, you know you're my candidate."[29] Humphrey would laugh good-naturedly, but something held him back from running. Later that fall Humphrey was operated on for bladder cancer. In the heat of a close general election campaign, Ford still took the time to visit his old friend, who offered the President unexpected news. "Mr. President," Humphrey disclosed, "I want to confide in you. You're going to be getting some votes from the Humphrey family."

In an era in which the public was open to an unknown candidate who promised, in an obviously intended contrast to Nixon, to "never lie to you," Carter had fashioned an opening. Indeed, he built a sizable thirty-three-point lead in the polls over Ford through the summer, though the margin had closed to thirteen points by the close of the Republican convention. This left a good deal of ground for Ford to try to make up, but after the successful convention, Ford seemed ready to meet the challenge.

At his first Cabinet meeting after the G.O.P. convention, at the end of August, the President seemed reinvigorated. He told the Cabinet he was ready to make bold moves. He laid out guidelines for foreign and domestic policy, declaring, "I won't be timid." He told the Cabinet: "I don't want anyone to hesitate to make recommendations because they think they aren't politically palatable."[30] It may have been an election year, but Ford was encouraged by his success at the convention and wanted to get back to the business of doing the right things for the country, rather than focusing on the politics of the presidential race. The Cabinet was told to keep governing well and that the politics would take care of itself.

From Ford's perspective, his admonition to pursue good policies for the country over what may or may not have seemed to be good politics extended to a Strategic Arms Limitation (SALT) arms control agreement, which the President badly wanted to achieve. Some of us at the Department of Defense remained concerned that the terms, as they then stood, were not good enough, and might be improved. As the Democratic candidate for President, Carter was blasting the President on the campaign trail for failing to come to an agreement with the Soviets. But, despite the President's strong desire for an agreement, Ford held with the military and civilian recommendations from the Department of Defense and kept working with Kissinger to try to achieve better terms.

By early September, Ford's focus turned to his first debate with Governor Carter, which was scheduled for the end of the month. To help him prepare, the President wanted a detailed list, with dates and locations, of "where Carter said what." He undoubtedly believed that his considerable knowledge of the federal government, particularly national security issues and the federal budget, would compare favorably to Carter's. The President approached his preparation with a focus on details, asking to be reminded of the costs of specific initiatives—for instance, the cost of an Army division and various missile systems.[31] As with all of the federal departments, at Defense we provided the White House with whatever they needed for preparation. Meeting with Cheney on a Saturday, I asked Dick what else they needed. "Just creativity, really," he responded.[32]

Though public opinion polls were still showing Carter with a sizable lead, I was told the Ford campaign's internal polling was showing the margin closing to single digits. Cheney reported that the President was relaxed and pleased with the way the campaign was going. I hoped that would put him in a confident mood for his first debate.

Dean Burch, a senior White House advisor and one of the GOP's most knowledgeable campaign experts, and his wife came over to our house to watch the first debate, which was broadcast from Philadelphia on September 23. The President did well, though I was concerned that he may have lost some momentum in that Carter did better than I had expected and committed no major mistakes. Still, watching their exchanges on television, something seemed off about Carter. When I met with the President a few days later, he mentioned the importance of the closing statements in the debates, and that he was thinking about some useful analogies or anecdotes. He was considering ways to be able to contrast his positions with Carter's.[33]

Though the election was looming, I was focused on leading a sizable government department, and I was interested in the President's guidance. We discussed his thoughts about the Defense Department.[34] I brought up a specific issue that was on my mind. Echoing his concerns during his primary contest with Reagan, I had heard he was interested in precisely how we ought to be characterizing the fact that the Soviets had been investing heavily and were trending up, while the United States had seen our advantage narrowing.

I said to the President, "I'm telling the truth the way I'm saying it."

"That's fine," the President responded, "but we ought to be positive about what the Congress has done." I agreed with him. The President had persuaded the Democrat-controlled Congress to boost U.S. military investments, thereby reversing a long-standing downward trend relative to the Soviet Union, and he was rightly proud of that accomplishment, as he fully deserved to be.

We needed to find the right balance.[35]

As it happened, the phrasing on this issue, while important, would not be Ford's major foreign policy headache. The headache would come on October 6, 1976, at a crucial moment during the second presidential debate, when Ford was asked a question by panelist Max Frankel of *The New York Times*:

> Mr. President, I'd like to explore a little more deeply our relationship with the Russians. They used to brag back in Khrushchev's day that because of their greater patience and because of our greed for—for business deals that they would sooner or later get the better of us. Is it possible that despite some setbacks in the Middle East, they've proved their point? Our allies in France and Italy are now flirting with Communism. We've recognized the permanent Communist regime in East Germany. We've virtually signed, in Helsinki, an agreement that the Russians have dominance in Eastern Europe. We've bailed out Soviet agriculture with our huge grain sales. We've given them large loans, access to our best technology and if the Senate hadn't interfered with the Jackson Amendment, maybe we—you would've given them even larger loans. Is that what you call a two-way street of traffic in Europe?

The President replied that we have "negotiated with the Soviet Union since I've been President from a position of strength." Citing several examples, he dwelt on his signing of the Helsinki Accords, over which he'd been criticized for some months. "In the case of Helsinki," he said, "thirty-five nations signed an agreement, including the Secretary of State for the Vatican—I can't under any circumstances believe that the . . . His Holiness, the Pope, would agree by signing that agreement that the thirty-five nations have turned over to the Warsaw Pact nations the domination of the . . . Eastern Europe." Then Ford finished with a statement that would have become instantly viral, if the internet had existed back in 1976. "There is no Soviet domination of Eastern Europe and there never will be under a Ford administration."

Taken aback, Frankel pressed Ford. "Did I understand you to say, sir, that the Russians are not using Eastern Europe as their own sphere of influence in occupying most of the countries there . . . ?" In response, Ford doubled down on his comment:

> I don't believe, uh—Mr. Frankel that uh—the Yugoslavians consider themselves dominated by the Soviet Union. I don't believe that the Romanians consider themselves dominated by the Soviet Union. I don't believe that the Poles consider themselves dominated by the Soviet Union. . . . the United States does not concede that those countries are under the domination of the Soviet Union. As a matter of fact, I visited Poland, Yugoslavia and Rumania to make certain that the people of those countries understood that the president of the United States and the people of the United States are dedicated to their independence, their autonomy and their freedom.

This was a statement that would dog the President for the rest of the 1976 presidential campaign. Few people listening to that debate could have imagined what Gerald Ford was thinking. It was certainly clear and well understood that the Soviet Union was in fact still subjugating Eastern Europe and that those captive nations were part of the Warsaw Pact. Watching the debate with Joyce at home however, I knew immediately what the President was thinking, what he had meant to say, and indeed what, as it turned out, he was absolutely convinced he had said.

The source of Ford's answer was his strong conviction that someday the captive nations would be freed. What he was thinking and without question what he meant to say, and what he was absolutely convinced he had said, was that he did not and would not concede that the countries in Eastern Europe would be "permanently" subjugated. The problem was he had left out the word *permanently*. What he intended to convey was that he was confident that their subjugation by the Soviets would not be permanent and that he held out hope for liberty among the people of those oppressed nations.

I knew well his line of thinking went back to our days in the Congress, when many members of Congress, Democrats and Republicans alike, would mark annual Captive Nations Week by drawing attention to the plight of those nations that were caught in the grip of the Soviet Union's totalitarian rule. On the occasion of Captive Nations Week back in 1969, for example, then Congressman Gerald R. Ford had observed: "There is a truth that no arms and no occupation can kill. The truth is that within the hearts of the enslaved peoples there burns a love of liberty which is a constant threat to their rulers—a yearning for freedom which will ultimately prevail." Ford even cited specifically the Polish protesters in the city of Poznan who had been gunned down by Communist forces in 1956. He concluded by declaring that "America must never accept the view that freedom is foreclosed for the now-enslaved peoples of the world."

I and many other members of Congress who made remarks in the U.S. House of Representatives each year during Captive Nations Week would regularly make similar statements, referring to our hope for freedom for the people of these nations in the future. In various ways, we were saying that we believed someday those countries would be free, that we did not "concede" that they would remain "permanently" subjugated.

Looking back, there was an incident during Ford's preparation for his first debate in September that may have foreshadowed this mistake. During a discussion, he mentioned he had been going over statements made by Communist leaders in the mid-1940s, when a number of them vowed to be independent of Moscow. Even though he knew today that they were not truly independent, as far back as the 1940s, they aspired to be.[36]

For whatever reason, the President did not quickly realize that he had left out the word *permanently*. I was told later that Cheney and Scowcroft, who were with Ford at the debate, had met with the President immediately after his debate and forcefully attempted to explain how his remark was being received. Only after several attempts were they able to get the President to recognize the gaps between what he was firmly convinced he had conveyed and what he had actually said and how it was being understood. But by the time they were able to convince him, too much time had passed.

It was Cheney and Scowcroft who met with the media right after the debate. The first question asked was simply: "Are there Soviet troops in Poland?" Scowcroft, of course, answered "Yes," and then provided an estimate of how many Soviet troops were in Poland before he was snidely asked by a reporter: "Do you think that would imply some Soviet dominance to Poland?"

He explained to the media that what the President knew well and meant. Cheney went on to add that the "policy of his administration is that we are interested in separate, independent autonomous relationships with governments like Yugoslavia, Romania and Poland."[37] President Ford finally explained as much the next day, and told reporters that the United States "firmly supports the aspirations for independence of the nations of Eastern Europe."[38]

The President's reluctance to immediately correct his mistake had made the problem linger. Before the second debate, Ford had pulled almost even with Carter, and was behind by only two points. Carter's lead moved back up to six.

Carter was not without his errors on the campaign trail, however. For one, he gave an ill-advised interview to *Playboy* magazine, which ran in its November 1976 issue, in which he made the comment, "I've looked on a lot of women with lust. . . . I've committed adultery in my heart many times."[39] His personal comment was probably intended to convey his openness, but it was perhaps better suited to a private conversation. Carter raised objections to a Ford campaign ad that contrasted the cover of the *Playboy* magazine featuring Carter's interview with the cover of *Newsweek* carrying an article on Ford. The President had responded simply: "I don't think the President of the United States ought to have an interview in a magazine featuring photographs of unclad women."[40] Some voters, particularly in the South, seemed to agree. As Dick Cheney noted in a memo to the President, "Governor Carter has begun to campaign more actively in the South which you take as an indication that he too is aware of the problems he has in the once solid South."[41]

On October 22, the day of their final debate, I had breakfast with Henry Kissinger. Kissinger told me he was pleased with the relationship between our two departments. Once again, though, he suggested the possibility that he was ready to leave government. But if the President won, I hoped he would be willing to stay on. And if he stayed, I believed there was a lot of good we could do.

That evening, the Dean Burches had the G. H. W. Bushes, Joyce and me, and a few others for dinner and to watch the final debate, which turned out to be easily the best of the three for the President. He was relaxed—he was "letting it roll." The voters apparently thought so, too. After that debate, the President pulled even with Carter in the polls once again. On a personal level, I was pleased for him. After rough spots that were inevitable in an instant presidency, he had become an excellent President—thoughtful, confident, and decisive—and I was convinced he would lead the country ably were he elected to a full term of his own.

Election Day generally seems to be a quiet day. And I had a less-than-typical day as Secretary of Defense. I brought our three young children to the White House in the morning to see President Ford arrive, marking the official end of his campaign. Later, I went by helicopter to the Aberdeen Proving Ground in Maryland. After a brief stop en route due to an oil leak, we arrived and I had a look at some military equipment. I briefly drove one of our M-60 tanks as well as a German Leopard tank—quite a change from flying S2F Trackers as a reservist naval aviator. I even tried my hand at tank gunnery, landing three or four rounds on or at least near the target.

I returned home that evening in time to watch the election returns with our family. In the final Gallup poll before Election Day, President Ford was shown as having pulled ahead by a point, besting Carter 49–48. After being buffeted by the Republican primary contest, a tough convention, and a general election campaign somewhat overshadowed by his innocent mistake, he still had a chance to come out ahead. Later that night Joyce and I briefly stopped at the election night gathering at the Sheraton Park Hotel before leaving the crowds behind and getting home sometime after midnight. We were in bed before 2:00 a.m., believing the President still had a chance, but knowing it would be close.

It was so close, in fact, that nobody was able to call the race until around three-thirty in the morning. Governor Carter had won by two percentage points in the popular vote. To add a final unfortunate note, President Ford had lost his voice from the campaigning and was unable to make his concession remarks, so he stood by as Betty read them.

To friends of the President, the final outcome was heartbreaking. Ford had been fighting from the minute he took office—fighting the ghosts of the Watergate scandal and the ghosts of the unhappy ending of the Vietnam War, working to counter an aggressive Soviet Union, taking important steps to improve a faltering economy, fashioning and directing his new White House team, and then fending off Governor Reagan, and in the end losing in a close contest to Carter. In the movies, the good guy—and Jerry Ford was the quintessential good guy—who after fighting against all odds, wins in the end. That Gerald Ford had come so close made his loss even harder to accept.

MEETING WITH THE PRESIDENT
November 3, 1976
Had good healthy view of [the loss] and demonstrated himself to be the kind of man we have known he is.[42]

Gerald Ford, of course, spent most of his time in the days and weeks that followed his narrow loss bucking everyone else up, doing his job as President, wishing President-elect Jimmy Carter well, ensuring a smooth transition for the new incoming President, and ending his decades of public service on a high note. To one friend who said sadly, "Damnit, we should have won," and wondered where things went wrong, Ford said bluntly, "Hey, there are more important things to worry about than what happens to Jerry Ford."[43] The President was not bitter. There were no recriminations. He cast no blame on others. He wasn't going to dwell on the what-ifs, though he was human and occasionally they must have crossed his mind. What if he had handled the pardon of Nixon differently? What if Reagan hadn't challenged him?

Some years later, the former President came to Illinois for a speech and to personally deliver a golden retriever puppy to Joyce and me. In the car taking us from the airport where I greeted him, he handed me a copy of his memoir, *A Time to Heal: The Autobiography of Gerald R. Ford*, saying with a smile, "Don, you're not going to like it." I asked why. He said, "Because I blame Brezhnev and you for our not getting a SALT deal." I said with a smile, "Mr. President, I can live with that."

It was left to Ford's son, Jack, to sum up the President's philosophy of life and politics. "If you can't lose as graciously as you had planned to win," Jack said, "then you shouldn't have been in the thing in the first place."[44] Ford quoted that line proudly. It was exactly what he felt.

Everyone who was Jerry Ford's friend when he entered the White House remained a friend when he left it—an achievement that is all too rare in Washington, D.C. In time, of course, the American people would come to value Ford's admirable qualities and appreciate his long service. He was, as one observer once put it, the President we always wanted that we didn't know we had.

Epilogue

The great gray hull of steel rose twenty-five stories before us. We gathered in front to pay our respects at the waterline. Above us, the flight deck of America's newest and largest naval vessel covered a full five acres. Deep within the one hundred thousand tons of metal were two nuclear reactors ready to surge to life. The ship spanned the length of three football fields, territory her namesake had known well.[1]

On hand to commemorate the christening of the USS *Gerald R. Ford* on November 9, 2013, were his four children, with his daughter Susan taking a lead role in the proceedings. Henry Kissinger was there—his notable German accent no less prominent with age. Ford's two former White House Chiefs of Staff—former Vice President Dick Cheney and I—were in attendance as well. Filling out the crowd of naval personnel and dignitaries were a good many of President Ford's former Cabinet, staff, colleagues from his years in government, and friends.[2]

When Cheney spoke, he invoked the Watergate scandal that had propelled Ford into the presidency, affirming that President Ford had handled the unprecedented challenge of preserving the union and healing the nation "better than anybody else could have."

In his remarks, Dr. Kissinger, who had earned Ford's greatest respect for his skillful foreign policy leadership, attested he "loved"
Ford, pointedly noting that this was "a feeling not every President
inspires."

President Ford had been gone for nearly seven years when the
formidable naval vessel that bears his name was christened. I did not
have to wonder what he would have thought about that impressive
occasion, the military bands and crisp uniforms of hundreds of military personnel arrayed around him. Over the Thanksgiving holiday
in 2006, while serving my second tour as Secretary of Defense, this
time in the administration of George W. Bush, I had called former
President Gerald R. Ford just to visit. He had sounded frail on the
phone. At ninety-three, he had become the longest-living former
U.S. President in American history.

Since we had each left Washington, D.C., back in 1977 after
spending a good many years serving together, first in the Congress
and then in the White House, our lives had taken distinctly different paths. Ford had settled into the comfortable but active life of an
elder statesman, while making time for some well-deserved hours on
the golf course. I had gone on to spend more than two decades in the
business world, and then went back into government to join my old
colleague and friend Dick Cheney in the administration of George
W. Bush.

Over the intervening years, Ford and I had talked on the phone
and been together in person periodically. But at the time of my call in
2006, I had not seen him for some time. I came away from our conversation concerned about his health, so Joyce and I decided to leave
our home in New Mexico and head west to Ford's home in Rancho
Mirage, California, to pay him a visit.

As we were greeted at the front door, I heard the President
shout, "Rummy!" His voice was booming—however frail he might
have been, that much was still indomitable. He was in his living

room, just down from the front hall, sitting back in a reclining arm-chair on wheels and giving us his big warm smile.

Though the ship to bear his name was still many years away from construction, I had been able to bring with me a rendition of what the USS *Gerald R. Ford* would look like once completed, and handed him a baseball cap with the ship's name emblazoned on the front, which he immediately put on. The aircraft carrier–based World War II veteran was deeply moved by his country's tribute.

It was a tribute well deserved. That the ship would be an aircraft carrier was particularly fitting, and not just because he had served on an aircraft carrier in the Pacific—the USS *Monterey*—during World War II. The new nuclear-powered vessel would carry the Ford name and the American flag across the oceans of the world as a massive, floating symbol of American strength and will—qualities that, fortunately for our country, the ship's namesake had demonstrated in his long service.

As the thirty-eighth President of the United States, Gerald Ford had restored the balance of our faltering republic in what was its most divisive moment since the Civil War. His was a historic accomplishment, not fully appreciated even then. This book is most certainly not a biography of his life. Rather, what I have hoped to do with this book is give a sense of what it was like to be there, during one of our nation's most tempestuous times, at Gerald Ford's side. He, along with those who served with him, tried mightily to right America's ship of state. In the end, it can be said that is what his leadership was able to achieve.

Of course, it didn't always feel that way for those in the Ford administration. Policy debates are in some ways inevitable challenges whenever a collection of strong-willed personalities find themselves packed together. And nobody should be surprised at the fact that Washington, D.C., can be a magnet for sizable personalities.

Gerald Ford's saving grace, however, was that he was *not* a big personality—not when he was in Congress, not when he moved through the ranks of leadership in the U.S. House of Representatives, not as the Vice President, and not when serving as President of the United States. His calm, thoughtful, and steadfast nature was remarkable in Washington, D.C., even in his own day, and some might assert even more so now. That may well have been how he was able to keep a strong hand on the wheel throughout the tumultuous years he led the nation.

While our country seemed to lurch from crisis to crisis at home and abroad, and those in the Ford administration did their best to stay ahead of problems and deal with those as they came up, Ford himself remained steady. When faced with a difficult decision, he sought and took the counsel of all sides and ultimately made the decision that he believed would be best for his country, regardless of his or anyone else's personal feelings. We always knew we could count on him for that.

Aside from the natural humility that was ingrained in him as a product of the American heartland and likely from his experiences in World War II, there was, I think, another wellspring for the modest, prudent nature that Ford brought to the Oval Office. He was the "accidental President," and he remembered that.

It is common in inaugural addresses for new presidents to declare—possibly with varying degrees of conviction—that they are going to be a President not simply in the service of the party that elected them, but in the service of all Americans. Though Gerald Ford did not have the opportunity to make a proper inaugural address, he made this promise, too—and in his case he meant every word.

He understood from the beginning that he had taken the reins during an emergency, a constitutional crisis unlike anything our country had faced before. He was President, but he did not have a mandate from voters who had endorsed him in an election. But he understood the American people and their desire and indeed need for stable, competent leadership, and that was to be Ford's priority—not scoring partisan points.

"I am acutely aware," Ford told the American people after being sworn in by Chief Justice Berger in the East Room of the White House, "that you have not elected me as your President by your ballots, and so I ask you to confirm me as your President with your prayers.

"I have not campaigned either for the presidency or the vice presidency," Ford reminded the nation. "I have not subscribed to any partisan platform." From the outset, Ford looked at his presidency not as a time to further a political agenda but as a mission to bring trust and confidence back to the American government at a time when much of the public was convinced Washington had given up on both.

At the same time, Ford never lost touch with his personal convictions. These remained as strong as they had been when he had helped navigate the Civil Rights Act through Congress back in the 1960s. Whether he was dealing with Soviet leaders on his terms, concluding the nation's involvement in Vietnam, or finding ways to strengthen the economy at home, Ford was guided by the principles that had sustained him throughout his personal and professional life.

Perhaps the greatest source of that sustenance, though, was his wife. Betty Ford was open and honest, and understood better than most that all of us are human, and all of us have flaws. That made her a steadfast pillar of support for a husband who valued it every single day.

As much as Vice President Ford had never expected to find himself thrust into the role of President, Betty Ford had not expected to be the First Lady, either. But she didn't let it change her in any way. She continued to provide advice to her husband and to those of us who served him—and whether we had asked for it or not, we always appreciated it. She never held back, and President Ford valued her counsel above anyone else's.

Given these qualities, it surprised none of us that Betty Ford went on to make such a name for herself helping millions of people around the country. She never met the vast majority, but she didn't have to meet people personally to understand their struggles. She understood that no human being was broken beyond repair, and her faith in that simple principle sustained an institution that in turn has saved lives and is still doing so today.

The Ford children—Mike, Jack, Steve, and Susan—brought a liveliness to the White House and helped to keep their dad grounded. A family man to the core, Jerry Ford, with his pipe and sweaters and penchant for plaid pants, projected the image of the quintessential "American dad" at a time when the country needed something so familiar and so comforting. Indeed, for a brief period he led our country out of his suburban home on Crown View Drive in Alexandria, Virginia. That house is now on the National Register of Historic Places, which describes it as "typical of middle-class housing in the northern Virginia suburbs of Washington," a "prosperous but unpretentious house and neighborhood."[3]

That was Gerald Ford. As a neighbor of mine put it, as we were discussing the former President shortly after his death, "He was one of us." Despite his holding the highest office in the land, pretension never once clouded his mind. Even though never elected to the vice presidency or the presidency, he knew he owed his best work to all of the folks in the middle-class suburbs, on the farms of the Great Plains, and in the inner cities. They hadn't chosen him, but they were still counting on him. And around the world, our allies and our enemies waited to see what this unassuming man would do with the smoldering wreckage of America's prestige he had inherited after Watergate.

Ford understood this calling from the moment he took office, and it sustained him through every day of his presidential service. President Kennedy's term is nostalgically referred to as "the thousand days"—President Ford had fewer than nine hundred. But each one of those days was spent working toward the goal of getting his country back on the right track and restoring the faith of its people.

That was why Gerald Ford never shied away from opportunities to meet our country's Cold War adversaries—to show them that America hadn't been hobbled by internal chaos and was as strong and ready to face the Communist threat as it had ever been. It was why he aggressively attacked inflation and worked to create more jobs and opportunities for American workers struggling in the tough economy of the 1970s.

Knowing Gerald Ford's dedication firsthand made the 1976 presidential campaign season especially tough for me. Gerald Ford was a good man who deserved to be elected President in his own right. His narrow victory in the Republican primary and his razor's-width loss to Governor Carter after the polls had narrowed dramatically before the general election were outcomes disappointing for the man who had served so well. But, that's politics—and even in defeat, Gerald Ford's graciousness proved an example for us all.

His humility was with him to the end, as it had been from his days as a star center on the University of Michigan Wolverines' football team. On the college gridiron, Ford proved that you didn't have to play one of the crowd-pleasing positions like quarterback or running back or wide receiver in order to be voted team captain. Even a humble center could earn that honor if he was good at his job, earned the trust of his teammates, and inspired his team to victory.

Decades later, Ford proved that you didn't have to have an outsized personality, movie-star charisma, or even Machiavellian cunning to be a truly great political leader at a most challenging time. You simply had to earn the people's trust and inspire and lead them in their hour of need. And once again, the center held.

Timeline

July 1913　Gerald Ford is born in Omaha, Nebraska

Spring 1935　Ford graduates from the University of Michigan with a BA in Economics and turns down offers from the Detroit Lions and Green Bay Packers to play professional football to instead work as an assistant varsity football coach and boxing coach at Yale University

Spring 1941　Ford graduates from Yale Law School in the top third of his class

December 1941　Pearl Harbor is attacked

May 1943　Ford is assigned to a new aircraft carrier, the USS *Monterey*

February 1946　Ford honorably discharged from the Navy

September 1948　Ford defeats four-term incumbent Bartel Jonkman in Michigan primary election for the U.S. Congress

October 1948　Ford marries Elizabeth Ann "Betty" Bloomer

November 1948　Ford is elected to the U.S. Congress to represent the Fifth District of Michigan with 60.5% of the vote

January 1963　Ford is elected Republican Conference Chairman in the U.S. House of Representatives

TIMELINE

November 1963 President John F. Kennedy is assassinated

January 1965 Ford is elected Minority Leader of the U.S. House of Representatives (73–67)

July 1969 Neil Armstrong becomes the first man to walk on the moon

1970 Average cost of a gallon of gas: $0.36; average cost of a gallon of milk: $1.15

June 1972 Five burglars break into the Democratic National Headquarters at the Watergate Hotel in Washington, D.C.

January 1973 The trial of the Watergate burglars begins in Washington, D.C.; the defendants plead guilty in federal court

October 1973 Vice President Spiro Agnew resigns and pleads no contest to accepting bribes and income tax evasion

President Richard Nixon nominates Ford as Vice President

December 1973 Ford is sworn in as Vice President by President Richard Nixon under the 25th Amendment after the Senate approved his nomination 92–3 and the House approves 387–15 in November

January 1974 Average cost of a gallon of gas: $0.53; average cost of a gallon of milk: $1.57

March 1974 Most Arab states involved in the oil embargo against the United States agree to end the ban

July 1974 U.S. House Judiciary Committee approves two Articles of Impeachment against President Richard Nixon

August 1974 Richard Nixon becomes the first U.S. President ever to resign the presidency. Chief of Staff Alexander Haig delivers President Nixon's letter of resignation to Secretary of State Henry Kissinger at 11:35 a.m. Ford takes the oath of office at noon in the East Wing. Rumsfeld lands at Dulles Airport at 1:55 p.m. to be met by his former assistant, Richard B. Cheney.

President Ford selects Nelson Rockefeller as his Vice President

TIMELINE

September 1974 Ford pardons Nixon

U.S. Government announces clemency for draft evaders and military deserters

October 1974 Ford appears before the House Judiciary subcommittee on Criminal Justice to respond to questions concerning his pardon of Nixon—the first President since Abraham Lincoln to testify before a congressional committee

Ford makes his first foreign trip as President of the United States to Nogales, Magdalena de Kino (Mexico)

November 1974 Ford visits Japan, South Korea, and Russia

Ford travels to the Soviet Union to meet with General Secretary Leonid Brezhnev in Vladivostok and signs the SALT-2 treaty to reduce each side's numbers and types of nuclear weapons

December 1974 Nelson Rockefeller is sworn in as Vice President of the United States

January 1975 Ford signs an Executive Order establishing a Commission on CIA Activities within the United States and appoints Vice President Rockefeller as the Chairman of the Commission

Average cost of a gallon of gas: $0.57; average cost of a gallon of milk: $1.57

April 1975 Cambodia falls to the Khmer Rouge

Ford orders the evacuation of American personnel and high-risk South Vietnamese nationals from Saigon in Operation Frequent Wind as a response to advancing North Vietnamese forces, bringing an end to U.S. involvement in the Vietnam War

May 1975 SS *Mayaguez* is captured less than a month after the Khmer Rouge take control of Phnom Penh

July 1975 Apollo 18 and Soyuz 19 make the first U.S./U.S.S.R. link-up in space

Ford is the first U.S. President to visit the former Nazi concentration camp Auschwitz in Poland

Ford goes on his second European trip and signs the Helsinki Accords on European Security and Cooperation

Ford announces his candidacy for the 1976 presidential election

September 1975 Lynette "Squeaky" Fromme, a follower of Charles Manson, attempts to assassinate Ford on the grounds of the California State Capitol in Sacramento, California

Second assassination attempt on Ford by Sara Jane Moore in San Francisco, California

November 1975 Former California Governor Ronald Reagan enters the race for the Republican presidential nomination, challenging incumbent President Gerald Ford

January 1976 Average cost of a gallon of gas: $0.60; average cost of a gallon of milk: $1.65

February 1976 Ford defeats Ronald Reagan in the New Hampshire primary with 51% of the vote

April 1976 Steve Wozniak and Steve Jobs create Apple Computer in the garage of Steve Jobs's parents' house in Cupertino, California

July 1976 Ford speaks at Valley Forge and Independence Hall at America's Bicentennial Celebration

Former Georgia Governor Jimmy Carter wins the Democratic nomination for President

Viking I lands on Mars

August 1976 Ford is nominated at the Republican Convention, beating former Governor Ronald Reagan; Ford selects Senator Robert Dole of Kansas as his running mate

September 1976 The first televised debate between Gerald Ford and Jimmy Carter is held

November 1976 Jimmy Carter wins the election with 297 electoral votes and 40,828,929 popular votes to Ford's 240 electoral votes and 39,148,940 popular votes

January 1977 Jimmy Carter becomes President of the United States; in his inaugural address he states, "For myself and for our Nation, I want to thank my predecessor for all he has done to heal our land."

August 1999 Ford is awarded the Presidential Medal of Freedom by President Bill Clinton

May 2001 Ford receives the Profile in Courage Award from the John F. Kennedy Library for his decision to pardon Richard Nixon

December 2006 President Gerald R. Ford dies at age 93

July 2011 Betty Ford dies at age 93

November 2013 The U.S. aircraft carrier *Gerald R. Ford* is christened

Notes

AUTHOR'S NOTE

1 "Former President Gerald Ford's Legacy Remembered." *PBS NewsHour.* December 27, 2006. http://www.pbs.org/newshour/bb/remember-july-dec06-ford _12-27/.

2 William Butler Yeats, "The Second Coming."

1. THE LONG NATIONAL NIGHTMARE

1 Gerald R. Ford, *A Time to Heal: The Autobiography of Gerald R. Ford* (New York: Harper & Row, 1979), 27.

2 Christopher Klein, "The Last Hours of the Nixon Presidency, 40 Years Ago." *History.* August 8, 2014. http://www.history.com/news/the-last-hours-of-the -nixon-presidency-40-years-ago.

3 http://www.nytimes.com/learning/general/onthisday/big/0808.html?mcubz=3.

4 http://www.washingtonpost.com/wp-srv/national/longterm/watergate/articles /080974-3.htm.

5 "President Nixon's Resignation Address." C-SPAN. August 8, 1974. https:// www.c-span.org/video/?320753-1/president-nixons-resignation-address.

6 "President Nixon's Resignation Address." C-SPAN. August 8, 1974. https:// www.c-span.org/video/?320753-1/president-nixons-resignation-address.

7 "President Nixon's Resignation Address." C-SPAN. August 8, 1974. https:// www.c-span.org/video/?320753-1/president-nixons-resignation-address.

8 "President Nixon's Resignation Address." C-SPAN. August 8, 1974. https:// www.c-span.org/video/?320753-1/president-nixons-resignation-address.

9 W. Landis Jones (ed.), *The Public Papers of Governor Wendell H. Ford, 1971– 1974* (Lexington, Kentucky: The University Press of Kentucky, 1978), 347.

10 "Historical Inflation Rates: 1914–2016." US Inflation Calculator. http://www .usinflationcalculator.com/inflation/historical-inflation-rates/.

11 "American National Election Studies." Stanford University and the University of Michigan. http://www.electionstudies.org/.

12 "Public Trust in Government: 1958–2015." Pew Research Center. November 23, 2015. http://www.people-press.org/2015/11/23/public-trust-in-government -1958-2015/.

13 "Presidential Approval Ratings—Gallup Historical Statistics and Trends." Gallup. http://www.gallup.com/poll/116677/presidential-approval-ratings-gallup-historical -statistics-trends.aspx.

14 David E. Hoffman, "Secret archive offers fresh insight into Nixon presidency." *Washington Post*. October 11, 2015. https://www.washingtonpost.com/news /post-politics/wp/2015/10/11/secret-archive-offers-fresh-insight-into-nixon -presidency/?utm_term=.4e3f40033a3b. James T. Patterson, *Grand Expectations: The United States, 1945–1974* (New York: Oxford University Press, 1996), 742. Richard Reeves, *President Nixon: Alone in the White House* (New York: Simon & Schuster, 2001), 298.

15 http://www.politico.com/magazine/story/2015/06/richard-nixon-watergate -drunk-yom-kippur-war-119021.

16 Lou Cannon, *Governor Reagan: His Rise to Power* (New York: Public Affairs, 2003), 385.

17 "President Nixon's Resignation Address." C-SPAN. August 8, 1974. https:// www.c-span.org/video/?320753-1/president-nixons-resignation-address.

18 Harvey Starr, *Henry Kissinger: Perceptions of International Politics* (Lexington, Kentucky: The University Press of Kentucky, 1984), 19.

19 Walter Isaacson, *Kissinger: A Biography* (New York: Simon & Schuster, 1992), 366.

20 Henry Kissinger, *Years of Upheaval: The Second Volume of His Classic Memoirs* (New York: Simon & Schuster, 1982), 68.

21 Gerald R. Ford, *A Time to Heal: The Autobiography of Gerald R. Ford* (New York: Harper & Row, 1979), 129.

22 Henry Kissinger, *Years of Renewal: The Concluding Volume of His Memoirs* (New York: Simon & Schuster, 1999), 22–23.

23 Gerald R. Ford, *A Time to Heal: The Autobiography of Gerald R. Ford* (New York: Harper & Row, 1979), 31.

24 Henry Kissinger, *Years of Renewal: The Concluding Volume of His Memoirs* (New York: Simon & Schuster, 1999), 22–23.

25 Gerald R. Ford, *A Time to Heal: The Autobiography of Gerald R. Ford* (New York: Harper & Row, 1979), 30.

26 Henry Kissinger, *Years of Renewal: The Concluding Volume of His Memoirs* (New York: Simon & Schuster, 1999), 22.

27 Gerald R. Ford, *A Time to Heal: The Autobiography of Gerald R. Ford* (New York: Harper & Row, 1979), 30.

28 Larry King and Irwin Katsof, *Powerful Prayers: Conversations on Faith, Hope, and the Human Spirit with Today's Most Provocative People* (Los Angeles: Renaissance Books, 1998), 68.

29 Bob Greene, *Fraternity: A Journey in Search of Five Presidents* (New York: Crown Publishers, 2004), 315–16.

30 Andrew Downer Crain, *The Ford Presidency: A History* (Jefferson, North Carolina: McFarland & Company, 2009), 33.

31 "Ford Promises That He and Kissinger Will Continue Nixon's Foreign Policy." *New York Times.* January 15, 1975, 4.

32 "Ford Promises That He and Kissinger Will Continue Nixon's Foreign Policy." *New York Times.* January 15, 1975, 4.

33 "A Transcript of Remarks Made by Vice President Ford." *New York Times.* August 9, 1974, 2.

34 Gerald R. Ford, *A Time to Heal: The Autobiography of Gerald R. Ford* (New York: Harper & Row, 1979), 29.

35 Henry Kissinger, *Years of Renewal: The Concluding Volume of His Memoirs* (New York: Simon & Schuster, 1999), 27.

36 Rumsfeld. Memorandum for the File. February 12, 1975.

37 James M. Cannon, *Time and Chance: Gerald Ford's Appointment with History* (Ann Arbor, Michigan: The University of Michigan Press, 1998), 197.

38 Gerald R. Ford, *A Time to Heal: The Autobiography of Gerald R. Ford* (New York: Harper & Row, 1979), 107, n1.

39 Henry Kissinger, *Years of Renewal: The Concluding Volume of His Memoirs* (New York: Simon & Schuster, 1999), 27.

40 Barry Werth, *31 Days: Gerald Ford, the Nixon Pardon and a Government in Crisis* (New York: Anchor Books, 2006), 112.

2. "GIVE ME HELL"

1 Rumsfeld. "Meeting with the President." Memorandum. November 30, 1974, and December 1, 1974.

2 James Whitcomb and Claire Whitcomb, *Real Life at the White House: 200 Years of Daily Life at America's Most Famous Residence* (New York: Routledge), 401. Rick Perlstein, *The Invisible Bridge: The Fall of Nixon and the Rise of Reagan* (New York: Simon & Schuster, 2014), 278.

3 "Nixon Resigns." *The Washington Post.* August 9, 1974, 1.

4 "Nixon Resigns." *The Washington Post.* August 9, 1974, 1.

5 Gerald R. Ford, *A Time to Heal: The Autobiography of Gerald R. Ford* (New York: Harper & Row, 1979), 39.

6 Henry Kissinger, *Years of Renewal: The Concluding Volume of His Memoirs* (New York: Simon & Schuster, 1999), 26.

7 Gerald R. Ford, *A Time to Heal: The Autobiography of Gerald R. Ford* (New York: Harper & Row, 1979), 124–25.

8 Gerald R. Ford, "Remarks Upon Taking the Oath of Office as President." East Room, White House. Washington, D.C., August 9, 1974. Gerald R. Ford Presidential Library & Museum. https://www.fordlibrarymuseum.gov/library /speeches/740001.asp.

9 Secretary of State Henry Kissinger to U.S. Ambassador to NATO Donald Rumsfeld. Telegram. August 9, 1974.

10 Rumsfeld. Memorandum. August 1974.

11 Rumsfeld. Memorandum. August 1974.

12 Rumsfeld. Memorandum. August 9, 1974.

13 Rumsfeld. Memorandum. August 1974.

14 Rumsfeld. Memorandum. August 1974.

15 Gerald R. Ford, *A Time to Heal: The Autobiography of Gerald R. Ford* (New York: Harper & Row, 1979), 23–24.

16 Author Interview with Henry Kissinger, November 12, 2014.

17 Gerald R. Ford, *A Time to Heal: The Autobiography of Gerald R. Ford* (New York: Harper & Row, 1979), 126.

18 Gerald R. Ford, *A Time to Heal: The Autobiography of Gerald R. Ford* (New York: Harper & Row, 1979), 126.

19 Gerald R. Ford, *A Time to Heal: The Autobiography of Gerald R. Ford* (New York: Harper & Row, 1979), 126–27.

20 Rumsfeld. Memorandum. August 9, 1974.

21 Henry Kissinger, *Years of Renewal: The Concluding Volume of His Memoirs* (New York: Simon & Schuster, 1999), 27.

22 Rumsfeld. "Meeting with the President." Memorandum. October 1, 1974.

23 Donald Rumsfeld, *Known and Unknown: A Memoir* (New York: Sentinel, 2011), 167.

24 Rumsfeld. "Memorandum of Conversation with President." Memorandum. September 22, 1974.

25 Donald Rumsfeld, *Known and Unknown: A Memoir* (New York: Sentinel, 2011), 168.

26 Rumsfeld. Memorandum. August 9, 1974.

27 http://www.politico.com/magazine/story/2015/06/richard-nixon-watergate -drunk-yom-kippur-war-119021.

28 Leon Jaworski to Julius Klein. Letter. March 7, 1975.

29 Rumsfeld. Memorandum. August 9, 1974.

30 Robert Goldwin to Donald Rumsfeld. Memorandum. October 3, 1974.

31 James Cannon, *Gerald R. Ford: An Honorable Life* (Ann Arbor, Michigan: The University of Michigan Press, 2013), 264.

32 Rumsfeld. Memorandum. August 9, 1974.

33 Gerald R. Ford, *A Time to Heal: The Autobiography of Gerald R. Ford* (New York: Harper & Row, 1979), 127.

34 James Robenalt, *January 1973: Watergate, Roe v. Wade, Vietnam, and the Month That Changed America Forever* (Chicago: Chicago Review Press, 2015), 11–12.

35 Gerald R. Ford, *A Time to Heal: The Autobiography of Gerald R. Ford* (New York: Harper & Row, 1979), 131.

36 Rumsfeld. Memorandum. August 10, 1974.

37 Rumsfeld. Memorandum. August 10, 1974.

38 Rumsfeld. Memorandum. August 10, 1974.

39 Rumsfeld. Memorandum. August 10, 1974.

40 Gerald R. Ford, *A Time to Heal: The Autobiography of Gerald R. Ford* (New York: Harper & Row, 1979), 131.

41 Anthony Lewis, "The Age of Nixon." *New York Times*. August 10, 1974, 29.

42 "Tragedy and Triumph." *New York Times*. August 11, 1974, 182.

43 "Presidential Approval Ratings—Gallup Historical Statistics and Trends." Gallup. http://www.gallup.com/poll/116677/presidential-approval-ratings-gallup-historical-statistics-trends.aspx.

3. THE PARDON

1 Rumsfeld. "Meeting with the President." Memorandum. October 9, 1974.

2 Benton L. Becker. "History and Background of Nixon Pardon." Memorandum. September 9, 1974. Gerald R. Ford Presidential Library & Museum. https://www.fordlibrarymuseum.gov/library/document/0238/1126646.pdf.

3 Matt Schudel, "Benton L. Becker, negotiator of Ford's pardon of Nixon in 1974, dies at 77." *Washington Post*. August 4, 2015. https://www.washingtonpost.com/local/obituaries/benton-l-becker-negotiator-of-fords-pardon-of-nixon-in-1974-dies-at-77/2015/08/04/eda22892-3ac0-11e5-8e98-115a3cf7d7ae_story.html?utm_term=.8b4562e885f4.

4 Matt Schudel, "Benton L. Becker, negotiator of Ford's pardon of Nixon in 1974, dies at 77." *Washington Post*. August 4, 2015. https://www.washingtonpost.com/local/obituaries/benton-l-becker-negotiator-of-fords-pardon-of-nixon-in-1974-dies-at-77/2015/08/04/eda22892-3ac0-11e5-8e98-115a3cf7d7ae_story.html?utm_term=.8b4562e885f4.

5 Gerald R. Ford, *A Time to Heal: The Autobiography of Gerald R. Ford* (New York: Harper & Row, 1979), 165–66.

6 Benton L. Becker. "History and Background of Nixon Pardon." Memorandum. September 9, 1974. Gerald R. Ford Presidential Library & Museum. https://www.fordlibrarymuseum.gov/library/document/0238/1126646.pdf.

7 Matt Schudel, "Benton L. Becker, negotiator of Ford's pardon of Nixon in 1974, dies at 77." *Washington Post*. August 4, 2015. https://www.washingtonpost .com/local/obituaries/benton-l-becker-negotiator-of-fords-pardon-of-nixon -in-1974-dies-at-77/2015/08/04/eda22892-3ac0-11e5-8e98-115a3cf7d7ae_story .html?utm_term=.8b4562e885f4.

8 Gerald R. Ford, *A Time to Heal: The Autobiography of Gerald R. Ford* (New York: Harper & Row, 1979), 168.

9 Benton L. Becker. "History and Background of Nixon Pardon." Memorandum. September 9, 1974. Gerald R. Ford Presidential Library & Museum. https://www.fordlibrarymuseum.gov/library/document/0238/1126646.pdf.

10 Benton L. Becker. "History and Background of Nixon Pardon." Memorandum. September 9, 1974. Gerald R. Ford Presidential Library & Museum. https://www.fordlibrarymuseum.gov/library/document/0238/1126646.pdf.

11 Gerald R. Ford, *A Time to Heal: The Autobiography of Gerald R. Ford* (New York: Harper & Row, 1979), 168.

12 Matt Schudel, "Benton L. Becker, negotiator of Ford's pardon of Nixon in 1974, dies at 77." *Washington Post*. August 4, 2015. https://www.washingtonpost .com/local/obituaries/benton-l-becker-negotiator-of-fords-pardon-of-nixon -in-1974-dies-at-77/2015/08/04/eda22892-3ac0-11e5-8e98-115a3cf7d7ae_story .html?utm_term=.8b4562e885f4.

13 Gerald R. Ford, *A Time to Heal: The Autobiography of Gerald R. Ford* (New York: Harper & Row, 1979), 169–70.

14 Matt Schudel, "Benton L. Becker, negotiator of Ford's pardon of Nixon in 1974, dies at 77." *Washington Post*. August 4, 2015. https://www.washingtonpost .com/local/obituaries/benton-l-becker-negotiator-of-fords-pardon-of-nixon -in-1974-dies-at-77/2015/08/04/eda22892-3ac0-11e5-8e98-115a3cf7d7ae_story .html?utm_term=.8b4562e885f4.

15 Matt Schudel, "Benton L. Becker, negotiator of Ford's pardon of Nixon in 1974, dies at 77." *Washington Post*. August 4, 2015. https://www.washingtonpost .com/local/obituaries/benton-l-becker-negotiator-of-fords-pardon-of-nixon -in-1974-dies-at-77/2015/08/04/eda22892-3ac0-11e5-8e98-115a3cf7d7ae_story .html?utm_term=.8b4562e885f4.

16 Matt Schudel, "Benton L. Becker, negotiator of Ford's pardon of Nixon in 1974, dies at 77." *Washington Post*. August 4, 2015. https://www.washingtonpost

.com/local/obituaries/benton-l-becker-negotiator-of-fords-pardon-of-nixon
-in-1974-dies-at-77/2015/08/04/eda22892-3ac0-11e5-8e98-115a3cf7d7ae_story
.html?utm_term=.8b4562e885f4.

17 Benton L. Becker. "History and Background of Nixon Pardon." Memorandum. September 9, 1974. Gerald R. Ford Presidential Library & Museum.
https://www.fordlibrarymuseum.gov/library/document/0238/1126646.pdf.

18 Benton L. Becker. "History and Background of Nixon Pardon." Memorandum. September 9, 1974. Gerald R. Ford Presidential Library & Museum.
https://www.fordlibrarymuseum.gov/library/document/0238/1126646.pdf.

19 Benton L. Becker. "History and Background of Nixon Pardon." Memorandum. September 9, 1974. Gerald R. Ford Presidential Library & Museum.
https://www.fordlibrarymuseum.gov/library/document/0238/1126646.pdf.

20 Benton L. Becker. "History and Background of Nixon Pardon." Memorandum. September 9, 1974. Gerald R. Ford Presidential Library & Museum.
https://www.fordlibrarymuseum.gov/library/document/0238/1126646
.pdf.

21 Carl Feldbaum and Peter Kreindler. "Factors to be Considered in Deciding
Whether to Prosecute Richard M. Nixon for Obstruction of Justice." Memorandum. August 9, 1974. Watergate.info. http://watergate.info/1974/08/09
/jaworski-memorandum-on-prosecuting-nixon.html.

22 Carl Feldbaum and Peter Kreindler. "Factors to be Considered in Deciding
Whether to Prosecute Richard M. Nixon for Obstruction of Justice." Memorandum. August 9, 1974. Watergate.info. http://watergate.info/1974/08/09
/jaworski-memorandum-on-prosecuting-nixon.html.

23 John Herbers, "Ford Gives Pardon to Nixon, Who Regrets 'My Mistakes.'"
New York Times. September 9, 1974, 1.

24 Gerald R. Ford, *A Time to Heal: The Autobiography of Gerald R. Ford* (New
York: Harper & Row, 1979), 158.

25 Rumsfeld. Memorandum. October 5, 1974.

26 Lester David, *The Lonely Lady of San Clemente: The Story of Pat Nixon* (New
York: Crowell, 1978), 7.

27 "Patricia Nixon, Wife of Former President, Dies at 81." *Los Angeles Times*.
June 23, 1993.

28 "Nixon's fear of dying in hospital." Associated Press. September 15, 1974.

29 Rumsfeld. Memorandum. October 29, 1974.

30 Gerald R. Ford, *A Time to Heal: The Autobiography of Gerald R. Ford* (New
York: Harper & Row, 1979), 161.

31 Gerald R. Ford, *A Time to Heal: The Autobiography of Gerald R. Ford* (New
York: Harper & Row, 1979), 162.

32 Gerald R. Ford, *A Time to Heal: The Autobiography of Gerald R. Ford* (New York: Harper & Row, 1979), 161.

33 Gerald R. Ford, *A Time to Heal: The Autobiography of Gerald R. Ford* (New York: Harper & Row, 1979), 161.

34 Found in Barry Werth, *31 Days: Gerald Ford, the Nixon Pardon, and a Government in Crisis* (New York: Anchor Books), 318.

35 Gerald R. Ford, *A Time to Heal: The Autobiography of Gerald R. Ford* (New York: Harper & Row, 1979), 175.

36 Gerald R. Ford, "Remarks on Signing a Proclamation Granting Pardon to Richard Nixon." White House, Washington, D.C. September 8, 1974. https://www.fordlibrarymuseum.gov/library/speeches/740060.asp.

37 Gerald R. Ford, "Remarks on Signing a Proclamation Granting Pardon to Richard Nixon." White House, Washington, D.C. September 8, 1974. https://www.fordlibrarymuseum.gov/library/speeches/740060.asp.

38 David Hume Kennerly, "In the Room When Ford Pardoned Nixon." David Hume Kennerly. September 8, 2014. http://kennerly.com/blog/room-ford-pardoned-nixon.

39 David Hume Kennerly, "In the Room When Ford Pardoned Nixon." David Hume Kennerly. September 8, 2014. http://kennerly.com/blog/room-ford-pardoned-nixon.

40 http://content.time.com/time/subscriber/article/0,33009,908675-4,00.html.

41 Patrick Flanary, "How the Nixon Pardon Strained a Presidential Friendship." ProPublica. December 13, 2011. https://www.propublica.org/article/presidential-pardons-how-the-nixon-pardon-strained-a-presidential-friendshi.

42 "Carter: Nixon pardon okay, after conviction." United Press International. August 6, 1976.

43 John Herbers, "Ford Gives Pardon to Nixon, Who Regrets 'My Mistakes.'" *New York Times*. September 8, 1974. http://www.nytimes.com/learning/general/onthisday/big/0908.html.

44 Anthony Lewis, "Watergate Aftermath." *New York Times*. November 28, 1974, 33.

45 Tom Wicker, "Nixon and Ford." *New York Times*. December 7, 1973, 41.

46 Found in Stanley I. Kutler (ed.), *Watergate: A Brief History with Documents* (Malden, Massachusetts: Wiley-Blackwell, 2010), 206.

47 Benton L. Becker. "History and Background of Nixon Pardon." Memorandum. September 9, 1974. Gerald R. Ford Presidential Library & Museum. https://www.fordlibrarymuseum.gov/library/document/0238/1126646.pdf.

48 "The Nixon pardon in constitutional retrospect." *Constitution Daily*. National Constitution Center. September 8, 2016. http://blog.constitutioncenter.org/2016/09/the-nixon-pardon-in-retrospect-40-years-later.

49 "The Nixon pardon in constitutional retrospect." *Constitution Daily*. National Constitution Center. September 8, 2016. http://blog.constitutioncenter.org /2016/09/the-nixon-pardon-in-retrospect-40-years-later.

50 Douglas Brinkley, *Gerald R. Ford: The American Presidents Series: The 38th President, 1974–1977* (New York: Times Books, 2007), 71.

51 http://content.time.com/time/subscriber/article/0,33009,908675-4,00.html.

52 John Herbers, "Ford Gives Pardon To Nixon, Who Regrets 'My Mistakes.'" *New York Times*. September 8, 1974. http://www.nytimes.com/learning/general /onthisday/big/0908.html.

53 Joel Roberts, "Polls: Ford's Image Improved Over Time." CBS News. December 27, 2006. http://www.cbsnews.com/news/polls-fords-image-improved -over-time/.

54 Jeffrey M. Jones, "Gerald Ford Retrospective." Gallup. December 29, 2006. http://www.gallup.com/poll/23995/gerald-ford-retrospective.aspx.

55 Rumsfeld. "Memorandum of Conversation with President." Memorandum. October 24, 1974.

56 Gerald R. Ford to Donald Rumsfeld. Telegram. September 18, 1974.

57 Rumsfeld. "Memorandum of Conversation with President." Memorandum. September 22, 1974.

58 Gerald R. Ford, *A Time to Heal: The Autobiography of Gerald R. Ford* (New York: Harper & Row, 1979), 184.

59 Gerald R. Ford, *A Time to Heal: The Autobiography of Gerald R. Ford* (New York: Harper & Row, 1979), 185.

60 Gerald R. Ford, *A Time to Heal: The Autobiography of Gerald R. Ford* (New York: Harper & Row, 1979), 185.

61 https://www.fordlibrarymuseum.gov/library/document/0314/1552748.pdf.

62 Donald Rumsfeld to Dick Cheney. Letter. November 16, 1974.

63 Donald Rumsfeld to Dick Cheney. Memorandum. February 27, 1975.

64 Donald Rumsfeld, "Safe in Haig's Office." Memorandum. September 29, 1974. Dick Cheney, "Safe." Memorandum. September 29, 1974.

65 Donald Rumsfeld to Phil Buchen. Memorandum. September 29, 1974. Dick Cheney to Phil Buchen. Memorandum. October 3, 1974.

66 Donald Lowitz. Memorandum. November 1, 1974.

67 Rumsfeld. Memorandum. October 4, 1974.

68 Don Lowitz to Donald Rumsfeld. "Gifts to the President and His Family by White House Staff Members." Memorandum, October 10, 1974.

69 John Herbers, "Reports of Nixon Ill Health Are Questioned by Visitors." *New York Times*. September 10, 1974. http://www.nytimes.com/1974/09/10/archives /reports-of-nixon-ill-health-are-questioned-by-visitors-reports-of.html.

70 Everett R. Holles, "Haig Denies That He Urged Ford to Pardon Nixon." *New York Times*. September 18, 1974. http://www.nytimes.com/1974/09/18/archives /haig-denies-that-he-urged-ford-to-pardon-nixon-denies-any-warning.html.

71 http://www.nytimes.com/1974/09/15/archives/terhorst-says-ford-spent-inordinate -time-on-haig-on-transfer-of.html?_r=0.

72 http://www.nytimes.com/1974/09/15/archives/terhorst-says-ford-spent-inordinate -time-on-haig-on-transfer-of.html?_r=0.

73 http://www.nytimes.com/1974/09/18/archives/haig-denies-that-he-urged -ford-to-pardon-nixon-denies-any-warning.html.

74 http://www.nytimes.com/1974/09/18/archives/haig-denies-that-he-urged -ford-to-pardon-nixon-denies-any-warning.html.

75 Rumsfeld, Note for the File, December 9, 1974.

4. PUBLIC ENEMY NUMBER ONE

1 Rumsfeld. "Meeting with the President." Memorandum. November 6, 1974.

2 George Gallup, Jr., *The Gallup Poll: Public Opinion, 1998* (Wilmington, Delaware: Scholarly Resources Inc.), 61.

3 Judith Stein, "Politics and Policies in the 1970s and Early Twenty-first Century: The Linked Recessions." In Leon Frink, Joseph A. McCartin, and Joan Sangster (eds.), *Workers in Hard Times: A Long View of Economic Crises* (Urbana, Illinois: University of Illinois Press, 2014), 145.

4 Frank M. Magill (ed.), *Chronology of Twentieth-Century History: Business and Commerce, Volume II* (New York: Routledge, 2013), 1,036.

5 http://www.presidency.ucsb.edu/ws/index.php?pid=5963.

6 Gerald R. Ford, "Address to a Joint Session of the Congress." House of Representatives, Washington, D.C. August 12, 1974. Found at www.presidency.ucsb.edu.

7 Gerald R. Ford, "Address to a Joint Session of the Congress." House of Representatives, Washington, D.C. August 12, 1974. Found at www.presidency.ucsb .edu.

8 https://www.fordlibrarymuseum.gov/library/document/0047/phw19740919- 10.pdf.

9 Gerald R. Ford, "Address to a Joint Session of the Congress." House of Representatives, Washington, D.C. August 12, 1974. Found at www.presidency.ucsb .edu.

10 Gerald R. Ford, *A Time to Heal: The Autobiography of Gerald R. Ford* (New York: Harper & Row, 1979), 191.

11 Gerald R. Ford, "Address to a Joint Session of the Congress." House of Representatives, Washington, D.C. August 12, 1974. Found at www.presidency.ucsb .edu.

12 Sam Frizell, "Could a 40-Year-Old Bank Collapse Have Saved the U.S. Economy?" *Time*. October 8, 2014. time.com.

13 Ron Nessen, *Making the News, Taking the News: From NBC to the Ford White House* (Middletown, Connecticut: Wesleyan University Press, 2011), 123–24.

14 Alan Greenspan, *The Age of Turbulence: Adventures in a New World* (New York: Penguin, 2007), 66.

15 Rumsfeld. "Meeting with the President." Memorandum. October 8, 1974.

16 Ron Nessen, *Making the News, Taking the News: From NBC to the Ford White House* (Middletown, Connecticut: Wesleyan University Press, 2011), 98.

17 See, for example, *Wall Street Journal* on October 11, 1974.

18 Rumsfeld. "Meeting with the President." Memorandum. November 30, 1974, and December 1, 1974.

19 Gerald R. Ford, *A Time to Heal: The Autobiography of Gerald R. Ford* (New York: Harper & Row, 1979), 193–94.

20 Ron Nessen, *Making the News, Taking the News: From NBC to the Ford White House* (Middletown, Connecticut: Wesleyan University Press, 2011), 124.

21 Rumsfeld. "Meeting with the President." Memorandum. October 8, 1974.

22 Found in Mark J. Rozell, *The Press and the Ford Presidency* (Ann Arbor, Michigan: The University of Michigan Press, 1992), 65.

23 Gerald R. Ford, *A Time to Heal: The Autobiography of Gerald R. Ford* (New York: Harper & Row, 1979), 194.

24 Found in John Robert Greene, *The Presidency of Gerald R. Ford* (Lawrence, Kansas: University Press of Kansas, 1995), 72.

25 "WIN Is Losing." *Washington Post*. December 20, 1974.

26 "WIN Is Losing." *Washington Post*. December 20, 1974.

27 Meg Jacobs, *Panic at the Pump: The Energy Crisis and the Transformation of American Politics in the 1970s* (New York: Hill and Wang, 2016), 134.

28 Found in Beth Ingold and Theodore Windt (eds.), *Essays in President Rhetoric* (Dubuque, Iowa: Kendall/Hunt, 1992), 316.

29 "WIN Is Losing." *Washington Post*. December 20, 1974.

30 Rumsfeld. "Meeting with the President." Memorandum. October 7, 1974.

31 Rumsfeld. Memorandum for the File. October 10, 1974.

32 Rumsfeld. "Meeting with the President." Memorandum. December 10, 1974.

33 Robert Werner to Donald Rumsfeld. Letter. December 11, 1974.

34 Rumsfeld. Memorandum. November 6, 1974.

35 Rumsfeld. Memorandum. October 10, 1974.

36 Rumsfeld. "Meeting with the President." Memorandum. November 5, 1974.

37 Rumsfeld. "Meeting with the President." Memorandum. October 8, 1974.

38 Kiron K. Skinner, et al., *The Strategy of Campaigning: Lessons from Ronald Reagan & Boris Yeltsin* (Ann Arbor, Michigan: The University of Michigan Press, 2007), 105.

39 Kiron K. Skinner, et al., *The Strategy of Campaigning: Lessons from Ronald Reagan & Boris Yeltsin* (Ann Arbor, Michigan: The University of Michigan Press, 2007), 105.

40 Rumsfeld. Memorandum. November 6, 1974.

41 Donald Rumsfeld to Gerald R. Ford. "Proposed TV Address to the Nation." Memorandum. January 10, 1975.

42 Gerald R. Ford, "Address to a Joint Session of the Congress." House of Representatives, Washington, D.C. January 15, 1975. Found at www.presidency.ucsb.edu.

43 Gerald R. Ford, "Address to the Nation on Energy and Economic Programs." January 13, 1975. Found at www.presidency.ucsb.edu.

44 Clyde Rapp to Donald Rumsfeld. Letter. January 14, 1975.

45 Rumsfeld. "Meeting with the President." Memorandum. January 21, 1975.

46 John Robert Greene, *The Limits of Power: The Nixon and Ford Administrations* (Bloomington, Indiana: Indiana University Press, 1992), 210.

47 Gerald R. Ford, *A Time to Heal: The Autobiography of Gerald R. Ford* (New York: Harper & Row, 1979), 204.

48 Ron Nessen, *Making the News, Taking the News: From NBC to the Ford White House* (Middletown, Connecticut: Wesleyan University Press, 2011), 127.

49 Ron Nessen, *Making the News, Taking the News: From NBC to the Ford White House* (Middletown, Connecticut: Wesleyan University Press, 2011), 98.

50 Yanek Mieczkowski, *Gerald Ford and the Challenges of the 1970s* (Lexington, Kentucky: The University Press of Kentucky, 2005), 194.

5. CHOOSING ROCKEFELLER

1 Rumsfeld. "Meeting with the President." Memorandum. December 19, 1974.

2 Rick Perlstein, *Nixonland: The Rise of a President and the Fracturing of America* (New York: Scribner, 2008), 304.

3 Ron Nessen, *Making the News, Taking the News: From NBC to the Ford White House* (Middletown, Connecticut: Wesleyan University Press, 2011), 79.

4 Rumsfeld. "1968 Nixon Meeting to Discuss Vice Presidential Nomination." Confidential Memorandum. August 8, 1968.

5 Rumsfeld. Memorandum. August 20, 1974.

6 Gerald R. Ford, *A Time to Heal: The Autobiography of Gerald R. Ford* (New York: Harper & Row, 1979), 107.

7 http://www.nytimes.com/1973/10/13/archives/move-is-surprise-house-gop-leader-would-be-the-40th-vice-president.html.

8 Rumsfeld. Memorandum 2. August 20, 1974.

9 Gerald R. Ford, *A Time to Heal: The Autobiography of Gerald R. Ford* (New York: Harper & Row, 1979), 29.

10 http://www.politico.com/story/2012/12/this-day-in-politics-085261.

11 http://www.nytimes.com/2006/12/31/nyregion/31rocky.html.

12 Gerald R. Ford, *A Time to Heal: The Autobiography of Gerald R. Ford* (New York: Harper & Row, 1979), 142.

13 Gerald R. Ford, *A Time to Heal: The Autobiography of Gerald R. Ford* (New York: Harper & Row, 1979), 118.

14 http://www.nytimes.com/2006/12/31/nyregion/31rocky.html.

15 http://www.nytimes.com/1974/08/21/archives/presidents-instincts-shaped -decision-poker-face-approach-remember.html.

16 Lee Edwards to Donald Rumsfeld. "President Ford and Conservatives." Memorandum. November 6, 1974.

17 http://www.nytimes.com/1974/08/21/archives/a-turn-in-gop-tide-nomination -of-rockefeller-completes-quick.html.

18 http://www.nytimes.com/1974/10/06/archives/rockefeller-gave-kissinger -50000-helped-2-others-he-denies-any.html?mcubz=3&_r=0.

19 http://www.nytimes.com/1974/10/13/archives/rockefeller-says-hes-responsible -on-goldberg-book-sends-telegram-to.html?mcubz=3.

20 http://www.nytimes.com/1974/10/13/archives/rockefeller-says-hes-responsible -on-goldberg-book-sends-telegram-to.html?mcubz=3.

21 Rumsfeld. "Meeting with the President." Memorandum. October 1, 1974.

22 Rumsfeld. "Meeting with the President." Memorandum. December 19, 1974.

23 Rumsfeld. "Meeting with the President." Memorandum. December 21, 1974.

24 Rumsfeld. "Meeting with the President." Memorandum. December 21, 1974

6. MORNING COATS AND WOLF FURS: FORD ABROAD

1 Rumsfeld. Memorandum for the File. November 20, 1974.

2 Gerald R. Ford, *A Time to Heal: The Autobiography of Gerald R. Ford* (New York: Harper & Row, 1979), 211.

3 John Herbers, "8-Day Asia Trip Will Be Ford's First Major Test in Personal Diplomacy." *New York Times*. November 17, 1974, 12.

4 Yanek Mieczkowski, *Gerald Ford and the Challenges of the 1970s* (Lexington, Kentucky: The University Press of Kentucky, 2005), 283.

5 Frank Cormier, "Ford Visits Japanese Tourist Sites." Associated Press. *Kentucky New Era*. November 21, 1974, 3A.

6 Richard Halloran, "Hirohito and Tanaka Greet Ford in Tokyo." *New York Times*. November 19, 1974, 3.

7 Peter J. Katzenstein, *Rethinking Japanese Security: Internal and External Dimensions* (New York: Routledge, 2008), 91.

8 Found in Tara John, "Here's What Happened During the First U.S. Presidential Trip to Japan." *Time*. May 24, 2016. time.com.

9 Richard Halloran, "Hirohito and Tanaka Greet Ford in Tokyo." *New York Times*. November 19, 1974, 1, 3.

10 John Roderick, "Ford's Tokyo Arrival Solves Historic Absurdity." Associated Press. *The Eagle* (Bryan, TX). November 18, 1974, 6.

11 Richard Halloran, "Hirohito and Tanaka Greet Ford in Tokyo." *New York Times*. November 19, 1974, 1.

12 Ron Nessen, *Making the News, Taking the News: From NBC to the Ford White House* (Middletown, Connecticut: Wesleyan University Press, 2011), 129.

13 Gerald R. Ford, *A Time to Heal: The Autobiography of Gerald R. Ford* (New York: Harper & Row, 1979), 210.

14 Yanek Mieczkowski, *Gerald Ford and the Challenges of the 1970s* (Lexington, Kentucky: The University Press of Kentucky, 2005), 43.

15 Ron Nessen, *Making the News, Taking the News: From NBC to the Ford White House* (Middletown, Connecticut: Wesleyan University Press, 2011), 129.

16 Gerald R. Ford, *A Time to Heal: The Autobiography of Gerald R. Ford* (New York: Harper & Row, 1979), 211.

17 Gerald R. Ford, *A Time to Heal: The Autobiography of Gerald R. Ford* (New York: Harper & Row, 1979), 210.

18 Gerald R. Ford, *A Time to Heal: The Autobiography of Gerald R. Ford* (New York: Harper & Row, 1979), 210.

19 Gerald R. Ford, *A Time to Heal: The Autobiography of Gerald R. Ford* (New York: Harper & Row, 1979), 211.

20 Gerald R. Ford, *A Time to Heal: The Autobiography of Gerald R. Ford* (New York: Harper & Row, 1979), 211.

21 Catherine Mayer, "Why Is Donald Rumsfeld on This Package of Spicy Peanuts?" *Time*. December 7, 2011. world.time.com.

22 "Top 10 Embarrassing Diplomatic Moments." *Time*. content.time.com.

23 Fox Butterfield, "President Tours Old Kyoto and Samples Some of Its Elegance." *New York Times*. November 22, 1974, 16.

24 Frank Cormier, "Ford Visits Japanese Tourist Sites." Associated Press. *Kentucky New Era*. November 21, 1974, 3A.

25 Fox Butterfield, "President Tours Old Kyoto and Samples Some of Its Elegance." *New York Times*. November 22, 1974, 16.

26 Gerald R. Ford, *A Time to Heal: The Autobiography of Gerald R. Ford* (New York: Harper & Row, 1979), 212.

27 "Geishas tend Ford dinner." Associated Press. *The Newark Advocate*. November 21, 1974, 34.

28 Frank Cormier, "Ford Visits Japanese Tourist Sites." Associated Press. *Kentucky New Era*. November 21, 1974, 3A.

29 John Herbers, "Ford and Tanaka Note Joint Tasks." *New York Times*. November 21, 1974, 18.

30 Richard Halloran, "Ford Is in Korea; Hails Close Link." *New York Times*. November 22, 1974, 16.

31 Gerald R. Ford, "Remarks on Arrival at Seoul, Republic of Korea." November 22, 1974. www.presidency.ucsb.edu.

32 Richard Halloran, "Ford Is in Korea; Hails Close Link." *New York Times*. November 22, 1974, 16. Aldo Beckman, "Thousands Cheer Ford Arrival in South Korea." *Chicago Tribune*. November 22, 1974, 18.

33 Rumsfeld. Memorandum for the File. November 21, 1974. Richard W. Johnson, "New Army Game." *Sports Illustrated*. July 21, 1975, 34.

34 Gerald R. Ford, *A Time to Heal: The Autobiography of Gerald R. Ford* (New York: Harper & Row, 1979), 212.

35 Gerald R. Ford, *A Time to Heal: The Autobiography of Gerald R. Ford* (New York: Harper & Row, 1979), 213.

36 Richard Halloran, "Ford Is in Korea; Hails Close Link." *New York Times*. November 22, 1974, 16.

37 Peter Lisagor, "Ford Flies to Orient." *The Pittsburgh Press*. November 17, 1974, 1.

38 Rumsfeld. Memorandum for the File. November 23, 1974.

39 Rumsfeld. Memorandum for the File. November 22, 1974.

40 Rumsfeld. Memorandum for the File. November 23, 1974.

41 https://www.bloomberg.com/view/articles/2013-08-23/the-secret-bromance-of-nixon-and-brezhnev.

42 Gerald R. Ford, *A Time to Heal: The Autobiography of Gerald R. Ford* (New York: Harper & Row, 1979), 213.

43 Rumsfeld. Memorandum for the File. November 22, 1974.

44 Gerald R. Ford, *A Time to Heal: The Autobiography of Gerald R. Ford* (New York: Harper & Row, 1979), 214.

45 Gerald R. Ford, *A Time to Heal: The Autobiography of Gerald R. Ford* (New York: Harper & Row, 1979), 214.

46 Gerald R. Ford, *A Time to Heal: The Autobiography of Gerald R. Ford* (New York: Harper & Row, 1979), 214.

47 Ron Nessen, *Making the News, Taking the News: From NBC to the Ford White House* (Middletown, Connecticut: Wesleyan University Press, 2011), 130.

48 Ron Nessen, *Making the News, Taking the News: From NBC to the Ford White House* (Middletown, Connecticut: Wesleyan University Press, 2011), 131.

49 Hedrick Smith, "Ford-Brezhnev Talks." November 22, 1974. *New York Times*, 7.

50 Rumsfeld. Memorandum for the File. November 22, 1974.

51 Gerald R. Ford, *A Time to Heal: The Autobiography of Gerald R. Ford* (New York: Harper & Row, 1979), 218.

52 Ron Nessen, *Making the News, Taking the News: From NBC to the Ford White House* (Middletown, Connecticut: Wesleyan University Press, 2011), 132.

53 Rumsfeld. "Meeting with the President." Memorandum. November 26, 1974.

54 Gerald R. Ford, *A Time to Heal: The Autobiography of Gerald R. Ford* (New York: Harper & Row, 1979), 219.

55 "Wolf-Skin Fur Coat." Gerald R. Ford Presidential Library & Museum. www.fordlibrarymuseum.gov.

56 Ron Nessen, *Making the News, Taking the News: From NBC to the Ford White House* (Middletown, Connecticut: Wesleyan University Press, 2011), 133.

57 Found in Mark J. Rozell, *The Press and the Ford Presidency* (Ann Arbor, Michigan: The University of Michigan Press, 1992), 78.

58 Rumsfeld. Memorandum for the File. November 20, 1974.

59 John Herbers, "Ford and Tanaka Note Joint Tasks." *New York Times*. November 21, 1974, 18. John Herbers, "Ford Asks Japan to Help Combat Economic Stress." *New York Times*. November 20, 1974, 3.

60 Rumsfeld. Memorandum for the File. November 20, 1974.

7. NEITHER CONFIRM NOR DENY:
THE *GLOMAR EXPLORER* AND THE CRISIS IN THE CIA

1 Rumsfeld. "Meeting with the President." Memorandum. March 19, 1975.

2 Rumsfeld. "Meeting with the President." Memorandum. March 19, 1975.

3 "Sunken Ship Deal by CIA, Hughes Told." *Los Angeles Times*. February 7, 1975, 1.

4 [Author excised], "Project Azorian: The Story of the *Hughes Glomar Explorer*." *Studies in Intelligence*. Secret. Excised copy. Fall 1985. Found at The National Security Archive, The George Washington University. nsarchive.gwu.edu.

5 [Author excised], "Project Azorian: The Story of the *Hughes Glomar Explorer*." *Studies in Intelligence*. Secret. Excised copy. Fall 1985. Found at The National Security Archive, The George Washington University. nsarchive.gwu.edu.

6 "Full text of 'Declassified Articles from the CIA Journal *Studies in Intelligence*.'" archive.org.

7 Rumsfeld. "Meeting with the President." Memorandum. August 10, 1974.

8 Seymour Hersh, "Huge CIA Operation Reported in U.S. Against Antiwar Forces, Other Dissidents in Nixon Years." *New York Times*. December 22, 1974, 1.

9 James A. Wilderotter. "CIA Matters." Memorandum. January 3, 1975. George Washington University, National Security Archive.

10 James A. Wilderotter. "CIA Matters." Memorandum. January 3, 1975. George Washington University, National Security Archive.

11 Rumsfeld. "Meeting with the President." Memorandum. February 7, 1975.

12 Rumsfeld. "Meeting with the President." Memorandum. February 7, 1975.

13 Rumsfeld. "Meeting with the President." Memorandum. March 17, 1975.

14 Rumsfeld. "Meeting with the President." Memorandum. October 7, 1974.

15 Rumsfeld. "Meeting with the President." Memorandum. January 3, 1975.

16 Rumsfeld. "Meeting with the President." Memorandum. January 3, 1975.

17 Rumsfeld. "Meeting with the President." Memorandum. January 4, 1975.

18 Rumsfeld. "Meeting with the President." Memorandum. January 3, 1975.

19 "Allegations of CIA Domestic Activities." Memorandum. January 3, 1975. Gerald R. Ford Presidential Library and Museum.

20 Rumsfeld. Memorandum. January 4, 1975.

21 Rumsfeld. Memorandum. January 4, 1975.

22 Rumsfeld. Memorandum, January 4, 1975.

23 Rumsfeld. Memorandum. January 4, 1975.

24 Rumsfeld. Memorandum. January 4, 1975.

25 Alex E. Hindman, *Gerald Ford and the Separation of Powers: Preserving the Constitutional Presidency in the Post-Watergate Period* (Lanham, Maryland: Lexington Books, 2017), 153.

26 Dick Cheney to Donald Rumsfeld. Memorandum. February 28, 1975.

27 Rumsfeld. "Meeting with the President." Memorandum. January 29, 1975.

28 "Sunken Ship Deal by CIA, Hughes Told." *Los Angeles Times*. February 7, 1975, 1.

29 Rumsfeld. "Meeting with the President." Memorandum. March 19, 1975.

30 Rumsfeld. "Meeting with the President." Memorandum. March 19, 1975.

31 Memorandum of Conversation; Ford Library, National Security Adviser, Box 8, January 23, 1975—Ford, Kissinger. history.state.gov.

32 Rumsfeld. "Meeting with the President." Memorandum. March 19, 1975.

33 Rumsfeld. "Meeting with the President." Memorandum. March 10, 1975.

34 Rumsfeld. "Meeting with the President." Memorandum. March 19, 1975.

35 Nicholas Daniloff, *Of Spies and Spokesmen: My Life as a Cold War Correspondent* (Columbia, Missouri: University of Missouri Press, 2008), 242.

36 Seymour Hersh, "CIA Salvage Ship Brought Up Part of Soviet Sub Lost in 1968, Failed to Raise Atom Missiles." *New York Times*. March 19, 1975, 1.

37 Rumsfeld. "Meeting with the President." Memorandum. March 20, 1975.

38 "Project AZORIAN." Central Intelligence Agency. November 21, 2012. www.cia.gov.

8. THE REAGAN SHADOW

1 Rumsfeld. "Meeting with the President." Memorandum. March 7, 1975.

2 Rumsfeld. "Meeting with the President." Memorandum. November 4, 1974.

3 Rumsfeld. "Meeting with the President." Memorandum. October 9, 1974.

4 Rumsfeld. "Meeting with the President." Memorandum. October 28, 1974.

5 Rumsfeld. "Meeting with the President." Memorandum. November 30, 1974, and December 1, 1974.

6 Rumsfeld. "Meeting with the President." Memorandum. November 4, 1974.

7 Rumsfeld. "Meeting with the President." Memorandum. February 3, 1975.

8 Rumsfeld. "Meeting with the President." Memorandum. February 6, 1975.

9 Rumsfeld. "Meeting with the President." Memorandum. February 18, 1975.

10 Rumsfeld. "Meeting with the President." Memorandum. February 17, 1975.

11 Rumsfeld. "Meeting with the President." Memorandum. February 17, 1975.

12 Rumsfeld. "Meeting with the President." Memorandum. October 25, 1974.

13 Rumsfeld. "Meeting with the President." Memorandum. March 24, 1975.

14 Rumsfeld. "Meeting with the President." Memorandum. April 1, 1975.

15 Richard Reeves, "G.O.P.: Ford Says It Is His, But It Isn't Yet." *New York Times*. March 16, 1975, 4.

16 https://www.fordlibrarymuseum.gov/library/exhibits/campaign/016800303 -001.pdf.

17 "Ronald Reagan Announcement for Presidential Candidacy." November 20, 1975. The Reagan Library. reaganlibrary.archives.gov.

18 Rumsfeld. "Meeting with the President." Memorandum. February 26, 1975.

19 Rumsfeld. "Meeting with the President." Memorandum. April 1, 1975.

9. THE FALL OF VIETNAM

1 Rumsfeld. "Meeting with the President." Memorandum. March 31, 1975.

2 Rumsfeld. "Meeting with the President." Memorandum. March 29, 1975.

3 Rumsfeld. "Meeting with the President." Memorandum. March 27, 1975.

4 Rumsfeld. "Meeting with the President." Memorandum. March 3, 1975.

5 Rumsfeld. "Meeting with the President." Memorandum. March 3, 1975.

6 Rumsfeld. "Meeting with the President." Memorandum. March 27, 1975.

7 Rumsfeld. "Meeting with the President." Memorandum. April 1, 1975.

8 Gerald R. Ford, "Remarks to the Veterans of Foreign Wars Annual Convention, Chicago, Illinois." Chicago, Illinois. August 19, 1974. www.presidency .ucsb.edu.

9 Gerald R. Ford, "Remarks Announcing a Program for the Return of Vietnam Era Draft Evaders and Military Deserters." Washington, D.C. September 16, 1974. www.presidency.ucsb.edu.

NOTES

10 Rumsfeld. "Meeting with the President." Memorandum. January 16, 1975.

11 Rumsfeld. "Meeting with the President." Memorandum. February 6, 1975.

12 Rumsfeld. "Meeting with the President." Memorandum. January 17, 1975.

13 Rumsfeld. "Meeting with the President." Memorandum. January 27, 1975.

14 Gerald R. Ford, "Special Message to the Congress Requesting Supplemental Assistance for the Republic of Vietnam and Cambodia." Washington, D.C. January 28, 1975. www.presidency.ucsb.edu.

15 Rumsfeld. "Meeting with the President." Memorandum. February 14, 1975.

16 Rumsfeld. "Meeting with the President." Memorandum. January 30, 1975.

17 Rumsfeld. "Meeting with the President." Memorandum. February 14, 1975.

18 John P. Murtha, *From Vietnam to 9/11: On the Front Lines of National Security* (University Park, Pennsylvania: Pennsylvania State University Press, 2006), 24–25.

19 Testimony before U.S. Senate Foreign Relations Committee, Hearings on Supplemental Assistance to Cambodia, February 24, 1975.

20 Rumsfeld. "Meeting with the President." Memorandum. April 1, 1975.

21 David Coleman, "NSC Meetings in the Nixon Administration." History in Pieces. historyinpieces.com.

22 Rumsfeld. "Meeting with the President." Memorandum. February 25, 1975.

23 Rumsfeld. "Meeting with the President." Memorandum. April 1, 1975.

24 Rumsfeld. "Meeting with the President." Memorandum. April 1, 1975.

25 Author Interview with Henry Kissinger, November 12, 2014.

26 Rumsfeld. "Meeting with the President." Memorandum. March 18, 1975.

27 Rumsfeld. "Meeting with the President." Memorandum. October 23, 1974.

28 David Kennerly, Interview with the author, May 19, 2015.

29 Gerald R. Ford, *A Time to Heal: The Autobiography of Gerald R. Ford* (New York: Harper & Row, 1979), 254.

30 Rumsfeld. "Meeting with the President." Memorandum. April 2, 1975.

31 Rumsfeld. "Meeting with the President." Memorandum. April 14, 1975.

32 Rumsfeld. "Meeting with the President." Memorandum. April 10, 1975.

33 Rumsfeld. "Meeting with the President." Memorandum. April 1, 1975.

34 Gerald R. Ford. "The President's News Conference." April 3, 1975. The American Presidency Project. www.presidency.ucsb.edu.

35 Gerald R. Ford, *A Time to Heal: The Autobiography of Gerald R. Ford* (New York: Harper & Row, 1979), 253.

36 Rumsfeld. "Meeting with the President." Memorandum. April 4, 1975.

37 Rumsfeld. "Meeting with the President." Memorandum. April 1, 1975.

38 Gerald R. Ford, et al. Joint Leadership Meeting. Memorandum. Early April 1975.

39 James Reston, "Jackson's Latest Scoop." *New York Times*. April 9, 1975, 43.

40 Ron Nessen to Donald Rumsfeld. "Some Thoughts." Memorandum. April 10, 1975.

41 Rumsfeld. "Meeting with the President." Memorandum. April 10, 1975.

42 Gerald R. Ford, *A Time to Heal: The Autobiography of Gerald R. Ford* (New York: Harper & Row, 1979), 255.

43 Rumsfeld. "Meeting with the President." Memorandum. April 14, 1975.

44 Gerald R. Ford, et al. "Cabinet Meeting." Memorandum. April 16, 1975.

45 Michael H. Hunt (ed.), *A Vietnam War Reader: A Documentary History from American and Vietnamese Perspectives* (Durham, North Carolina: The University of North Carolina Press, 2010), 190.

46 Rick Perlstein, *The Invisible Bridge: The Fall of Nixon and the Rise of Reagan* (New York: Simon & Schuster, 2014), 427.

47 Rumsfeld. "Meeting with the President." Memorandum. April 22, 1975.

48 Gerald R. Ford. "Address at a Tulane University Convocation." Tulane University, New Orleans, Louisiana. April 23, 1975. The American Presidency Project. www.presidency.ucsb.edu.

49 Richard L. Madden, "Ford Says Indochina War Is Finished for America." *New York Times*. April 24, 1975, 1.

50 Rumsfeld. "Meeting with the President." Memorandum. April 24, 1975.

51 Rumsfeld. "Meeting with the President." Memorandum. April 24, 1975.

52 Rumsfeld. "Meeting with the President." Memorandum. April 24, 1975.

53 Rumsfeld. "Meeting with the President." Memorandum. April 30, 1975.

54 Rumsfeld. "Meeting with the President." Memorandum. April 30, 1975.

55 Ron Nessen, *It Sure Looks Different From the Inside* (Chicago: Playboy Press, 1978), 113.

56 Rumsfeld. "Meeting with the President." Memorandum. April 30, 1975.

57 Gerald R. Ford, *A Time to Heal: The Autobiography of Gerald R. Ford* (New York: Harper & Row, 1979), 257.

58 Rumsfeld. "Meeting with the President." Memorandum. April 25, 1975.

59 Rumsfeld. "Meeting with the President." Memorandum. April 14, 1975.

60 Rumsfeld. "Meeting with the President." Memorandum. April 14, 1975.

61 Rumsfeld. "Meeting with the President." Memorandum. April 25, 1975.

62 Gerald R. Ford, *A Time to Heal: The Autobiography of Gerald R. Ford* (New York: Harper & Row, 1979), 257.

63 Rumsfeld. "Meeting with the President." Memorandum. May 1, 1975.

10. FORD AT THE HELM: THE SS *MAYAGUEZ* CRISIS

1 Rumsfeld. "Meeting with the President." Memorandum. May 12, 1975.

2 Gerald R. Ford, *A Time to Heal: The Autobiography of Gerald R. Ford* (New York: Harper & Row, 1979), 275.

3   Rumsfeld. "Meeting with the President." Memorandum. July 12, 1975.

4   Rumsfeld. "Meeting with the President." Memorandum. June 23, 1975.

5   Rumsfeld. "Meeting with the President." Memorandum. May 12, 1975.

6   Rumsfeld. "Meeting with the President." Memorandum. May 12, 1975.

7   Rumsfeld. "Meeting with the President." Memorandum. May 12, 1975.

8   Rumsfeld. "Meeting with the President." Memorandum. May 12, 1975.

9   Rumsfeld. "Meeting with the President." Memorandum. May 12, 1975.

10 Gerald R. Ford, *A Time to Heal: The Autobiography of Gerald R. Ford* (New York: Harper & Row, 1979), 276.

11 Rumsfeld. "Meeting with the President." Memorandum. May 12, 1975.

12 Rumsfeld. "Meeting with the President." Memorandum. May 12, 1975.

13 Rumsfeld. "Meeting with the President." Memorandum. May 12, 1975.

14 Rumsfeld. "Meeting with the President." Memorandum. May 12, 1975.

15 Rumsfeld. "Meeting with the President." Memorandum. May 12, 1975.

16 Donald Rumsfeld, *Known and Unknown: A Memoir* (New York: Sentinel, 2011), 211.

17 Rumsfeld. "Meeting with the President." Memorandum. May 12, 1975.

18 Rumsfeld. "Meeting with the President." Memorandum. May 13, 1975.

19 Rumsfeld. "Meeting with the President." Memorandum. May 13, 1975.

20 Rumsfeld. "Meeting with the President." Memorandum. May 13, 1975.

21 Rumsfeld. "Meeting with the President." Memorandum. May 13, 1975.

22 Rumsfeld. "Meeting with the President." Memorandum. May 13, 1975.

23 Rumsfeld. "Meeting with the President." Memorandum. May 13, 1975.

24 Donald Rumsfeld to Gerald R. Ford. "Cambodia." Memorandum. May 14, 1975.

25 Rumsfeld. "Meeting with the President." Memorandum. May 13, 1975.

26 Rumsfeld. "Meeting with the President." Memorandum. May 13, 1975.

27 Rumsfeld. "Meeting with the President." Memorandum. May 13, 1975.

28 Rumsfeld. "Meeting with the President." Memorandum. May 13, 1975.

29 Gerald R. Ford, *A Time to Heal: The Autobiography of Gerald R. Ford* (New York: Harper & Row, 1979), 278.

30 Gerald R. Ford, *A Time to Heal: The Autobiography of Gerald R. Ford* (New York: Harper & Row, 1979), 278.

31 Rumsfeld. "Meeting with the President." Memorandum. May 14, 1975.

32 Gerald R. Ford, *A Time to Heal: The Autobiography of Gerald R. Ford* (New York: Harper & Row, 1979), 279.

33 Rumsfeld. "Meeting with the President." Memorandum. May 14, 1975.

34 Rumsfeld. "Meeting with the President." Memorandum. May 14, 1975.

35 Gerald R. Ford, *A Time to Heal: The Autobiography of Gerald R. Ford* (New York: Harper & Row, 1979), 282.

36 Rumsfeld. "Meeting with the President." Memorandum. May 14, 1975.

37 Gerald R. Ford, *A Time to Heal: The Autobiography of Gerald R. Ford* (New York: Harper & Row, 1979), 283.

38 Gerald R. Ford, *A Time to Heal: The Autobiography of Gerald R. Ford* (New York: Harper & Row, 1979), 283.

39 Rumsfeld. "Meeting with the President." Memorandum. May 16, 1975.

40 Rumsfeld. "Meeting with the President." Memorandum. May 16, 1975.

41 Rumsfeld. "Meeting with the President." Memorandum. May 20, 1975.

42 Rumsfeld. "Meeting with the President." Memorandum. May 20, 1975.

43 Rumsfeld. "Meeting with the President." Memorandum. May 20, 1975.

44 Jeffrey M. Jones, "Gerald Ford Retrospective." Gallup. December 29, 2006. http://www.gallup.com/poll/23995/gerald-ford-retrospective.aspx.

11. COMMANDER IN CHIEF

1 Rumsfeld. "Meeting with the President." Memorandum. May 9, 1975.

2 Gerald R. Ford to Henry Kissinger. Letter. January 30, 1975.

3 Severn Palydowycz, Kenneth Wanio, and John Burtyk to Gerald R. Ford. Letter. October 3, 1975.

4 Richard Lewis, "Space age: end of act one." *New Scientist*. July 31, 1975, 265.

5 Rumsfeld. "Meeting with the President." Memorandum. June 23, 1975.

6 Rumsfeld. "Meeting with the President." Memorandum. June 27, 1975.

7 Rumsfeld. "Meeting with the President." Memorandum. October 9, 1975.

8 Rumsfeld. "Meeting with the President." Memorandum. July 9, 1975.

9 Rumsfeld. "Meeting with the President." Memorandum. July 9, 1975.

10 Rumsfeld. "Meeting with the President." Memorandum. April 30, 1975.

11 Dick Cheney to Donald Rumsfeld. "Solzhenitsyn." Memorandum. July 8, 1975.

12 http://www.nytimes.com/1975/07/17/archives/kissinger-sees-perils-in-solzhenitsyns-views-secretary-says-meeting.html.

13 http://www.nytimes.com/1975/07/18/archives/ford-now-trying-to-arrange-solzhenitsyn-meeting.html.

14 http://www.nytimes.com/1975/07/18/archives/ford-now-trying-to-arrange-solzhenitsyn-meeting.html.

15 Gerald R. Ford, *A Time to Heal: The Autobiography of Gerald R. Ford* (New York: Harper & Row, 1979), 298.

16 Rumsfeld. "Meeting with the President." Memorandum. July 17, 1975.

17 http://www.nytimes.com/1975/07/12/archives/notes-on-people-congress-urged-to-invite-writer.html.

18 Rumsfeld. "Meeting with the President." Memorandum. July 9, 1975.

19 Rumsfeld. "Meeting with the President." Memorandum. July 11, 1975.

20 Rumsfeld. "Meeting with the President." Memorandum. July 11, 1975.

21 Rumsfeld. "Meeting with the President." Memorandum. March 6, 1975.

22 Rumsfeld. "Meeting with the President." Memorandum. February 27, 1975.

23 Rumsfeld. "Meeting with the President." Memorandum. July 23, 1975.

24 Rumsfeld. "Meeting with the President." Memorandum. July 23, 1975.

25 Gerald R. Ford, *A Time to Heal: The Autobiography of Gerald R. Ford* (New York: Harper & Row, 1979), 298.

26 Ron Nessen, *Making the News, Taking the News: From NBC to the Ford White House* (Middletown, Connecticut: Wesleyan University Press, 2011), 178.

27 Daniel J. Sargent, *A Superpower Transformed: The Remaking of American Foreign Relations in the 1970s* (New York: Oxford University Press, 2015), 219.

28 https://www.bostonglobe.com/ideas/2015/06/06/how-handshake-helsinki -helped-end-cold-war/YggtezKJGdM7d7jv8uEy5I/story.html.

29 Rumsfeld. "Meeting with the President." Memorandum. February 16, 1976.

30 Gerald R. Ford, *A Time to Heal: The Autobiography of Gerald R. Ford* (New York: Harper & Row, 1979), 299–300.

31 Rumsfeld. "Meeting with the President." Memorandum. February 16, 1976.

32 Rumsfeld. "Meeting with the President." Memorandum. February 15, 1976.

33 Rumsfeld. "Meeting with the President." Memorandum. February 16, 1976.

34 Rumsfeld. "Meeting with the President." Memorandum. January 8, 1976.

35 Rumsfeld. "Meeting with the President." Memorandum. July 18, 1975.

36 Rumsfeld. "Meeting with the President." Memorandum. July 21, 1975.

37 Rumsfeld. "Meeting with the President." Memorandum. July 21, 1975.

38 Rumsfeld. "Meeting with the President." Memorandum. January 2, 1976.

39 Rumsfeld. "Meeting with the President." Memorandum. January 2, 1976.

40 Rumsfeld. "Meeting with the President." Memorandum. January 2, 1976.

41 Rumsfeld. "Meeting with the President." Memorandum. January 14, 1976.

42 Rumsfeld. "Meeting with the President." Memorandum. January 19, 1976.

43 Rumsfeld. "Meeting with the President." Memorandum. January 19, 1976.

12. ASSASSINS' TARGET

1 Rumsfeld. "Meeting with the President." Memorandum. August 26, 1975.

2 Rumsfeld. "Meeting with the President." Memorandum. August 29, 1975.

3 https://www.cbsnews.com/news/the-remarkable-mrs-ford/.

4 Rumsfeld. "Meeting with the President." Memorandum. August 9, 1975.

5 Rumsfeld. "Meeting with the President." Memorandum. August 27, 1975.

6 Rumsfeld. "Meeting with the President." Memorandum. March 3, 1975.

7 "Ford Assassination Attempts Recalled." Associated Press. *Washington Post.* December 27, 2006.

8 http://www.nytimes.com/1975/09/06/archives/ford-safe-as-guard-seizes-a
-gun-woman-pointed-at-him-on-coast.html.

9 Rumsfeld. "Meeting with the President." Memorandum. September 5, 1975.

10 http://www.sacbee.com/news/local/history/article2596754.html.

11 Rumsfeld. "Meeting with the President." Memorandum. September 11, 1975.

12 Ron Nessen, *Making the News, Taking the News: From NBC to the Ford White House* (Middletown, Connecticut: Wesleyan University Press, 2011), 181.

13 Rumsfeld. "Meeting with the President." Memorandum. September 22, 1975.

14 http://www.nytimes.com/1975/09/24/archives/man-who-deflected-gun-asserts
-im-not-a-hero.html.

15 http://www.nytimes.com/1975/09/24/archives/man-who-deflected-gun-asserts
-im-not-a-hero.html.

16 http://www.nytimes.com/1975/12/21/archives/for-sara-moore-brilliant-roles
-enriched-a-drab-life.html.

17 Ron Nessen, *Making the News, Taking the News: From NBC to the Ford White House* (Middletown, Connecticut: Wesleyan University Press, 2011), 182.

18 Rumsfeld. "Meeting with the President." Memorandum. September 23, 1975.

19 Rumsfeld. "Meeting with the President." Memorandum. September 23, 1975.

20 http://www.nytimes.com/1975/10/01/archives/miss-moore-tried-to-call-ford
-guards-five-times-miss-moore-tried-to.html.

21 http://www.nytimes.com/1975/09/24/archives/ford-resists-growing-pressure
-to-curb-his-public-appearances-guard.html.

22 Rumsfeld. "Meeting with the President." Memorandum. September 22, 1975.

23 Rumsfeld. "Meeting with the President." Memorandum. September 24, 1975.

24 Rumsfeld. "Meeting with the President." Memorandum. September 26, 1975.

25 Rumsfeld. "Meeting with the President." Memorandum. September 23, 1975.

26 Ron Nessen, *Making the News, Taking the News: From NBC to the Ford White House* (Middletown, Connecticut: Wesleyan University Press, 2011), 184.

13. THE (SO-CALLED) HALLOWEEN MASSACRE

1 Donald Rumsfeld and Richard Cheney. Memorandum for the President. October 24, 1975.

2 Rumsfeld. "Meeting with the President." Memorandum. October 22, 1975.

3 Rumsfeld. "Meeting with the President." Memorandum. October 22, 1975.

4 Rumsfeld. "Meeting with the President." Memorandum. June 11, 1975.

5 Rumsfeld. "Meeting with the President." Memorandum. September 24, 1975.

6 Gerald R. Ford, *A Time to Heal: The Autobiography of Gerald R. Ford* (New York: Harper & Row, 1979), 320.

7 Gerald R. Ford, *A Time to Heal: The Autobiography of Gerald R. Ford* (New York: Harper & Row, 1979), 323.

8 Samuel Kernel and Samuel L. Popkin (eds.), *Chief of Staff: Twenty-Five Years of Managing the Presidency* (Berkeley: University of California Press, 1986), 175.

9 Rumsfeld. "Meeting with the President." Memorandum. March 4, 1975.

10 Rumsfeld. "Meeting with the President." Memorandum. August 5, 1975.

11 Rumsfeld. "Meeting with the President." Memorandum. February 1, 1975.

12 Rumsfeld. "Meeting with the President." Memorandum. April 28, 1975.

13 Rumsfeld. "Meeting with the President." Memorandum. July 10, 1975.

14 Rumsfeld. "Meeting with the President." Memorandum. October 22, 1975.

15 Rumsfeld. "Meeting with the President." Memorandum. September 17, 1975.

16 Rumsfeld. "Meeting with the President." Memorandum. October 22, 1975.

14. RUMBLE FROM THE RIGHT

1 Rumsfeld. "Meeting with the President." Memorandum. April 6, 1976.

2 Rumsfeld. "Meeting with the President." Memorandum. May 21, 1975.

3 Rumsfeld. "Meeting with the President." Memorandum. June 17, 1975.

4 Bob Teeter to Dick Cheney, "Analysis of Early Research." November 12, 1975. https://www.fordlibrarymuseum.gov/library/exhibits/campaign/002700157-001.pdf.

5 Gerald R. Ford: "The President's News Conference." February 17, 1976. http://www.presidency.ucsb.edu/ws/?pid=5569.

6 Rumsfeld. "Meeting with the President." Memorandum. February 18, 1976.

7 http://www.nytimes.com/1976/02/21/archives/reagan-discloses-ford-cabinet-bid-countering-rivals-attack-on-him.html.

8 http://www.nytimes.com/1976/02/21/archives/reagan-discloses-ford-cabinet-bid-countering-rivals-attack-on-him.html?_r=0.

9 http://www.nytimes.com/1976/02/21/archives/reagan-discloses-ford-cabinet-bid-countering-rivals-attack-on-him.html?_r=0.

10 http://www.nytimes.com/1976/02/21/archives/nixon-trip-revives-issue-vexing-to-ford-in-primary-nixon-trip.html.

11 Bob Teeter to Dick Cheney, "Analysis of Early Research," November 12, 1975. https://www.fordlibrarymuseum.gov/library/exhibits/campaign/002700157-001.pdf.

12 "Ronald Reagan Announcement for Presidential Candidacy." November 20, 1975. https://reaganlibrary.archives.gov/archives/reference/11.20.75.html.

13 Gerald R. Ford. "Address in Minneapolis Before the Annual Convention of the American Legion." August 19, 1975. http://www.presidency.ucsb.edu/ws/?pid=5174.

14 Gerald R. Ford. "Address in Minneapolis Before the Annual Convention of the American Legion." August 19, 1975. http://www.presidency.ucsb.edu /ws/?pid=5174.

15 Gerald R. Ford. "Address in Minneapolis Before the Annual Convention of the American Legion." August 19, 1975. http://www.presidency.ucsb.edu /ws/?pid=5174.

16 http://www.nytimes.com/1975/12/29/archives/detentes-supporters-under-fire -in-the-us-faced-with-a-formidable.html?nytmobile=0.

17 http://www.nytimes.com/1975/12/29/archives/detentes-supporters-under-fire -in-the-us-faced-with-a-formidable.html?nytmobile=0.

18 Gerald R. Ford: "Interview for an NBC News Program on American Foreign Policy," January 3, 1976. http://www.presidency.ucsb.edu/ws/?pid=6132.

19 Rumsfeld. "Meeting with the President." Memorandum. February 24, 1976.

20 Gerald R. Ford, *A Time to Heal: The Autobiography of Gerald R. Ford* (New York: Harper & Row, 1979), 367.

21 Gerald R. Ford, *A Time to Heal: The Autobiography of Gerald R. Ford* (New York: Harper & Row, 1979), 367.

22 Rumsfeld. "Meeting with the President." Memorandum. February 27, 1976.

23 Rumsfeld. "Meeting with the President." Memorandum. February 27, 1976.

24 Rumsfeld. "Meeting with the President." Memorandum. February 27, 1976.

25 Rumsfeld. Memorandum for the File. January 30, 1976.

26 http://www.nytimes.com/1976/03/04/archives/reagan-to-press-attacks-on -ford-he-will-stress-failures-of-us.html?_r=0.

27 Rumsfeld. "Meeting with the President." Memorandum. March 4, 1976.

28 Gerald R. Ford: "Remarks and a Question-and-Answer Session at the Everett McKinley Dirksen Forum in Peoria," March 5, 1976. http://www.presidency .ucsb.edu/ws/?pid=5672.

29 http://www.nytimes.com/2008/03/15/opinion/15clymer.html.

30 https://history.state.gov/milestones/1977-1980/panama-canal.

31 Rumsfeld. "Meeting with the President." Memorandum. February 18, 1975.

32 Rumsfeld. "Meeting with the President." Memorandum. February 18, 1975.

33 http://www.politico.com/magazine/story/2016/04/1976-convention-oral -history-213793?paginate=false.

34 Rumsfeld. Memorandum of Conversation. March 29, 1976.

35 Rumsfeld. Memorandum for the File. January 6, 1976.

36 Rumsfeld. "Meeting with the President." Memorandum. April 1, 1976.

37 http://www.nytimes.com/1976/04/01/archives/reagan-says-kissinger-yields-u -s-leadership-to-russians.html?_r=0.

38 Rumsfeld. "Meeting with the President." Memorandum. April 1, 1976.

39 Rumsfeld. "Meeting with the President." Memorandum. April 6, 1976.
40 Rumsfeld. "Meeting with the President." Memorandum. April 6, 1976.

15. LAST CAMPAIGN

1 Rumsfeld. "Meeting with the President." Memorandum. September 8, 1976.
2 https://apnews.com/1a98fa0647824cb29100144deed02855/76-window-ugliness
   -gop-contested-convention.
3 http://www.cbsnews.com/videos/cary-grant-introduces-betty-ford-at-the
   -1976-gop-convention/.
4 James Sterba, "Visiting Diplomats Get New Idea of U.S.," *New York Times*,
   August 20, 1976.
5 "Giant Elephants Flop As Gimmick," *Pittsburgh Post-Gazette*, August 17, 1976.
6 http://www.gallup.com/poll/23995/gerald-ford-retrospective.aspx.
7 Gerald R. Ford, *A Time to Heal: The Autobiography of Gerald R. Ford* (New
   York: Harper & Row, 1979), 397.
8 https://www.nytimes.com/politics/first-draft/2016/04/27/ted-cruzs-early-vice
   -presidential-pick-has-echoes-of-ronald-reagan/.
9 Gerald R. Ford, *A Time to Heal: The Autobiography of Gerald R. Ford* (New
   York: Harper & Row, 1979), 394.
10 Gerald R. Ford, *A Time to Heal: The Autobiography of Gerald R. Ford* (New
   York: Harper & Row, 1979), 394.
11 Gerald R. Ford, *A Time to Heal: The Autobiography of Gerald R. Ford* (New
   York: Harper & Row, 1979), 348.
12 http://archives.chicagotribune.com/1976/07/28/page/5/article/reagan-gambles
   -all-in-schweiker-choice.
13 Gerald R. Ford, *A Time to Heal: The Autobiography of Gerald R. Ford* (New
   York: Harper & Row, 1979), 395.
14 There was another name that was decidedly not on my list but which the
   President had decided to include on his: my own. The same day I turned in
   my list of possible running mates to the President, I received a call from Phil
   Buchan, the White House Counsel, informing me that I was being considered.
   Around the same time, I was confronted with a matter more urgent than the
   possibility of the vice presidency. Some weeks before the convention, I discovered a visible lump on my throat. Shortly before, I had heard from my mother
   about a newspaper article on the recent discovery of tumors in adults who had
   undergone radiation therapy for tonsillitis as children, as I had. When I first
   went to the White House physician's office to get checked out, they didn't find
   anything. But now, with the big lump erupting in my neck while this was
   still fresh in my mind, I wasn't taking any chances. On August 6, I met with

another doctor and learned that I was going to have to have surgery to remove a tumor on my thyroid. The first available date—August 16—was the day the convention would be kicking off in Kansas City. I concluded my chances of being selected had dropped significantly, not least because we wouldn't know if the bulge in my neck was cancerous until after the convention. Fortunately, it wasn't.

15 Adam Wren, "'It Was Riotous': An Oral History of the GOP's Last Open Convention," *Politico*, April 5, 2016. http://www.politico.com/magazine/story/2016/04/1976-convention-oral-history-213793.

16 Quoted in Adam Wren, "'It Was Riotous': An Oral History of the GOP's Last Open Convention," *Politico*, April 5, 2016. http://www.politico.com/magazine/story/2016/04/1976-convention-oral-history-213793.

17 This wasn't the first time during the campaign season that Rockefeller drew unwanted headlines. At one point, while addressing a southern Republican state chairman, Rockefeller snapped, "You got me out, you sons of bitches. Now get off your ass!"

18 Quoted in Adam Wren, "'It Was Riotous': An Oral History of the GOP's Last Open Convention," *Politico*, April 5, 2016. http://www.politico.com/magazine/story/2016/04/1976-convention-oral-history-213793.

19 Quoted in Adam Wren, "'It Was Riotous': An Oral History of the GOP's Last Open Convention," *Politico*, April 5, 2016. http://www.politico.com/magazine/story/2016/04/1976-convention-oral-history-213793.

20 Quoted in Adam Wren, "'It Was Riotous': An Oral History of the GOP's Last Open Convention," *Politico*, April 5, 2016. http://www.politico.com/magazine/story/2016/04/1976-convention-oral-history-213793.

21 Gerald R. Ford, *A Time to Heal: The Autobiography of Gerald R. Ford* (New York: Harper & Row, 1979), 398.

22 Quoted in Adam Wren, "'It Was Riotous': An Oral History of the GOP's Last Open Convention," *Politico*, April 5, 2016. http://www.politico.com/magazine/story/2016/04/1976-convention-oral-history-213793.

23 http://www.newsweek.com/delegate-battle-1976-reagan-almost-unseated-ford-449843.

24 Gerald R. Ford, *A Time to Heal: The Autobiography of Gerald R. Ford* (New York: Harper & Row, 1979), 400.

25 Gerald R. Ford: "Remarks in Kansas City Upon Accepting the 1976 Republican Presidential Nomination," August 19, 1976. http://www.presidency.ucsb.edu/ws/?pid=6281.

26 "Republican National Convention." August 19, 1976. Reagan Library. https://reaganlibrary.archives.gov/archives/reference/8.19.76.html.

27 "Republican National Convention." August 19, 1976. Reagan Library. https://reaganlibrary.archives.gov/archives/reference/8.19.76.html.

28 https://www.fordlibrarymuseum.gov/library/exhibits/campaign/020500224 -001.pdf.

29 Gerald R. Ford, *A Time to Heal: The Autobiography of Gerald R. Ford* (New York: Harper & Row, 1979), 377.

30 Rumsfeld. Meeting with the President. Memorandum. August 30, 1976.

31 Rumsfeld. Meeting with the President. Memorandum. September 7, 1976.

32 Rumsfeld. Meeting with the President. Memorandum. September 7, 1976.

33 Rumsfeld. Meeting with the President. Memorandum. September 30, 1976.

34 Rumsfeld. Meeting with the President. Memorandum. September 30, 1976.

35 Rumsfeld. Meeting with the President. Memorandum. September 30, 1976.

36 Rumsfeld. Meeting with the President. Memorandum. September 17, 1976.

37 Press Conference, October 6, 1976. https://www.fordlibrarymuseum.gov/library /exhibits/campaign/020500300-001.pdf.

38 http://www.nytimes.com/1976/10/08/archives/ethnic-groups-score-ford-on -europe-view-many-are-astonished-by.html?_r=0.

39 http://www.pbs.org/newshour/spc/character/glossaries/carter.html.

40 http://www.nytimes.com/1976/10/22/archives/ford-and-carter-forces-dispute -gop-ad-showing-playboy-cover.html.

41 https://www.fordlibrarymuseum.gov/library/exhibits/campaign/002400398 -001.pdf.

42 Rumsfeld. Meeting with the President. Memorandum. November 3, 1976.

43 Gerald R. Ford, *A Time to Heal: The Autobiography of Gerald R. Ford* (New York: Harper & Row, 1979), 435.

44 Gerald R. Ford, *A Time to Heal: The Autobiography of Gerald R. Ford* (New York: Harper & Row, 1979), 436.

EPILOGUE

1 https://www.upi.com/Navy-christens-worlds-most-expensive-warship-the -Gerald-R-Ford/70081384109591.

2 http://www.weeklystandard.com/the-good-ship-gerald-ford/article/767149.

3 https://npgallery.nps.gov/pdfhost/docs/NHLS/Text/85003048.pdf.

Acknowledgments

When President Ford knew that his life was drawing to a close, he called on some of his associates to deliver his eulogy. One was the man who defeated him for the presidency in 1976 and who had since become a friend, former President Jimmy Carter. Ford's request of his successor was, of course, true to form for a gentleman who instinctively always put friendship over politics.

Among the other friends he called on the phone to ask if they would deliver eulogies at his funeral services were Dick Cheney, Henry Kissinger, and me, each of whom had worked closely with him during his presidency. This was one of the honors of my life, and I thought carefully about what I might say as Gerald R. Ford moved into history. Yet even on the day of his service, as I gazed out at the many who had gathered to mourn him and shared the grief of millions of Americans who never had the pleasure of knowing Gerald R. Ford personally, I knew somewhere in the back of my mind that I hadn't finished offering President Ford the tribute I felt he deserved. With this book, these many years later, I finally complete that mission—a mission that began when we first met back in November 1962 in the U.S. House of Representatives, now more than half a century ago.

To that end, it is appropriate to begin these acknowledgments by mentioning him first, that very special man, along with his loving wife, Betty, and their children and grandchildren. Gerald R. Ford and his family answered the call of history when Americans needed them most, and this country will never be able to or need to fully repay that debt.

In putting this book together, I relied on a talented group of individuals. I first met Matt Latimer and Keith Urbahn when they were young speechwriters at the Department of Defense. I have amused them on occasion, always with a smile, by suggesting that back then they were young lumps of clay who have been molded and shaped over the years to become the models of excellence we benefit from today. I am deeply grateful to them for their help and patience on this project.

Matt, without you, this book would not exist. Beyond being a friend, you are an outstanding writer, and I am deeply indebted to you for making it all happen. Matt pored over my archive, including the nearly two thousand action memos I dictated during Gerald Ford's 895-day presidency, and has skillfully extracted the essence of what took place during that historic and unprecedented period in our country's history. Matt took my cryptic, unedited memos that had been dictated in real time and for an entirely different purpose and has helped to weave them into the story of the Ford presidency.

Keith, my thanks for your assistance in many ways, but particularly for your leadership at Javelin, the fine company you and Matt founded. I salute the first-rate team you have assembled at Javelin, including those who have also helped on this book: Dylan Colligan, Dr. Jonathan Bronitsky, and Vanessa Santos. The name Javelin, incidentally, was adopted by Keith from the Secret Service code name that had been assigned to my wife, Joyce, during my time as Chief of Staff in the Ford White House.

This project proves the truth of the phrase "It takes a village." We have been ably supported by my outstanding personal staff, which included my enormously talented Chief of Staff, Remley Johnson, who has ably assisted in this project in too many ways to recount. She has done it all with skill and unfailing good humor. And my thanks also to Linda Shepard, Rebecca Robison, and Abigail Hundley, each of whom has helped to keep this project on track in a variety of ways, by poring over the literally hundreds of memos from my meetings with Gerald R. Ford over some five decades, assisting with photographs, correspondence, and other material, providing useful suggestions and edits, or helping my schedule stay in order so that we could complete this enjoyable project.

My appreciation also to the many people who graciously took the time to recount for me their recollections of Gerald Ford, whom they had known well, including Fred Barnes, Red Cavaney, Secretary Bill Coleman, Senator Robert Dole, Dr. Alan Greenspan, Secretary Carla Hills, Jerry Jones, Dr. Henry Kissinger, Tom Korologos, Jack Marsh, David Mathews, Ron Nessen, Terry O'Donnell, Judge Larry Silberman, Ron Walker, Brenda Williams, and Frank Zarb.

I owe a very special thanks to David Hume Kennerly, the Pulitzer Prize–winning former White House photographer, who generously assisted and allowed us to select from the thousands of photos he took as Gerald Ford's official photographer and friend.

A number of people were of special assistance in reading and commenting on drafts of this book and offering insights and criticisms have helped to improve it. My thanks to former Congressman Pete Biester, who had served with Gerald Ford and me in the Congress back in the 1960s, and my friend and former college classmate the distinguished historian Dr. Jean Edward Smith.

Two of those readers were particularly valuable, since they shared a great many of the experiences recounted in this book. They are our longtime friends former Vice President Dick Cheney and his wife, Dr. Lynne Cheney, each of whom are, of course, accomplished authors many times over. Dick's role in the Ford administration, first as my deputy White House Chief of Staff and then as my seasoned and enormously talented successor, was central to the success of President Ford's administration. Dick was there every day with his always steady, skillful, and good-humored presence. Dick, thank you for your consistently sound advice, your encouragement, and your greatly valued friendship over these many years. Our country has been better for your long service in the Congress, White House, Cabinet, and the Vice Presidency.

My thanks also to the Gerald R. Ford Presidential Library and Museum for their assistance in this project, and importantly in their daily efforts to assure that the memory of President Ford is kept alive for the coming generations of Americans.

I want to also thank the team at Simon & Schuster and in particular my editor, Mitchell Ivers, who in addition to his enthusiasm for this project provided a number of thoughtful and helpful suggestions. My appreciation as well to President and Publisher Jon Karp, Richard Rohrer, Cary Goldstein, Caitlyn Reuss, Hannah Brown, Kristen Lemire, Al Madocs, and Jackie Seow.

Despite the many hundreds of hours that have been put into the drafting, redrafting, researching, and editing of this book, it is perhaps inevitable that some errors may have crept into this book and certainly some differences in recollections. As regrettable as it is to accept this reality, the responsibility for any errors is mine.

My wife, Joyce Rumsfeld, played the role I've come to rely on during our journey since our time in high school in the 1940s and our now more than sixty-three years of marriage—advisor, inner gyroscope, and friend. Our children, Valerie, Marcy, and Nick, have been with us every step of the way through our years of public service and they each have made fascinating but occasionally challenging times easier.

The effort involved in recounting this story, most important from studying my roughly two-thousand hastily dictated and never-edited memos from those years now long ago, has brought to mind memories of an especially challenging period in our nation's history. I like to think that this undertaking has been blessed with the spirit of Gerald Ford himself, and especially with his optimism, his steady hand, and his love of country. His belief in America, and in Americans, is what really helped the center hold when it counted.

It is fitting then, as President Ford closed out his memoirs, reflecting back on the day he departed Washington, D.C., after his tough election loss, that his words were in keeping with that spirit of hope and possibility: "The sun was shining brightly. I couldn't see a cloud anywhere, and I felt glad about that."

Rest in peace, Mr. President. And thank you.

List of Illustrations

1. Gerald Ford, Ann Arbor, Michigan, 1933 (Courtesy Gerald R. Ford Library)

2. Gerald Ford, Betty Ford, Jack, Steve, Susan, Michael, Gayle, Oval Office, August 9, 1974 (Courtesy Gerald R. Ford Library, White House photograph by Moore)

3. Gerald Ford, Don Rumsfeld, John O. Marsh, Bill Scranton, Clay Whitehead, Phil Buchen, Sen. Robert Griffin, Oval Office, August 15, 1974 (Courtesy Gerald R. Ford Library, White House photograph by David Hume Kennerly)

4. Bryce Harlow, Don Rumsfeld, Henry Kissinger, Cabinet Room, August 15, 1974 (Courtesy Gerald R. Ford Library, White House photograph by David Hume Kennerly)

5. Gerald Ford, Terry O'Donnell, Air Force One, August 19, 1974 (Courtesy Gerald R. Ford Library, White House photograph by David Hume Kennerly)

6. Gerald Ford, Alan Greenspan, Ayn Rand, Frank O'Connor, Oval Office, September 4, 1974 (Courtesy Gerald R. Ford Library, White House photograph by David Hume Kennerly)

7. Sen. J. William Fulbright (D-AR) & Sen. Hugh Scott (R-PA), Gerald Ford, White House Second Floor Family Dining Room, September 26, 1974 (Courtesy Gerald R. Ford Library, White House photograph by David Hume Kennerly)

8. Betty Ford, Gerald Ford, Bethesda Naval Hospital, October 4, 1974 (Courtesy Gerald R. Ford Library, White House photograph by David Hume Kennerly)

Index

INDEX